C000245224

A Guide to Salmon Flies

A GUIDE TO

SALMON FLIES

JOHN BUCKLAND and ARTHUR OGLESBY

THE CROWOOD PRESS

First published in 1990 by
The Crowood Press,
Ramsbury, Marlborough,
Wiltshire SN8 2HE

© John Buckland and Arthur Oglesby 1990

All rights reserved. No part of this publication may be reproduced or
transmitted in any form or by any means, electronic or mechanical,
including photocopy, recording, or any information storage and
retrieval system without permission in writing from the publishers.

British Library Cataloguing in Publication Data
Buckland, John
  A guide to salmon flies.
  1. Salmon & trout. Fly fishing. Flies
  I. Title   II. Oglesby, Arthur
  799.1'755

  ISBN 1 85223 246 3

Photography by Tony Pugh
Line-drawings by Charles Jardine

Typeset by Chippendale Type, Otley, West Yorkshire.
Printed and bound in Spain by Graficas Estella, S.A. (Navarra)

To our wives, Lavender and Gracie, without whom our lives would be
like life without fishing

Contents

Foreword

In my dictionary the word 'grand' is defined as 'splendid, magnificent, imposing, dignified'. Salmon fishing can thus be fairly described as a grand sport. Rich in traditions, literature and codes of conduct, it attracts to its ranks some of the nicest people I have ever met – and two of them, John Buckland and Arthur Oglesby, have, with the publication of this splendid book, added greatly to our knowledge of one of the most fascinating aspects of the sport.

A Guide to Salmon Flies is a shining example of an exhaustively researched work, and its importance to salmon fishers – wherever they pursue their sport – cannot be over-stressed. Classic salmon flies are things of great beauty, and the splendid illogicality of many of them detracts not one jot from their loveliness and sense of tradition. In this book we have them described and illustrated for us and future generations to marvel at. We also have many modern patterns, dowdy by comparison, but nonetheless great killers of fish.

Just why a salmon should take a fly is a mystery. I have on my desk as I write this a fly that caught me my only salmon so far this year (on the Spey, incidentally, fishing with Arthur Oglesby). It is a home-made thing with a silver body and blue hackle. It is not a handsome fly, but for some reason it gave me great confidence when I tied it on. Dangling it in the water it swam beautifully. It was easily seen, but not so easily as to appear out of place in the Spey's sparkling stream. And on about my tenth cast a fish took it.

Would that fish have taken, say, a Thunder & Lightning if I had offered one instead? It probably would have done, but no one can say for certain. And that is the beauty of salmon fishing and salmon-fly tying. The glorious uncertainty of whether the fish are in a taking mood and, if they are, what they will take exercises the minds of thousands of salmon fishers the world over. It is absorbing, infuriating and addictive.

A book like this, giving us at a glance such a wealth of patterns to admire and try, is long overdue. I am honoured not only to have been asked to contribute this foreword, but also to have fished extensively with both authors, masters of their craft and marvellous company in and out of the water.

Sandy Leventon
Editor, *Trout and Salmon*

Preface

When Arthur was first approached to write the definitive book on salmon flies he was slightly doubtful about the monumental task he was facing. Additionally, he has always been a bit of a heretic on the value of a huge range of salmon fly patterns, so he felt that a single author, particularly one so jaundiced, might not serve the subject as it deserved. Following a long and very happy liaison with John Buckland over other matters piscatorial and knowing of John's dedication to the intricacies of fly-tying and salmon-fly history, he felt that John would make the perfect partner to co-author this book. John would bring an enquiring mind and the capacity to sift through the many historical aspects of salmon flies and their design. Thus the bulk of the research fell into John's lap.

In all ways it proved to be an ideal partnership, with John cheerfully trying to reconcile his views with Arthur's. The result is an objective outlook on the selection of salmon flies. Indeed, even Arthur now agrees that since so many of our notable salmon anglers have given much thought to salmon fly design the subject cannot be treated lightly; we must have some rationale to enable us to choose a specific pattern or size for any given circumstance.

When salmon return from their rich spell of sea feeding and migrate into fresh water, they cease entirely to feed. On this basis, whatever we choose to offer them should be regarded with total uninterest. But history and experience tell us that salmon can occasionally be caught on a wide variety of fly patterns. So how do we establish this all-important question of logic in fly selection? Ancient lore – which, incidentally, often works very well – suggests that we use big flies in big, deep and cold water, and small flies in smaller, shrunken rivers, when the water is warmer and the fish have less water over their backs. Also in practice we have to remember that there is a whole range of techniques which occasionally defy the basic rules, but about which we must be very careful not to offer dogmatic opinions. The 'lore' or convention applies in all the countries which are the natural habitat of the Atlantic salmon and, broadly speaking, Spanish salmon react similarly to Icelandic salmon in the same conditions of water and weather.

In making your choice of fly pattern we think that it pays to be ever mindful of the laws of nature. Nothing in the wild which is preyed upon by other species has too garish an appearance. It usually has some form of natural camouflage and does not look out of place in its environment. In conditions of clear water, therefore, we feel that the choice of fly should be dictated by this fact. Do not select a fly which sticks out like a sore thumb and, as your flies get smaller, it is not a bad idea to make them more subdued in colour. In conditions of high, turbid water, however, you may well have to confront your fish with a more garish-looking lure. You may even have to intimidate your fish and thus present your lure where it will threaten the fish with an eyeball-to-eyeball collision course.

These considerations suggest that we should choose a colour of fly which matches the overall colour of the river bed. Some rivers run off acidic formations in the hills and mountains of our Scottish rivers. They have an overall brown colour, comparable to weak milkless coffee. For these rivers we like a fly which has a dark-brown or black appearance. Scotland's River Spey responds well to this type of fly and such patterns as the Thunder & Lightning, Munro Killer and Stoat's Tail may all prove effective. Other rivers, such as those flowing off bare rock or limestone, are frequently crystal-clear at times of normal flow and offer a high absorption of ultra-violet light. Sometimes these rivers have a blue or green tinge to them and we feel that flies of those hues may suit them better.

A basic rule we tend to adopt when selecting flies for our own use calls for brighter or garish-looking flies on very cold days when the water may be higher than normal and flies of subdued colour on warmer days when the water may be low and clear.

But – sadly – the final act of deluding the fish into taking your lure may have little to do with your choice of fly. It may simply be that you were in the right place at the right time. It may have something to do with the fly's size, but it is more likely that the paramount consideration is casting and presentation. Suggest to a man that he change his fly for a pattern of your choosing and he will frequently accept your advice, but tell him that his casting and presentation are at fault and you might well end up with a punch on the nose.

Preface

Despite our deliberations, however, there is the undeniable fact that salmon do not feed in freshwater and that whatever we seek to offer them must remain a matter for guesswork or supposition. Some writers suggest a host of reasons for a fish taking an angler's fly and such notions as anger, boredom, curiosity and memory reflex have all been bandied about from time to time. We suspect that the real answer does not exist, but it is interesting to ponder and, although Arthur tends to dodge most theories on the subject, he is prepared to join with John in as thorough an examination as we can reasonably undertake.

Arthur continually likens a salmon in fresh water to a half-sleeping cat which lies down in the sunshine and rarely bothers with much else that is going on around it. Of course, unlike the salmon, the cat will feed when it is hungry, but there are other times when it is provoked to attack something that it has no intention of eating. We are thinking specifically of blown leaves on the wind. Sometimes, and for no apparent reason, the cat will stir itself from a fitful sleep and then chase a blown leaf and dab it with a paw. The cat knows that the leaf is not edible and it does not pursue it for food. But some reflex is triggered by the sight of that fluttering leaf which induces the cat to go and chase it. We submit that it has nothing to do with the colour of the leaf or its size, but merely with its movement, coupled with the fact that it might vaguely resemble an ailing prey.

In the case of wild cats, which have to survive by being fleet of foot, might it not be that they have to be continually on the alert, even to the extent of having the odd practice session when they are not feeding? Salmon rely almost entirely on their speed of interception to get a meal. Might there not be some occasion when they take an angler's fly purely because their attack reflexes have triggered them into taking something that they neither want nor need as food?

In seeking to catch salmon, therefore, we think it paramount not only to learn to cast a fly to the very best of your ability, but also to learn to think like the hunter and study both wild and tame animals to get a sense for their behaviour rhythms. Arthur regularly studies or notes the feeding times of birds, other fish and animals. Indeed, he once confided to John that he fished the hardest when cattle in a field were up and about munching their way quickly from one end to the other and that when they lay down to chew their cud he would take a rest from fishing and go and have a dram in the hut.

In offering you nigh on 400 fly patterns we are aware of the awesome task there might be in choosing one for specific circumstances. But this is also a representative catalogue of flies, some of which have been much revered by their creators or their disciples. Who are we to say that any one pattern in this book would be better than another? The choice of any size or pattern remains with our readers and it is a mystery which will continue to exercise your mind every time you go fishing. This is one of the greatest fascinations in salmon fishing. It is a sport where the words 'never' and 'always' have no place and where the results of your theories are likely to be just as rewarding or otherwise as those of anyone else. All we have done is to remind you of the wealth of information on the subject of flies. We have tried to take a dispassionate approach to it, but in the end you must be the judge of that.

If our book helps you to catch more fish we will be delighted. In its own terms it should stand as an important book of reference – for the historian, for those who believe in the merits of the complex patterns, for the pragmatic 'modern' fishers, and for the fly tyers.

Acknowledgements

When we made it known that we were starting this book we met tremendous enthusiasm. Amateur fly tyers offered their services, the tackle trade was most welcoming, authors enthused for hours on the telephone, tackle collectors generously offered the loan of their flies, *the* British hookmaker expressed his delight at being able to assist. In the background the specialist angling book suppliers took immense pains to see that we could either obtain copies of valuable historical works or have access to them for research. On every side we met kindness and assistance. It is our sincere hope that our joint efforts are not a disappointment: a book as detailed as this is never finished – 'If only we could have found a particular fly collection in Ireland . . . read the earliest gamebooks . . . met some of the famous fishermen . . . '

Our publishers have kept us encouraged, and found for us our photographer, Tony Pugh. Using the modern technique of placing the flies on glass, with the background colour well lit, he has given us delightfully crisp, shadow-free illustrations to support our text.

Ted Hunter, of Anglers' Choice at Melrose, has researched modern Tweed patterns for us and tied them specially, using many aspects of special expertise.

From the topmost beats of the Tweed at Traquair, Peter Nield has tied for us patterns with 'extra attraction', having corresponded widely to help us.

Jess Miller in Dunkeld made us free of his own beautifully preserved collection of gut-eyed and classic flies. Their intrinsic value is immense; their value in demonstrating what the patterns *did* look like, not what modern tyers think they should look like, is incalculable.

Among the book experts, John and Judith Head in Salisbury maintained their kindly patience and we are particularly grateful for their help in supplying details of Spanish salmon flies.

Perhaps Ronald Coleby takes the highest accolade. His life was dogged by one semi-permanent visitor, which distracted him in the even tenor of his occupation but fired him to seek out books, journals, scientific papers, old catalogues and illustrations, so that he quite became part of our team. His was a most selfless participation which is immensely appreciated.

Salmon flies are difficult to think about without reference to George Mortimer Kelson at the turn of the century. He entrusted to Farlow's of Pall Mall the task of executing his fly patterns, making his rods and dressing his lines. This tradition has been reflected in the interest which their company's managing director, Alastair Baxter, and the staff have shown in our venture. Their participation is evidenced by their providing us with priceless fly-tying materials. They have our warmest thanks.

We were most generously allowed access to the entire run of *Trout and Salmon* magazine back numbers, and even housed by the editor and his wife in the course of our research at Peterborough. Our thanks are very much due to Sandy and Alison Leventon and also for the loan of books from Sandy's own library.

Not all the patterns could be borrowed from collections or lent by contributors. To our eternal gratitude, Alan Bramley at Partridge supplied us with a splendid selection of Bartleet and modern hooks – all so that we could reproduce as nearly as possible the styles and patterns we wished to illustrate.

John Ayers from Wales found for us some suitably contemporary tapered eyeless salmon irons, from his own collection.

Joseph Bates junior, with true unselfishness, has allowed us to quote extensively from his three invaluable books on this subject. Generous gestures of this sort have not only helped us bring this book to publication; they have greatly heartened both of us.

While we have enjoyed our discussions and research, all the work of translating the notes and drafts and bringing them together on the word processor to make them into a book has cheerfully been undertaken by Lavender Buckland. Her constant support and involvement certainly deserves at least a week's fishing at the best time and on the best of rivers.

Introduction

It is time to go. There is the irresistible call of salt water; the magic and mystery of spume and salt spray beckon. The parr forget their trout-like habit and don their silvery coat. Like autumn leaves, they sweep downstream in ribbons and schools and shoals until they reach the estuary. They head for the feeding grounds. They gorge on capelin and shrimps and sand-eel and then, one year, two years, three years later, head back to their waters of birth to fulfil their trust to reproduce their species. Densely muscled, their flesh packed with power and sustenance for their freshwater fast, they work their way into the fresh flow of their home river.

The salmon are running again.

The fisherman's year can be a long one – from mid-January on Scotland's mighty Tay to the end of November on the prolific Tweed. There is no more beautiful fish than a classic, bright, fresh-run springer. There is an imposing majesty about an autumn 30-pounder, and more and more fishermen are finding that their enjoyment in salmon fishing is enhanced by seeking their quarry with the fly.

What do salmon feed on in fresh water? In immature stages their feeding habits are those of a small trout, and in mature stages (which includes grilse) they have no requirement to feed, though they have been seen to take aquatic and terrestrial insects, frogs, mice and small fish. So two 'memory banks' in our quarry may help us: flies simulating insects may deceive the fish into taking; flies providing a predatory stimulus may incite the fish to attack.

It may be just some small aspect of the fly which triggers the take – reflection from tinsel, sympathetic harmony with colour of water and intensity of light, or sinuous movement. On some occasions practically anything with a hook can catch salmon; on other occasions the salmon will not take. An infinite variety of patterns – in size, concept, style and colour – has therefore been developed among anglers in search of the elusive 'guarantee' of a take. Sometimes very local inventions find a wide and popular currency; sometimes they have their one day of glory, which is never repeated or even echoed.

There are many intangibles about salmon flies. Fishing with faith and persistence with a choice of pattern seems to be more effective than choosing a fly randomly without much belief in its efficiency. Then there is telepsychology – actively directed mental concentration, willing the fish to take.

Persistence is a factor which adds quality to a fly. Every time a fly is changed, the water is not being fished. This produces a splendid contradiction: if a pattern does not have the properties that the fish want, it is better to try an alternative; or, it's the fly in the water that takes the fish. A further contradiction is that it is better to choose the right moments, known from observation and experience, and then, and then only, to fish. The doubting Thomases will argue that only by fishing persistently can you find the moments when the fish do take; if you sit on the bank you may well miss opportunities because the fly is not at work.

Many aspects of salmon fly design and style are discussed in these pages. The convention of naming patterns is extremely useful. The angler and the tackle merchant (and perhaps the fish?) recognise the colour blend and, among the traditional patterns, the style of tying that the name suggests. Modern tyers, who have moved flexibly from the tenets of the old tying instructions, find it more difficult to standardise dressings, names and styles. Variation from a standard should be included in the name – for example, the Hairwing Jock Scott will differ in translucency and mobility from a feather-dressed fly of that name. In theory the tying will echo all the colour blends of the feathered pattern, and will use suitable substitutes for the plumage which is now too rare and unobtainable.

The classic traditional salmon flies which sprang from the 1700s, evolved through the 1800s and reached their zenith just after the turn of the century do still have a part to play in our salmon fishing. They embody some of the essentials of fly choice and colour blend which history has shown to be particularly successful in taking salmon. Some aspects of their tying are not favoured in the light of modern salmon fishing experience with simpler flies – such as their opacity in some lights, which can be considered a disadvantage. Equally, the solid, blocky effect which many of these patterns produce *is* wanted on occasion. Once a traditional pattern became established, it was possible to produce it in quite a wide range of sizes. If the hook to be dressed was 6 inches long a set of wings would be tied in part way along the body in addition to the set at the head. Modern tyings may incorporate variations on the materials of the traditional dressings – for example, the longer-fibred bucktail may replace red squirrel hair. Occasionally this gives a different quality to the fly, for the stiffness of fibres is directly proportional to their length for the same diameter.

Perhaps none of this really matters, but it makes difficulties for those who describe flies. The white-winged Akroyd with two or even three sets of wings was still as true as possible to the Akroyd pattern. A Hairy Mary was never designed to be tied in large sizes, and cannot possess the same characteristics tied huge, medium, and minute since the original materials cannot extend to this wide range. The tyer does his best, and the concept of black body, blue throat hackle and brown hair wing on a 3-inch tube or Waddington will no doubt appear bearing the name Hairy Mary.

Those interested in the development of the salmon fly will find the words 'Irish flies' or 'gaudy Irish flies' often enough in texts from the 1800s. The Irish literature is rich in early salmon fishing and credits milliners with applying the exotic plumage of their trade to flies for spring fishing. The rivers Erne and Shannon have a well documented history through Newland and O'Gorman, and tyers of their day noted that golden pheasant crest feathers have a peculiar allure in the water. Yellow is also a favoured colour for spring fishing. The salmon would have little chance as a good bundle of crests over a yellow floss or wool or mohair body would be irresistible.

In the meantime, patterns were usually rather drab combinations of gleanings from moor, riverbank and farmyard. Not all had tinsel, and the suggestion is that this was adopted from military uniforms. Even Isaac Walton suggested pieces of Turkey carpet as a source of dyed wool, but there were a host of natural dyes to help the tyer attain the tint he wanted.

So the first definition of Irish flies is flies dressed with the brighter plumage, either alone or together with less exotic material. The next interpretation is that of Pryce-Tannatt, an Edwardian who tied the most exquisite traditional patterns but also recognised the value of sleekness. For him the Irish patterns of

his time (1914) had bodies of wool or seal's fur, throat hackles of coarse feather and overwings of bronze mallard – in other words, some of the simple trout flies given more complexity and dignity to make them salmon patterns.

Nowadays Irish patterns can be taken to mean a development of many of the standard combinations dressed in the shrimp style. A look at the fly-box of an experienced Irish fly fisher will show rank after rank of easily recognisable colour combinations, all in the shrimp style. It is a persuasive style and it has returned across the water to challenge the other main branch of progress, the Esmond Drury treble – a treble hook with a longer shank to permit the tying of the pattern directly on it. To the eye accustomed to the slender, diaphanous low-water tyings, the thickness of the metal body and the potentially chunky outline of a fly tied on an ED treble may be undesirable. Supporters claim, however, that hooking and holding are so superior to the single hook that on balance the ED treble makes a better fly. Certainly very many of the old dressings have been adapted and new dressings created for this style of hook – and many fish approve, to their cost.

Since there are so few fully productive English rivers there is no real category of English salmon flies, and the general patterns from the Scottish repertoire are used. These northern patterns then formed the basis of the transatlantic patterns.

The circle has turned. American and Canadian influence can now be seen in the patterns we use here, in Iceland and in Scandinavia, even though the British first took the sport of fly fishing to these countries. The distinctive style of the transatlantic patterns probably results from the fact that the exotic materials were not available, so tyers drew on local fauna to create simpler copies. The wide range of furs and hairs of differing lengths, rigidities and colourings provided a rich basis for experimentation. In the absence of hidebound tradition – genius is the product of an uncluttered mind – some exceptional patterns have been designed, none of which has much more than a couple of generations of history.

Fly fishing for salmon was introduced to Scandinavia by the wealthy English milords and they took traditional patterns of flies with them. The classical styles of tying were then continued by keen Scandinavian rod fishermen. Built-wing and married-wing flies abound in their repertoires, but few of their patterns have established themselves in British fly-boxes.

However, the new wave of American simplicity reached Scandinavia and enjoyed great success, and as many if not more fish are taken on what are now considered the American classics, such as the Rat series, as are taken on British or local classics. The Scandinavian fisher of the modern generation is also taking to the latest in tubes and Waddingtons, wherever they remain within the fishery regulations. Some regulations in some areas and some countries forbid the use of trebles. In most of the north-eastern seaboard of North America and Canada trebles are forbidden, and the development of simple, but not necessarily drab, patterns on single irons has continued apace, while single irons in this country have largely given way to the development of double and treble patterns.

The Salmon Fly

We will look at the salmon fly in its details and see if a nation or a locality places special emphasis on a particular constituent part.

The Tag   Certainly tags were not found on the early salmon flies. The first tags comprised just a turn or two of tinsel to the rear of the tail. Later they were made up of two parts: the turns of silver or gold tinsel followed by a turn or two of floss silk, usually of a lightish colour. In American tying recipes the tag is often called the tip. An examination of the trade patterns by Hardy's, Forrest and Farlow's shows that the tag (or tag and tip) was, for the most part, modest in emphasis and in quantity of material.

The Tail   The tails of the early salmon flies were stated to be like the tails of the insects which the artificials were to represent, so a few strands of dull materials often similar to those of the wing were chosen. A wool tuft was an alternative with more emphatic colour. When the golden pheasant became a fly-dressing bird in the late 1700s the play and translucence of its crest feathers were admired, and the feather has almost monopolised tail material ever since. The ruff feather at the side of the cock bird's neck, called the tippet, also had qualities of translucence and colour which led to its incorporation in tails, usually in conjunction with the crest or topping.

The Butt   The butt is the next item in the construction. It is more often found in the complex classics, and it has two roles, one major and one minor. The major role is to cover the turns of tying silk which tie off the tag, tie in the tail and tie in the body material and rib

material. A twist of black Berlin wool dubbed onto the tying silk reinforced it, and disguised what otherwise might have been an unsightly lump in the smoothness of the dressing. The minor role was to give a contrast, a colour break, between the tag and the body material. In time ostrich herl took the place of the black wool, and, as natural black feathers are thought by some to emit infra-red, there may be some extra element of attraction. However, in terms of durability wool is far harder-wearing, so the use of ostrich herl as a material was a retrograde step. On one or two patterns the butt is not black; scarlet is correct for the Doctors, for example.

The design of some of the early patterns includes a rearmost segment of the body in a contrasting colour. This could be considered a proto-tag or proto-butt. The same could be said of some American patterns such as the Black Bear Blue Butt. As the dressings which follow will show, this tendency increases with the use of touches of fluorescent material. Obviously now and again the minor role of the original butt has usurped the major.

The Body   The bodies of some of the earlier patterns were fairly nondescript – wools and dubbings of natural furs and underfurs. But there is an intensity of colour in these materials. They darken a little when wet but, with a rough (and intentionally pricked out) outline, light illuminates their edges and they do achieve quite a strong impression of colour. If pig's wool is used it gleams slightly less than mohair, but sinks deeper. Mohair is intermediate in sinking qualities and gloss, and seal's fur the least absorbent and the most bright.

The thinness of the body is limited only by the coarseness of the hook and the dexterity of the tyer. Thickness is entirely within his control. Dubbed bodies may be dense and almost opaque, or finely spun and carefully teased out to give a slender silhouette in a nimbus of colour.

The brightness of floss silk is somewhat reduced when wet. Often it was included for a few turns at the rear of the body before the various dubbings were applied. Being sleek, it offers little water resistance and thus sinks quite readily. Against the light it produces a dark silhouette; with side-lighting against other backgrounds its colours show well.

The first tinsel-bodied salmon fly is thought to have originated in about 1840. Shortly afterwards a quantity make their appearance with Silver Wilkinson, Silver Grey and Silver

Introduction

Doctor paving the way for other tinsel-bodied confections in gold or copper.

The Hackle Since the early salmon fly dressings had as their rationale the concept of imitation, the dressers included a suggestion of legs, either by picking out the dubbing strands or by palmering a hackle along the body, with possibly a second hackle at the throat, under the wing. A poultry hackle spiralled along the body is fairly vulnerable to wear and tear: a rib of metallic yarn wound on the same spiral stands fractionally proud and protects the hackle stalk as well as adding extra sparkle or glitter. It can even be wound on in the opposite direction to cross over and tie down the hackle stalk. Needless to say, the breadth of the rib and the number of turns round the body affect its appearance, and dressers note this as they create particular emphases.

The palmer hackle was not obligatory but it did offer mobile fibres along the undersides and flanks of the fly to give a pulsating semblance of life. The throat hackle could augment this, or on its own produce a suitable touch of mobility, colour or balance to the dressing. It is better to leave the description as 'throat' rather than 'throat hackle', as hair fibres are often used in some modern dressings.

The Wing The next component in all normal salmon flies is the wing. Some historians give the salmon fly three major eras, the criterion being the winging style. The early era has simple wings from domestic sources – mallard, poultry, goose, swan, turkey and other birds of easy abundance. The gaudy flies of the later era include complicated wings of more exotic plumage. Modern flies eschew feather for the wings. The early flies set the wings on at the same angle as the closed wings of the damselfly. The gaudy flies adopted the wing posture of the butterfly, folded vertically across the back. Both traditions stem from the idea that salmon flies represent insects, but this concept soon became more of a formula for thought than any attempt to copy nature. Within both eras, early and gaudy, there are plenty of patterns which do not conform to this generalisation. They will receive their fair mention, as will the moderns.

The winging material of the early patterns showed its underside to an upward-looking fish. The design – deliberately or fortuitously – is quite mobile, with the water of the stream and tension on the line inducing quite a lot of movement from the wingtips in a sort of scissors action. The Tweed flies of Scrope were tied with the wing upright. For attraction they depended more on contrast of body colours and well picked out dubbing and hackle. But there were no mixtures of feathers in the wing. This development is attributed to the Irish. Yet it took them some years to stylise wings into the vertical plane. They did not marry the strips but produced a loose conical bundle of feather, often overtopped with bronze mallard, which presented quite a broad swathe to the upward-looking fish. As the fibres were separate some light could creep in among them and the result was a less harsh silhouette. ('**Marrying**' is the term for interlocking the barbules which are the tiny hooks and eyes running along the feather barbs. Barbs of commensurate length taken from the same side of the feather, from the same side of the bird, will interlock – whether the birds chosen for their plumage are swan, turkey, bustard or wildfowl. By manipulation the tyer creates a band of feather material with bands of colour or mottle to his taste, or to accord with an established design.)

At about the turn of the century it seemed almost imperative that vertical wings – whether married, built, sheaths of married fibres overlapping, or whole feather – should be further ornamented – with sides (either short married sections of brighter waterfowl feathers or jungle cock neck feathers); with cheeks (body feathers of the blue chatterer or kingfisher or Indian crow, superimposed with one or two toppings); or with horns (tough springy fibres from macaw tail to protect the brittle jungle cock as well as add a coloured whisker of mobility to each side of the wing). The gaudy patterns could become very bright indeed.

The Head The head changed in style. Early flies might have a wool head, since small size was not important, or a herl head, which suffered in the same way as a herl butt. Nowadays a whip finish and a good coat or two or three of varnish is normal. Where the pattern suggests, for instance, red wool for the head, red varnish is used in place of the usual black.

An element of symmetry is found in most patterns – that is, the artificial will look the same from each side. As the natural insect has this attribute, it seemed no doubt logical to represent it. Wings are the most absorbing of the constituent parts, since so many designs have gone into their making – certainly until the modern age, when feather materials have yielded to other fibres. There is little doubt that many winging styles have run concurrently, either because the tyer found a style easier and less-time consuming or because it suited a theory. Chaytor speaks of the fly used on the Tyne with wings of wren tail feathers; we see the Gaudy Fly of Hansard and Bainbridge with whole feather wings, in this case, guinea-fowl hackles; and in Hansard we also see the Spring pattern with whole bittern feathers for the wings. (It is certainly easier to tie in two whole feathers than matching slips.) Bainbridge's wasp pattern had no wings – a forerunner of grubs – and at about the same date the King's Fisher fly, quite complicated in its dressing of the body and the hackle, was sometimes tied with a simple and symmetrical wing of a bunch of peacock herls.

The bunch of herls as a wing is still with us (though with a tenuous hold) – partly because it is easy to tie and partly because the sheen of peacock herl excites our admiration and we hope that salmon will find it equally attractive. With probably fairly unfounded reasoning a herl wing is considered to represent one of the crustacea, which in the deep sea have this colour. However, putting aside any specific observations, we can make some generalisations: herl is mobile, it is quite strong, it stays tied in quite well, and to our eyes it complements many body or hackle combinations beneath it. However, though herl is long and mobile – attributes of hair – it has little place in the modern development of flies. Hair now holds sway, in conjunction with modern synthetic fibres.

Whole feather wings have lasted well, right into this modern age. It might be thought that the stiff quills in whole feathers would make them unacceptable as a mouthful and thus likely to be swiftly ejected by a fish, yet the Matuka style of trout flies from New Zealand and Lionel Walker's Killer series use quilled whole feathers and remain popular. Those who are unhappy with webbed feathers use hackles, softer-stemmed feathers from the neck of the bird rather than from the body. The hackle fibres of domestic poultry do not have barbules and the feather has great translucency since each fibre is shiny rather than matt. Poultry hackle wings are relative newcomers in Britain, but in both Spain and Brittany they are standard.

Whole feathers with special qualities of bright colours are probably more attractive to the tyer than the fish, and the golden pheasant's bright neck feathers – tippets – were seized upon from about 1840 onwards, culminating in the modern and extremely successful General Practitioner

of Esmond Drury in the early 1950s. Set upright, like butterfly wings, the tippet offers a wonderful tawny-orange blaze of colour with sharply contrasting black bars. The Durham Ranger and its series look to many observers like surprisingly successful boiled-prawn imitations, but on a two-dimensional plane. Fly dressers – particularly Irish dressers – liked tippet as an underwing, either in strands or on the stem.

Big flies call for big feathers, however, and a tippet can be too small. The bright sword feathers found by the tail train of the golden pheasant are designed into some patterns – some dressings of the Gordon and some Eagles. They might not be the primary element, and the contemporary tyer of classic flies often turns to dyed cock poultry hackles to achieve much the same result with less bulk and more translucence. Where he can he replaces whole feathers with strands, but often this is only possible in the smaller sizes.

The built-wing fly – slips of wing or tail feather partially overlaid with married slips and then adorned with sides, cheeks and horns – has been fiercely condemned as the worst in fly dressing for its bulk and inanimate opacity. As a fly-dressing exercise these flies are exceptionally difficult. The Jock Scott, probably the most widely known of all classic salmon flies, is of this design; yet tied in appropriate size and by a tyer with an eye for proportion no criticism can be levelled at it. Complex as it is, it is also a surprisingly attractive harmony of colour and contrast. It certainly catches fish: did not M.G.F. McCorquodale, who killed over 8,000 fish on the Spey, prefer it to all other patterns? He would hardly have chosen a feather duster with few intrinsic qualities for his fishing.

Size is important: the fibres used in fly tying all have different stiffness-to-length ratios. A short stiff feather will not enhance a 'miniature' tying of a classical pattern. Somewhere – perhaps about 1½ – 2 inches – there is a perfect size for a complex built-wing salmon fly, in which fibres will have play, and a judicious tyer will have incorporated just the right balance of, say, blue and red and yellow against the more muted mottlings of the various gamebird feathers.

Substitute Materials

Some feather and hair materials which are listed in traditional patterns may now be so rare, endangered or expensive that they are no longer practical to use. There are also many

Introduction

modern manmade materials with characteristics which may be even more advantageous, strength often being one of their particular virtues.

Although it seems that natural colours have an attraction superior to dyed colours, it is difficult to prove. With fluorescent dyes easily applicable to furs, floss, hairs and feathers, extra attraction can readily be added. Poultry, in the domestic sense, is not endangered, and careful genetic programmes are breeding birds for the fly tyer rather than the table or for egg production. Some of the other galliforms have become rare, and, although the breeding of birds in captivity is increasing with success, the product from aviary and wildfowl collections satisfies only a small part of a hungering fly-tying market. Lucky tyers may have access to some of the rarer feathers; others of us must look to ordinary poultry and see what careful material selection, dyes and a little ingenuity can do. For instance, there is no real substitute for jungle cock; the flies we have tied for the book incorporate the genuine feathers derived from home-reared birds, courtesy of Farlow's.

The plastics industry has produced artificial fibres to take the place of feathers or hairs, as well as alternatives to traditional furs such as seal's fur, and has even usurped some of the tinsels. No longer are they stiff metals, hard to tie in neatly, and tending to tarnish. In the realm of dyeing, probably the greatest boon has been the advent of many-hued indelible marker pens. A naturally marked feather such as the rare argus can be copied convincingly on common goose, and, when this latter fibre is incorporated according to a pattern's demands, the tyer is satisfied, the aesthetics are satisfied and in such a case, as if it mattered, probably the fish approve also.

We cannot escape the fact that for cost and convenience the old complicated patterns are rarely tied. Neither author considers tying to be an art – it is merely a craft or an easily acquired skill. The exercise of this skill is immensely satisfying, and it is up to the tyer to decide how complicated or simple his patterns will be. In the patterns which follow or are discussed, there will be few colours, tones, tints or combinations which are not included, either simply or in extreme complication.

Hairwing Variations of Classic Patterns

The original featherwing tying had some logic (not necessarily particularly sound) behind it, a belief in a touch of red to stimulate a predator, a golden yellow which in the water looks like the rich olive of an insect, and so on. The body in its combination of colour and tone will also accord with the hackle and wing, so that the composite fulfils the designer's ideals. Normally the tyer who chooses to vary a full featherwing pattern varies the body quite extensively, as well as varying the wing. It should be possible to view the pattern dispassionately, to see if items should be omitted in both major sectors.

A complex body like that of the Jock Scott takes many materials and much time to tie. Its essence is yellow at the rear and black at the front. However, the yellow is veiled with diaphanous toucan – which breaks a hard silhouette – and the black is palmer-hackled, which again does something to break the silhouette and add some shining movement. We feel that a variant leaving the body as mere yellow and black silks would be an oversimplification, because possibly advantageous elements in the dressing are omitted.

The wing of this pattern is complex: the white-topped black turkey gives a strong silhouette at the head, tapering into near-translucence towards the tail. The married strips of coloured swan offer a median band of iridescence which is muted by natural mottles higher up in the construction of the wing – just as a natural minnow is darker on its back. Jungle cock may give the appearance of a fish's eye, or may just be an element of striking contrast. Chatterer retains its electric blueness underwater as no other blue feather does. The topping overlying the wing adds a shimmering translucency to soften the edges of the silhouette.

We all acknowledge that the prescribed ingredients of this pattern are rare, endangered and hard to obtain – in fact nowadays almost immoral to use. It is, however, possible to dress hairwing variations which retain much of the original character, and this should be done even if only to establish convention. If extremely random variations take place, the character and style of the fly can change so much that it will not accord with the known and accepted pattern. There comes a breakdown in communication, which leads to a breakdown in knowledge about the salmon, its whims, caprices and taking moods. Therefore, in giving dressings for the 'old faithfuls' we try to stay with the concept as far as possible. There is no need for more than just a few hairwing conversion patterns once we have explained the dressing and concept of the classic which is to be copied. The amateur is not under the same restraints of time as the professionals – and we never can get away from the fact that fly fashions often follow the easiest tying trends for the trade.

Singles v. Doubles v. Trebles

Interesting correspondence has arisen recently in *Trout and Salmon* about stretch in fly lines, and its detriment to hooking fish. In the letters was a laser-measured comparison of the cross-section of the hook at the point of the barb. A size 6 low-water double was figured as giving 60 per cent more resistance than a single Captain Hamilton standard wire. If two hooks are to be pulled in over their barbs as the fish takes there is plenty of resistance. If a treble is used all three may have to be pulled in at the same time, with trebled resistance. Countering this potential disadvantage is the greater likelihood of one hook out of three managing to take a hold, or one of the two. If that hook-hold slips there is another hook on a different plane available to take a grasp. Before drawing any conclusions we would really need an underwater video to see the stresses, leverages and angles to which a hook is subjected as a salmon is being played. Until then it will remain a point of subjective taste whether to use single, double or treble, though circumstance will dictate to a large extent.

The size of a double or treble will have a lower limit. Suitable gape is one of the criteria of a good fish hook. A single has a wider comparative gape than a double of the same size, which in turn has a wider gape than a treble of that size. If the double or the treble has its eye downturned to the plane of two hooks, in effect the gape is further reduced.

A single offers the best gape in the small sizes, followed by the double, followed by the treble. As the sizes approach the maximum, the single becomes the least effective first and the double next. There is no need to choose outsize trebles: large ones do as well or better than extra-large. We think this is worth mentioning. It is up to you to choose which patterns you tie and which you use.

George Selwyn Marryat summed up hooks with wit and elegance: 'the temper of an angel and the penetration of a prophet; fine enough to be invisible, and strong enough to kill a bull in a ten-acre field'.

The salmon fly is 90 per cent a wet fly and 90 per cent or more of wet flies are attractors, though they may have some resemblance to natural creatures thought to be potential food. Few patterns seem planned as direct imitations. The remaining 10 per cent are dry flies, or flies designed specifically to be fished on the surface film, probably making a wake or surface disturbance.

The various wet-fly styles emphasise different dimensions – the fly looks most substantial seen from sideways on, or from above or below, or end on. Some wings are tied in vertically. The nearest to horizontal are Dee strip wings (which can, incidentally, be imitated badly with tufts of hair). Hairwings tied thickly present considerable bulk seen from most angles, and when tied slender will at least appear reasonably symmetrical.

An advantage of the Esmond Drury trebles is that they can be entirely symmetrical in their dressing and can be fished either up-eye or down-eye. The hook in the Collie Dog dressing is so unobtrusive that the entire attraction of the fly lies in the sinuous flow of the hair. The tube fly and the Waddington share this quality of offering the same profile when seen from above, below or from the side, provided the materials are tied in an even fan. Again the hook is self-effacing, though occasionally silvered trebles are used for extra potential sparkle.

Modern compound wings include an underwing of hair, with some of the characteristics of tone, impression and colour of the traditional suggested by feather. Such a wing is tied more 'in the round', and with opaque materials gives a very much more solid impression, to the extent that a reduction in size may be called for. Less opaque materials tied in this style may have better diaphanous translucency than feather strands.

A difficulty arises when the materials are used sparse and long. What size is the fly? Is it to be judged by the dressing or the hook size? Increasingly, modern patterns using the more mobile hair fibres are to be tied 'twice the hook length', 'at least 1½ times the hook length', and so on. The dressing of patterns such as Crossley's Black Heron and some shrimp tyings also extends well beyond the bend.

Introduction

A.H.E. Wood's rating of size 6 as the standard size, once the water temperature reached and exceeded 48°F, is valuable both as a convention and as a comparison. Other fishermen have used it as a base from which to go up or down according to brightness of light and clarity, speed and depth of water. If the water is fast, deep and coloured the fly will be some sizes larger than a 6, and vice versa. With the ED trebles and their intrinsically thicker bodies, however, and the patterns with trailing filaments, the equation is slightly a question of guess and experience.

The wet fly in many of its forms may also be used in the surface film. Although the history and technique of the *riffling* or *Portland Creek* hitch are well known in the British Isles, there is little information on its regular place in the fisherman's repertoire. Early traditional patterns of salmon wet flies were tied on eyeless irons, with a loop of gut incorporated beneath the dressing to which the leader was attached. Old or maltreated flies would lack reliability, as the gut loop would degrade, yet the pattern and dressing might otherwise be in good order. A couple of hitches after the leader-loop knot is tied would guarantee that the fly and fish would not be lost. The result is that the fly swims in the surface film, riffling or cutting a wake by reason of its asymmetrical attachment. This does not deter fish from taking it, and in the Portland Creek it proved a more successful method than standard wet fly use, though all the other elements of a long line and delicate presentation were observed.

The short-line version of this is dibbling. Although some wet flies are used for this, some specific patterns or alterations of style have been developed, an example being the use of a tube fly in which the entry hole for its leader has been made one-third of its length from the head. Other patterns will be more heavily palmered or dubbed, or have a broader, thicker wing. With this technique, and with the use of the riffling hitch, the way the rod is manipulated has a great effect on the fly. For the most part the rod top is kept high to prevent the fly from submerging and losing its effect.

Dry flies may be allowed to 'dead drift' just like a trout dry fly presented on the surface to a feeding trout, or to walk across the water on hackle points, or they may be induced to drag.

Natural materials tend to retain their stiffness and sparkle better than when they are dyed, and many of the original dry patterns were therefore composed of natural red and grey hackles from quality cock capes. Deer hair, with its positive buoyancy, is also used in its natural colouring, ranging through the greyish browns as well as white. For the fisherman straining to see a dark fly against a dark background, the addition of white or dyed scarlet to the standard patterns helped to make the fly show up on the water. The increasing use of colour in dry-fly patterns seems to have served more to help the angler than to attract the fish.

Dry flies came to be tied both large – really large at about 2/0, which is the biggest fly that can be cast comfortably – and down through the sizes to trout size 16. It would be fair to say that the larger sizes often act as attractors, bringing potential target fish to show at the surface without necessarily being taken, before the angler works through size and silhouette until the fish does choose to take. Silhouette is considered of great importance, with thick-bodied 'buggy' flies apparently possessing much attraction even in small sizes.

There are plenty of specific salmon dry fly patterns: however many of the standard trout dry flies can be adapted to catching salmon, and the three imitations which immediately spring to mind are the mayfly in the streams of southern Britain, the stoneflies of North America, and the march browns where such insects abound.

Neither author is brave enough to suggest infallible choices of fly. Probably 90 per cent of the time it is not really important. Both accept that fly fishing involves a fly (not a worm) at one end of the line, and a philosopher (not a fool) at the other. There is a sense of completeness about devising and tying fly patterns, and finding that they prove successful. Equally, the satisfaction to be gained from the skills of fly tying is enough to make the striving for perfection an object in itself.

Salmon fishing, and especially salmon fishing with the fly, seems to both of us to be the very cream of angling. Why is salmon fishing so attractive? 'Because God made salmon just the right size.' It is a sporting fish, good-looking, and good to eat. It is a wild creature from wild places.

Bibliographical References

We give a full bibliography on page 268. However, in the text we mention some authors so regularly that full reference each time would lead to interminable repetition. So Kelson, Hale, Francis, Pryce-Tannatt, Jorgensen, Bates (*ASF*), Bates (*Art*), Hill, Lee Wulff (*AS*) and others, may appear as bare names; or, where they have several books, with an abbreviation of the title following their name.

The Fly

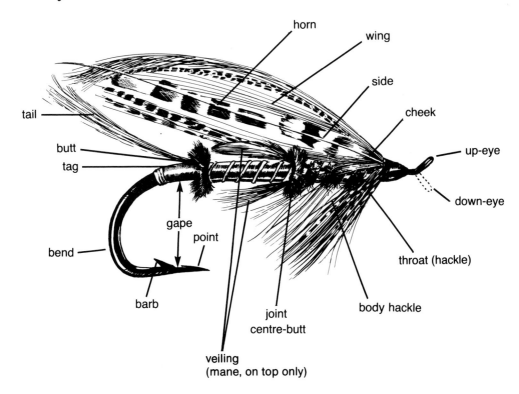

1 **Tag** tinsel, or tinsel plus floss, wool, etc.
2 **Tail** usually topping; can be floss or wool.
3 **Butt** black, or sometimes red, herl or wool.
4 **Body** wide variety of materials.
5 **Rib** usually tinsel.
6 **Veiling** toucan or Indian crow. A mane is tied on top only, in feather, silk, mohair, etc.
7 **Joint** or butt repeated (there may be several joints).
8 **Hackle** palmered usually tight against rearmost edge of rib.
9 **Throat** tied in before the wing.

10 **Wing** of whole feather, strips of feather, hair, artificial fibres, a mixture of any of these – or no wing at all.
11 **Collar** tied in after the wing.
12 **Sides** about half the length of the wing.
13 **Cheeks** about half the length of a side.
14 **Horns** hard fibres of macaw.
15 **Head** varnished black unless otherwise specified.

The terminology adapts itself for tubes and Waddingtons.

Introduction

Seen from behind with horizontal hookshank.

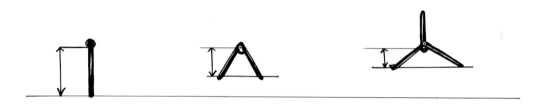

Redrawn with down-eye, the point made becomes even more graphic.

In the treble the 'double' axis of the hook has almost negligible gape.

We think this is worth mentioning: it will be up to you to choose which patterns you tie and which you use, but it would be a pity not to depict some of the facts about hooks.

HISTORIC AND CLASSIC FLIES

Historic Flies

There are no exact formulae for the earliest flies, and the texts which exist are usually ambiguous. Very few really early salmon flies seem to have been preserved.

The woodcuts and the other illustrations in the early books all have some element of artist's impression rather than true representation such as a photograph would give, and this is so even as late as Kelson in 1895, for the eight plates in *The Salmon Fly* are chromolithographs, with emphatic stylisation.

Earlier fishing historians have searched hard to present examples of what they consider the flies would have looked like. We have found the observations in the Lonsdale Library the most convincing, and base our interpretations along those lines.

This set includes an early 'gaudy' fly, some examples of Irish tying techniques and the first of the established hairwing patterns, which was the precursor of so many modern tyings.

1 King's Fisher

COMMENT

Peacocks were regularly included in Elizabethan menus. It comes as no surprise that their plumage attracted tyers, and this suited their theory that salmon liked bright flies of large size. This sort of thinking was current from the mid-1700s onwards. Since both salmon and pike can attain large sizes they were offered similar flies. For this style of winging, matching whole feathers are chosen. Here they are peacock eyes or moons, which are the tail coverts. For some contemporary patterns whole feathers from the jay's wings were matched to form the wings.

DRESSING

'This is also a Salmon fly, and it is seen at the same time as the Dragon Fly. The wings are made of a feather from the neck or tail of a peacock; the body of deep green mohair, warped with light green silk; and a jay's feather striped blue and white, wrapped under the wings. It may be thus varied: the wings of a dark shining green feather from the drake's wing; the body of green mohair warped with chocolate silk, and a bittern's hackle under the wings.' – (Charles Bowlker, *The Art of Angling*, 1747)

2 Mackintosh's Black Dog

COMMENT

An engaging comment from Mackintosh's book is that 'I caught one when angling with the fly at Castle-Menzies in the year 1765, that weighed fifty-four and a half pounds.' This is a big fish on modern tackle, let alone on an early reel and with a horsehair connection to the fly. In his *Driffield Angler* (1808) Mackintosh gave seven salmon patterns. Strip wings were explained, and tied on one by one. Golden pheasant was certainly a well-known and used material by his time. We have followed the replica dressed by Forrest for the Lonsdale Library for our representation of this pattern.

DRESSING

Tag: None.
Tail: None.
Body: Lead-coloured pig's wool from behind the ear.
Rib: Fine gold twist.
Wing: Bluish feather from heron wing intermixed with spotted reddish fibres of turkey tail.

1 King's Fisher   **2** Mackintosh's Black Dog   **3** Hansard's Spring Fly
4 Gaudy Fly   **5** Toppy   **6** Owenmore   **7** Yellow Parson   **8** Garry Dog

3 Hansard's Spring Fly

COMMENT

For many of the early patterns tyers did not detach two matching strips from a feather, but tied in matching whole feathers. However, replicas of this pattern mentioned by both Bainbridge and Hansard are tied either way.

George C. Bainbridge is widely credited with giving the first coloured plates of salmon flies. It seems, however, that there is almost certainly one precursor in Daniel's *Rural Sports* in the 1805 edition. There is also a whisper around that there is an Irish monograph on salmon flies from before the turn of the century, and it included coloured plates.

DRESSING

Tag: None.
Tail: None.
Body: Orange silk and worsted.
Rib: Broad gold twist.
Throat: Smoky dun.
Wing: Dark mottled brown feather of a bittern.
(The example illustrated is a replica of the 1816 pattern.)

4 Gaudy Fly

COMMENT

The plate in Bainbridge is quite clear, and it is not too difficult to follow the artist's impression, though with possibly some doubt about the set of the wings. The hook is drawn to be of fine wire and of round bend shape. It is long in the shank compared with the gape. In all the patterns illustrated the head is kept respectably small.

'So fastidious and whimsical are the Salmon at times, that the more brilliant and extravagant the fly, the more certain is the Angler of diversion.'

'Beads, which are sometimes used to represent the bright prominent eyes of the dragonfly, are reprehensible.'

DRESSING

Tag: None.
Tail: Strands of green peacock herl.
Body: Ostrich herl dyed the same red as the wing feather.
(**Rib:** 'Avoid introducing too great a weight of gold or silver'.)
Hackle: Bright yellow.
Throat: Strands of green peacock herl.
Wing: Dyed red hackles, or red macaw, enveloped by whole feathers of guinea-fowl.

5 Toppy

COMMENT

Scrope's book of 1843 is a delight for its content and style. He recorded the six most telling patterns of his time, which incidentally closely resemble the anonymous patterns listed by Younger three years earlier, also for the Tweed. The keen eye will spot such developments as a butt or tag and a tail. Scrope's companion flies are Kinmont Willie, Meg in her Braws, Meg wi' the Muckle Mouth, Michael Scott, and The Lady of Mertoun. He expressed a dislike of multiplying reels in favour of single-action, and related a tale of another angler with a wooden pirn, not attached to his rod but to his waist!

DRESSING

End of body: Crimson wool.
Tail: Yellow wool.
Body: Black bullock's hair.
Body hackle: Black cock.
Wing: White-tipped back turkey feather.
End of body: Small piece of red cock hackle.
Head: Crimson wool.

6 Owenmore

COMMENT

This is an example of a 'maned' fly, with tufts of winging-type material or veiling material sprouting at intervals along the top of the shank. Tag and tail are now established features of a fly, and they reign in some form for about 100 years before the fashion of reducing them or omitting becomes prevalent.

This is an Irish style, which did not catch on much, but a modern tyer may see considerable possibilities. We now have many materials with better properties than mohair; it allows a segmented wing with plenty of light passing between the segments.

DRESSING

Tag: Silver and light orange floss.
Tail: Topping and Indian crow.
Butt: Black herl.
Body: In five joints – black floss divided by yellow floss and silver tinsel.
Manes: First claret, second claret, third yellow, fourth claret and yellow mohair.
Throat: Olive-red rump of golden pheasant under jay.
Wing: Tippet strands, golden pheasant tail, brown mallard, topping.
Horns: Blue and yellow macaw.

7 Yellow Parson

COMMENT

The Parsons as a race contain a wide series of variations, but essentially they represent what were considered gaudy Irish flies by the conservative fishers on the British mainland. It may be that fashion dictated the design. Subsequent testing for luminosity by Wells in 1886 and Kingsmill Moore in 1960 attributed great visibility to toppings, a quality in a fly well suited for spring fish in cold and possibly coloured water. Golden pheasant tippet was later added to the wing. (In our section on Extra Attraction on page 212 we discuss more fully the value of topping in a fly.)

DRESSING

Tag: Gold twist and yellow floss.
Tail: Two toppings.
Body: Yellow floss.
Rib: Medium gold twist.
Hackle: Pale yellow.
Wing: About 15 toppings, curling upwards.
Collar: Jay.

8 Garry Dog

COMMENT

Hairwings have a longer history than many of us are aware. The classic among them is the Garry Dog, which originated with James Wright at Sprouston on the Tweed in the middle of the last century or a little later. This pattern is also referred to as the Minister's Dog, the Golden Dog, and the Yellow Dog. Garry was the name of the minister's dog whose hair was first used.

Newland had already suggested a hairwing in Ireland, and there was a pattern winged optionally with mohair, but none established itself as a standard.

DRESSING

Tag: Flat silver.
First tail: Topping.
Butt: Yellow floss, not wool or herl.
Second tail: Strip of ibis.
Body: Black floss.
Rib: Silver.
Throat: Dyed blue guinea-fowl.
Wing: Red hair under yellow hair in the proportion 1:2.

29

Classic Flies 1

The best known of the classics, and arguably the most successful, is the Jock Scott. Two dates of origin are suggested among the various authors, 1845 and 1850. The latter seems more likely. The brief obituary given in *The Field* in 1893 probably has the correct facts:

Jock Scott, for he was hardly known as John Scott, was born at Branxholme in 1817. When 13 he served two or three years with the Marquis of Lothian before he moved to the employ of Lord John Scott. It was while acting as fisherman to Lord John at Makerstoun he invented the pattern, something new and taking. The Jock Scott was the result, and, on trying it himself, he was so pleased with it that he gave a pattern to the late Mr Forrest, fishing tackle maker, Kelso . . . who named it after the inventor.

1 Jock Scott

COMMENT

One of the earliest patterns to include jungle cock (the Durham Ranger was the first) the Jock Scott is Tweedside fly. It is thought by many fly tyers and fishermen (and fish) to be the most effective harmony of colour and design in any elaborate salmon fly. There is a series – Red Jock, Blue Jock, Claret Jock, and Silver and Gold. Body colour and hackle are varied accordingly; the wing remains standard. Some fly-tying instructions suggest the Jock Scott wing for the Greenwell and the Dusty Miller.

Sometimes it is said that he devised it during a crossing of the North Sea to Norway with his employer. The date for this trip is given as 1845, and is occasionally embellished by adding he was sea-sick.

DRESSING

Tag: Oval silver and yellow floss. **Tail:** Topping and Indian crow. **Butt:** Black herl. **Body:** Rear half, primrose floss ribbed with fine oval silver, veiled above and below with six toucan feathers, followed by a butt of black herl; front half, black floss ribbed with flat silver (oval and flat on large sizes). **Hackle:** Black cock on the black floss. **Throat:** Guinea-fowl. **Wing:** Underwing, white-tipped black turkey; peacock wing, and yellow, scarlet and blue swan; speckled bustard, florican and golden pheasant tail; teal and barred summer duck; strands of green peacock herl; bronze mallard; topping. **Sides:** Jungle cock. **Cheeks:** Chatterer. **Horns:** B. & y. macaw.

2 Childers

COMMENT

This is a lovely old-fashioned full tying. The body tapers nicely to extra thickness towards the head, the throat hackle veils a vibrant flame, and the wing has just the right proportions in partially hiding the underwing of whole tippets. In 1853 Stoddart referred to the Childers as a new fly, but it does not establish its exact date, for he also calls the Butcher, the Parson and the Doctor new flies. Kelson thinks it was introduced in about 1850, and that initially it did not have the wing topping. Grimble noted its wide use in the Highland rivers; we read that the record Thurso fish (47 pounds) was taken on it.

DRESSING

Tag: Silver twist and light-blue silk. **Tail:** Topping with strands of red and blue macaw and pintail. **Butt:** Black herl. **Body:** Two turns of light-yellow silk, light-yellow seal fur, and three turns red seal fur at the throat. **Rib:** Silver lace and flat silver. **Hackle:** White furnace dyed yellow. **Throat:** Red hackle under wigeon. **Wing:** Tippet and golden pheasant tail, brown mottled turkey, Amherst tail, pintail, bustard, summer duck, green, blue and red swan, guinea fowl, brown mallard over, topping. **Cheeks:** Chatterer. **Horns:** B. & y. macaw.

1 Jock Scott   **2** Childers   **3** Brora   **4** Douglas Graham   **5** Torrish
6 Pale Torrish   **7** Alexandra   **8** Jonah

Historic and Classic Flies

3 Brora

COMMENT

This fully dressed pattern was popular in low-water guise on the Aberdeenshire Don some thirty years ago. It is pleasing to show an example in full regalia. We do not have a date for its origin. It is not found in Kelson, Pryce-Tannatt or Hale, but Bates lists it as an exhibition fly in his *Art of the Salmon Fly*.

DRESSING

Tag: Silver thread and lilac floss.
Tail: Topping and kingfisher above and below the shank.
Butt: Black herl.
Body: Rear half, oval silver veiled top and bottom with toucan; front half, black floss.
Rib: Oval silver over the black floss.
Throat: Black heron, long, to extend beyond the hook bend.
Wing: Two vertical strips of cinnamon turkey, with blue and white swan to their sides, and pintail to the sides of them.

4 Douglas Graham

COMMENT

This pattern appears in the early Hardy catalogues, and is usually included in the colour plates. It is not in Pryce-Tannatt or Kelson, but Hale includes it, with very little deviation from the pattern illustrated. The Indian crow veiling makes this a very expensive pattern to tie, as substitute material seldom achieves the gradation of yellow through to orangy red, nor does it have the attractive sheen.

DRESSING

Tag: Silver thread and dark claret floss.
Tail: Topping and Indian crow. **Butt:** Black herl. **Body:** Rear half, silver flat ribbed with oval silver and veiled with Indian crow top and bottom followed by a black herl butt; front half, dark-claret seal fur ribbed with fine oval silver and flat silver. **Hackle:** Dark-claret over the seal fur. **Throat:** Dyed blue guinea-fowl. **Wing:** Tippet strands and dark turkey; yellow, red, blue and cinnamon swan; bustard, golden pheasant tail, summer duck; mallard; topping. **Sides:** Jungle cock. **Horns:** B. & y. macaw.

5 Torrish

COMMENT

This and the following pattern are both Torrishes but there are many noticeable differences. The darker of the two seems to be the older dressing. There is also a mass of variations within each pattern.

On smaller patterns white-tipped black turkey forms the underwing and guinea-fowl replaces the argus. Sometimes all the dyed swans are placed next to each other.

We have a range of sizes, possibly tied by Hardy's, which are even darker in wing and hackle than in the plate.

DRESSING

Tag: Silver twist and yellow floss.
Tail: Topping and ibis (or Indian crow).
Butt: Black herl. **Body:** Rear half, oval silver, veiled with Indian crow above and below, followed by butt of black herl; front half, oval (or flat) silver, ribbed with oval silver. **Hackle:** Yellow, over the front half of the body.
Throat: Deep dyed orange. **Wing:** Two badger hackles back to back; yellow swan, bustard, red swan, Amherst tail, blue swan, argus; veiled teal. **Sides:** Jungle cock. **Cheeks:** Indian crow. **Horns:** B. & y. macaw.

6 Pale Torrish

COMMENT

There are many variations in this pattern, both in wing and in body. In 1913 Grimble gave the second half of the body as yellow mohair. Jorgensen gives the underwing as cinnamon turkey. The yellow joint hackle seems fairly common. Kelson attributes the Torrish pattern to Radcliffe; Grimble, to Donald Ross, keeper at Torrish on that river.

The Torrishes were favoured on the River Helmsdale. Salscraggie (written in a number of ways), an alternative name for this pattern, is one of the beats there. It is considered a good spring fly, and is also dressed in all hook styles.

DRESSING

Tag: Silver twist and yellow floss. **Tail:** Topping and (optional) tippet. **Butt:** Black herl. **Body:** Rear half, oval silver; joint, yellow hackle and black herl butt; front half, flat (or oval) silver, or yellow mohair, with ribbed oval silver. **Hackle:** Yellow, over the front half of the body. **Throat:** Yellow. **Wing:** White-tipped black turkey, or cinnamon turkey; yellow, blue and red swan; golden pheasant tail, bustard; two toppings. **Sides:** Jungle cock. **Cheeks (optional):** Indian crow. **Horns:** Blue and yellow macaw.

7 Alexandra

COMMENT

This tying seems to have been invented originally as a minnow imitation for brown trout. Its reputation, which seems partially unfounded, was such that many trout waters forbade its use. Subsequently it was used for sea trout, and then for salmon. It is now listed as a tying for steelhead. Pryce-Tannatt has a simpler pattern than this, but we have chosen our example as the earliest heavily weighted dressing we have found, and we can assure you there really is some weight to it. That is why the body is rather coarsely dressed.

DRESSING

Tag: Oval gold.
Tail: Topping, peacock herl strands and Indian crow.
Body: Flat silver.
Rib: Oval gold.
Throat: Natural black, with a tiny touch of red over, and shorter.
Wing: Two black hackles back to back, green peacock sword herls, and strips of red swan.
Sides: Jungle cock.

8 Jonah

COMMENT

It took us a moment to find some background for this pattern. It is recognised as a Tweed fly, and Kelson states that it is a favourite autumn fly there. According to Sir Herbert Maxwell, its name was given it for being three days and three nights in a fish's mouth.

For so simple a tying there is a surprising amount of slight variation. Kelson has it, Hale has it, and it is in the usual Hardy catalogues. W. Earl Hodgson pictures it in his model set of 72 patterns. Its elegant light-wire double reminds us that Kelson used to place *his* confidence in doubles.

DRESSING

Tag: Silver twist and yellow floss.
Tail: Topping and chatterer.
Butt: Scarlet wool.
Body: Flat silver.
Rib: Oval silver.
Throat: Light blue under guinea-fowl.
Wing: Peacock herl and ibis.
Sides (optional): Jungle cock.
Horns: Blue macaw (or red macaw).
Head: Scarlet wool.

Classic Flies 2

Now a note on George Mortimer Kelson, author of *The Salmon Fly: How to Dress It and How to Use It* (1895) and *Tips* (1901), as well as of many articles and wide correspondence. In fact the extent of his writings is still being investigated by fishing historians. With the help of Ron Coleby we have seen a run of *Land and Water* with inserted colour cards of flies. These have chromolithograph illustrations on one side and tying instructions and notes on the other. Some are similar to those in his main book, and others are less woodenly drawn in a freer artist's stylisation.

We know that Kelson was a regular correspondent to *The Field*, a contributor to the *Fishing Gazette*, though much of that material is more about how to fish than about flies, and he did write at one time for *Shooting Times*. He was an early member of the Flyfishers' Club, though little mention is made of him in their *History 1884–1934*.

1 Dunkeld

COMMENT

This is one of the relatively rare gold-bodied flies. In its simplest form it is little more than the trout pattern enlarged. We give the tying listed by Pryce-Tannatt and Jorgensen. Hale's is somewhat more simple. Our illustration shows a heavy emphasis on peacock secondary in the wing. Ephemera (Edward Fitzgibbon) noted this fly in 1850, seemingly rather yellow and heavily hackled. On the older tyings embossed gold was recommended for the body.

The other well-known gold fly in the classic style is the Sir Herbert, devised when Maxwell wished to confound his Tweed gillie.

DRESSING

Tag: Fine oval silver and light-orange floss.
Tail: Topping and jungle cock.
Butt: Black herl.
Body: Flat (or embossed) gold tinsel.
Rib: Oval gold.
Hackle: Orange, or light orange, or yellow.
Throat: Jay, or blue dyed guinea-fowl.
Wing: Scarlet, yellow and blue swan; peacock, bustard, florican, gold pheasant tail; bronze mallard; topping.
Sides: Jungle cock. **Cheeks (optional):** Chatterer. **Horns:** B. & y. macaw.

2 Green Highlander

COMMENT

This pattern seems to have started life as the Highlander of Francis Francis's recording of 1867. For a long time green has not been a popular colour for a salmon fly, so despite some use in the north of Scotland this pattern found most of its fame and success abroad – a prophet without honour in its own country. It is a bright fly and quite a contrast to many other patterns which favour black and orange. It has been adapted to tubes and Waddingtons and is even used on the lowland Tweed when autumn leaves camouflage the more usual choices of pattern.

DRESSING

Tag: Silver thread and canary floss.
Tail: Topping, pintail sprig and ibis sprig.
Butt: Black herl. **Body:** Two or three turns of yellow floss, then green seal fur. **Rib:** Silver lace (or oval) and flat silver. **Hackle:** Green, over the seal's fur. **Throat:** Yellow. **Wing:** Tippets back to back veiled with light and dark bustard, golden pheasant tail, dark mottled turkey, green swan, topping. **Sides:** Jungle cock (omitted in Hale). **Horns:** Blue and yellow macaw.

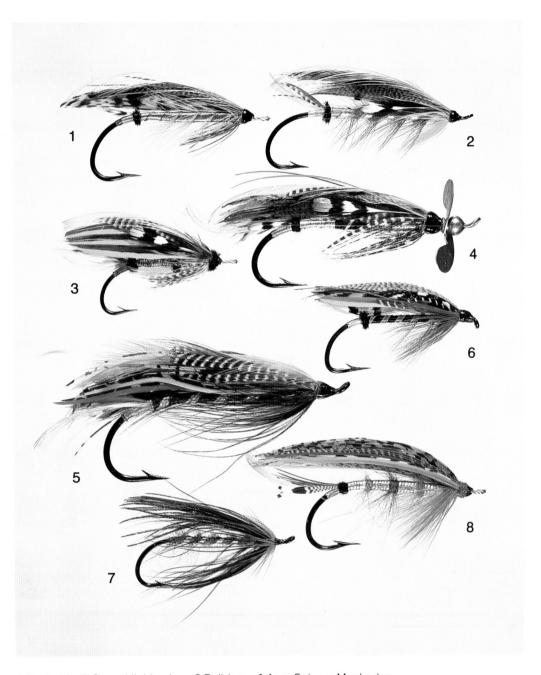

1 Dunkeld   **2** Green Highlander   **3** Bulldog   **4** Aaro Spinner Mar Lodge
5 Black Dog   **6** Black Dog   **7** Beauly Snowfly   **8** Garry Snowfly

3 Bulldog

COMMENT

Rather a handsome pattern, but, for all that, not listed in Hale, Kelson or Pryce-Tannatt. The Lonsdale Library puts it in context – a pattern designed by Strong of Carlisle before 1889, and one of the first 'gaudy' flies used on the Eden in Cumbria. It was to oust the traditional strip-wing Turkey patterns. Hardy's included it in their turn-of-the-century catalogues, even illustrating it tied in the Aaro spinner style. Sandeman had it in his list of recommended flies for Norway, and illustrated a rather dark version of it in *Angling Travels in Norway* (1895).

DRESSING

Tag: Silver thread and red-claret floss.
Tail: Topping and chatterer.
Butt: Black herl.
Body: Rear half, oval silver veiled top and bottom with toucan and butted with black herl; front half, blue floss ribbed with oval silver.
Hackle: Blue on the blue floss.
Throat: Tippet under yellow, black, yellow, black, yellow and black swan, with pintail and topping over.
Sides: Jungle cock. **Cheeks:** Chatterer.

4 Aaro Spinner Mar Lodge

COMMENT

Named after the one-time royal hunting lodge at the headwaters of the Aberdeenshire Dee, this pattern, according to Herbert Maxwell, was quite simple, and no rib was listed originally. Kelson, who attributed its invention to Lamont, affirms that it was a favourite Dee pattern, and includes Lamont's note: '1893, Her Royal Highness the Duchess of Fife has been most successful with the Mar Lodge fly. Apply to Garden, Aberdeen.'

The Aaro spinner was recommended by Hardy's for that mighty Norwegian river, and was a 20 per cent extra cost option.

DRESSING

Tag: Silver thread. **Butt:** Black herl.
Tail: Topping and two small jungle cock feathers.
Body: One-third flat silver, one-third black floss, one-third flat silver. **Rib:** Oval silver.
Throat: Guinea-fowl.
Wing: Underwing of yellow, red and blue swan; peacock wing, summer duck grey mallard, dark turkey, golden pheasant tail; bronze mallard; topping.
Sides: Jungle cock.
Horns: Blue and yellow macaw.

5 Black Dog

COMMENT

This is a traditional Tay pattern, not to be confused with Mackintosh's, shown on page 27. It is subject to so much and diverse variation that we show two examples, both with sufficient authority to merit their inclusion. This one is the most commonly found, though it has largely fallen out of use.

Hardy's tied something much like this fly as their standard, following the pattern which Kelson called an old standard of his father's, a useful high-water fly, and very good on the Spey and the Wye.

DRESSING

Tag: Silver thread and yellow floss.
Tail: Topping and ibis.
Butt: Black herl, or wool.
Body: Black floss.
Rib: A broad band made up of yellow floss flanked by oval silver.
Hackle: Black heron from the third rib.
Wing: Two orange hackles back to back, two jungle cock back to back, unbarred summer duck, light bustard, Amherst pheasant, swan dyed scarlet and yellow; two toppings.

6 Black Dog

COMMENT

If anything this is an older pattern than Kelson's. It is very similar to that of Francis Francis, yet when Forrest tied the flies for the plates in the 1920 edition of his *Book on Angling* he adopted the Kelson tying as their basis. Yet again there are variations within this second style, and the pattern described here has something of the Herbert Maxwell recipe.

DRESSING

Tag: Silver thread.
Tail: Topping.
Butt: Black herl.
Body: Black floss.
Rib: A broad band made up of red floss flanked by fine oval silver.
Throat: Long magenta cock (Maxwell specifies heron dyed crimson).
Wing: Tippet, yellow and red swan, golden pheasant tail, blue swan; grey mallard.
Sides: Swathe of guinea-fowl.

7 Beauly Snowfly

COMMENT

Richard Waddington once suggested that salmon are green/red colour-blind, that they feed on red prawns, and that flies winged with peacock herl might look somewhat prawn-like. They react to a prawn by either taking or fleeing, and Waddington observed that they react to herl-winged flies in the same way. There may be something in his theory.

   This is a long-standing pattern, with most of any variety there is in the treatment of the head: picked-out wool or mohair, even to the extent of making almost a collar of it, and using a collar hackle.

DRESSING

Tag and Tail: None.
Body: Pale-blue seal fur, dressed sparingly.
Rib: Broad flat silver and gold twist.
Hackle: Black heron from the third turn of rib, or as a throat.
Wing: Strands of peacock herl.
Head/Collar: Orange seal fur (or mohair, or a hackle collar).
(In *Halcyon* (1861) Wade calls it the Ness and Beauly Snowfly.)

8 Garry Snowfly

COMMENT

There is logic behind the design of a spring fly like this one. Many kelts or black fish may take in the spring, and their teeth play havoc with fly dressings. Damage can be minimised by the use of oval tinsel, which is strong, with seal's fur picked out at the joints to give colour instead of a hackle. (If hackles are included at the joints the fly is known as the Spirit Fly.)

   Maxwell suggest for the wing 'any fibres suitable and long enough for winging large flies, with yellow, pink and green dyed swan'. Our pattern is very close to the recipe given by Francis Francis.

DRESSING

Tag: Fine silver thread. **Tail:** Topping, summer duck and ibis. **Butt:** Black wool.
Body: Rear quarter, oval silver followed by a joint of light-blue seal fur, picked out; another quarter of oval silver, with a joint of claret seal fur; a quarter of oval silver with a joint of orange seal fur; a final quarter of oval silver and joint of yellow seal fur. **Throat:** Orange.
Wing: Underwing of sandy mottled turkey; orange and pink dyed swan, peacock secondary, red swan, bustard, green swan, and golden pheasant tail.

Classic Flies 3

Another important compiler whom we mention regularly in association with the classic patterns is J. H. Hale. The 1919 edition of his book *How to Tie Salmon Flies* is more valuable to us than the 1892 original because it enlarges the list of dressings from 40 to over 360. This was courtesy of John J. Hardy of Hardy Bros of Alnwick, who allowed him to borrow from his book *Salmon Fishing* (1907).

We don't know much about Hale. He is Major J. H. Hale (East Lancashire Regiment) on the title page of the revised second edition,

promoted by then from the Captain of the first edition.

He produced a well-organised and detailed book. Under 200 pages long, it contains excellent advice on materials and hooks, instructions on dying materials, and the massive list of dressings – and yet it measures a mere 4 inches by 6½. His system was to run the dressings across two-page spreads, with every colour and component reduced to initials or the shortest of abbreviations.

1 Dusty Miller

COMMENT

In his book *Salmon and Sea Trout in Wild Places* (1968) Sidney Spencer places this fly fifth and last in his list of special flies. He liked it best with a 'true pinky flame hackle', not the grey or the lime-green versions. For him it was *the* fly on bright days of sun or blinks of sun, when it had no equal. He used it as big as size 4/0 in Norway yet, like Herbert Maxwell, he also recommended it in the small sizes, particularly as a loch dropper.

Maxwell helped with Francis's compilation of flies for rivers and suggested this pattern for the Minnick. His pattern was rather simpler.

DRESSING

Tag: Silver twist and yellow floss.
Tail: Topping and Indian crow.
Butt: Black herl (or wool).
Body: Rear two-thirds, embossed silver; front third, orange floss. **Hackle:** Orange over the orange floss. **Throat:** Guinea-fowl.
Wing: White-tipped black turkey; teal, yellow, scarlet and orange swan, bustard, florican and golden pheasant tail; married strips of pintail and summer duck (or Amherst pheasant); brown mallard; topping.
Sides: Jungle cock.

2 Silver Grey

COMMENT

This was considered by conservative Tweed fishermen to be a 'gaudy Irish' fly, though it is attributed to the Sprouston tyer, James Wright, at about the time of the origination of the Durham Ranger and the Silver Wilkinson. It is lighter and more translucent than the Mar Lodge, yet not so bright as the Wilkinson. It has been described by some as the best small-fish imitation ever, and by others as an extremely good representation of a shrimp. Whichever, it has had tremendous success world-wide as a reliable silver pattern.

DRESSING

Tag: Silver twist and yellow floss.
Tail: Topping, unbarred summer duck and blue macaw.
Butt: Black herl.
Body: Flat silver. **Rib:** Oval silver.
Hackle: Silvery-white coch-y-bonddu.
Throat: Light wigeon.
Wing: Silver pheasant, bustard, golden pheasant tail, pintail, blue macaw, guinea-fowl, dyed yellow swan; bronze mallard; topping.
Sides: Jungle cock. **Horns:** B. & y. macaw.

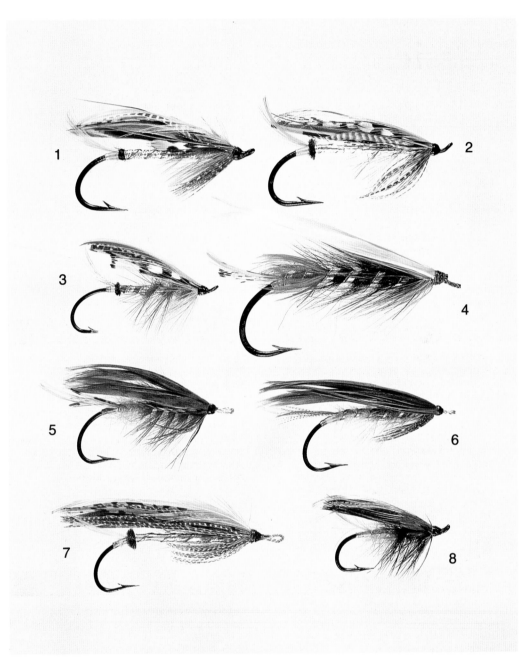

1 Dusty Miller **2** Silver Grey **3** Kate **4** White Wing
5 Claret Wasp **6** Blue Wasp **7** Sherbrook **8** Charlie

3 Kate

COMMENT

This is another of the gaudy flies which invaded the Tweed and spread. Kelson gives Mrs Courtney as the inventor, and under the name Courtney (or Daly, which was her maiden name) he also credits the following patterns: Namsen, Killarney Pet, Napoleon, Sundal Black, and Summer Duck. He notes that 'This is one of the best flies on the Tyne'. There are not that many red flies in the classic listings. Even in relatively recent years there is a feeling on some rivers that all-red flies clear a river. Lee Wulff includes such a tale in the Miscellany chapter in *The Atlantic Salmon*.

DRESSING

Tag: Fine oval silver and lemon floss.
Tail: Topping and chatterer.
Butt: Black herl.
Body: Crimson floss.
Rib: Oval silver.
Hackle: Crimson. **Throat:** Lemon.
Wing: Tippet strands, scarlet and yellow swan, golden pheasant tail, speckled bustard; teal and barred summer duck; bronze mallard over; topping.
Sides: Jungle cock.
Cheeks: Chatterer. **Horns:** B. & y. macaw.

4 White Wing

COMMENT

This is a redoubtable Tweed champion, a survival from an earlier age, and unrivalled for evening fishing – that was the opinion of Sir Herbert Maxwell, on whose pattern our illustration is based. However, from Ireland there is a contradictory claim – that white is bad at night and black is good. And that from a reverend. He was Henry Newland, who wrote *The Erne, its Legends and its Fly Fishing*.

More modern fishers would side with Maxwell. In 1958 Balfour-Kinnear was still recommending the White Wing for the time when the light begins to fade in the evening.

DRESSING

Tag: Fine oval silver.
Tail: Topping and tippet strands.
Body: Rear third, red, veiled with red ibis; front two-thirds, black, or dark blue (or equal segments of yellow, orange, claret and black seal fur).
Rib: Broad flat silver and silver twist.
Hackle: Black.
Throat: Blue.
Wing: Strips of white swan set horizontally.

5 Claret Wasp

COMMENT

Kelson attributed this pattern to Malloch, of the noted tackle shop in Perth. He recorded that it was a real favourite on the Earn, and popular on many other Scottish rivers. Hale gives the same dressing; Pryce-Tannatt does not have it. We feel that this is a transitional pattern – the last gasp of the horizontal strip wing just before all the complexities start to creep in, as indicated by the next pattern.

DRESSING

Tag: Silver twist and yellow floss.
Tail: Topping, summer duck (or wigeon) and ibis.
Body: Rear half, yellow; front half, claret seal fur.
Rib: Oval silver.
Hackle: Claret over the front half.
Throat: Jay, or dyed blue guinea-fowl.
Wing: Strips of cinnamon turkey, set horizontally.

6 Blue Wasp

COMMENT

Small details in this pattern differ among the compilers: Kelso and Hale omit the tag, and Pryce-Tannatt restricts it to the silver twist without the floss. The rib may be fine oval over the yellow and flat over the blue, or oval over both. The throat is lemon hackle with Pryce-Tannatt. Kelson and Hale offer sides.

The difficulty of obtaining turkey with white tips soon meant that plain turkey had to be used, and Pryce-Tannatt suggests that it should be set vertically. This fly is also recommended for the Earn, which Kelson asserts is a 'blue' river.

DRESSING

Tag: Silver twist and yellow floss (or none).
Tail: Topping, summer duck and ibis (or topping and strands of golden pheasant breast feather).
Body: Rear half yellow, front half light-blue seal fur.
Rib: Silver (oval or flat as described in text).
Hackle: Light-blue over the front half.
Throat: Guinea-fowl.
Wing: Cinnamon turkey with white tips and (optional) topping.
Sides: Summer duck (Kelson and Hale).

7 Sherbrook

COMMENT

Here is much the same colour scheme as the preceding fly, but the complexity has increased even further. This is Hale's pattern; Pryce-Tannatt includes even more material in the wing. Kelson said of it: 'A general standard in summer on the Dee, and a great favourite at Braemar.'

It was steadily in the tackle catalogues, occasionally illustrated with the Aaro spinner, or within the range of Ernest Crosfield's summer doubles series in Farlow's catalogues of the 1930s.

DRESSING

Tag: Silver twist and yellow floss.
Tail: Topping.
Butt: Black herl.
Body: Rear third, yellow floss; front two-thirds, light-blue floss.
Rib: Oval silver and flat silver.
Hackle: Light blue over the blue floss.
Throat: Wigeon.
Wing: Bustard, dark mottled turkey, golden pheasant tail and topping.
Horns: Scarlet ibis, or swan, or macaw.

8 Charlie

COMMENT

The theme of a black-and-yellow body recurs frequently. This was regarded as a sombre fly by Kelson, and thus useful as a foil to more showy patterns. He attributes its origination to Captain Dundas. A very similar fly is shown in Stoddart's *Angler's Companion*.

'Mr George Whitehead on the Tees in 1878 put on a cast with a Silver Doctor on the dropper and a Charlie on the tail. First time down the pool gave him five fish out of six hooked on the tail. He replaced the dropper with another Charlie and finished his day with 16 fish on the pattern, from 5½ to 22 pounds': Grimble.

DRESSING

Tag: Silver twist and light-yellow floss.
Tail: Topping.
Body: Rear half yellow, front half black seal fur.
Rib: Oval silver.
Hackle: Black over the black fur.
Throat: Jay or dyed blue guinea-fowl.
Wing: Tippet fibres, golden pheasant tail, teal; dark mottled turkey, bustard, wigeon, peacock wing, yellow, red and light-blue swan; mallard.
Cheeks: Chatterer.

Classic Flies 4

One personality not of the Victorian or Edwardian era is none the less extremely important in the compiling and recording of salmon flies. He is the late Joseph Bates Junior, whose love of Atlantic salmon fishing and salmon flies has made him the foremost of modern historians and researchers in this field. He has co-operated in our venture by allowing us to quote freely from his excellent *Atlantic Salmon Flies and Fishing* and his incomparable *The Art of the Atlantic Salmon Fly*, of 1970 and 1987 respectively. Not only did he look out the most recherché details in the development of the salmon fly on both sides of the Atlantic, he also put modern tyings from all sources on an authoritative footing. The modern student of the salmon fly will find both his volumes indispensable.

Sadly, as we go to press, we must record his death in late 1988.

1 Nicholson

COMMENT

This is one of the splendid hotchpotch flies from the Tay, where the style and character are determined but the ingredients are somewhat random. Earl Hodgson uses it to demonstrate the wide range of sizes in which a salmon fly is tied – from 4 inches, his Nicholson, down to a Dusty Miller of ⅝ inch. A plate rounds off his Model Collection of 72 patterns which he illustrates but omits the tyings. Wing and hackling resemble that other Tay pattern, the Black Dog. John Ashley-Cooper includes an illustration of it in *The Great Salmon Rivers of Scotland* without tracing its history and origin.

DRESSING

Tag: Silver twist. **Tail:** Topping, ibis and summer duck. **Butt:** Black herl. **Body:** In four sections – the rearmost and the next are the same: half red and half black floss, ribbed fine oval silver and flat silver equally separated; the next section is red floss, ribbed as above; the front is yellow floss, ribbed as above; each section butted with black herl and a wound turn of jay. **Throat:** Yellow under orange under very long black heron. **Wing:** Golden pheasant sword enveloped by jungle cock back to back; red, orange, blue and yellow swan; green peacock herl, pintail; topping. **Sides:** Jungle cock. **Horns:** Red macaw.

2 Sir Richard

COMMENT

On first impression this fly looks much like a Black Doctor, but does not have the Doctors' distinguishing mark of a red butt and head. In one of the fishing cottages on the banks of the Northumberland Tyne there is a carved wooden half-model salmon, recording and representing the capture of a thirty-nine pounder on 24 November 1885 from Sprouston Dub on the Tweed by Captain R. Waldie Griffith. It was part of a catch of 13 fish totalling 237 pounds, and the fly was a size 12 Sir Richard.

DRESSING

Tag: Silver twist and yellow floss.
Tail: Topping and Indian crow.
Butt: Black herl.
Body: Black floss.
Rib: Oval silver.
Hackle: None, or black cock, or black heron.
Throat: Guinea-fowl under blue jay.
Wing: Dark mottled turkey, red, yellow and blue swan, peacock wing, golden pheasant tail; mallard; topping.
Cheeks: Chatterer.
Horns: Blue and yellow macaw.

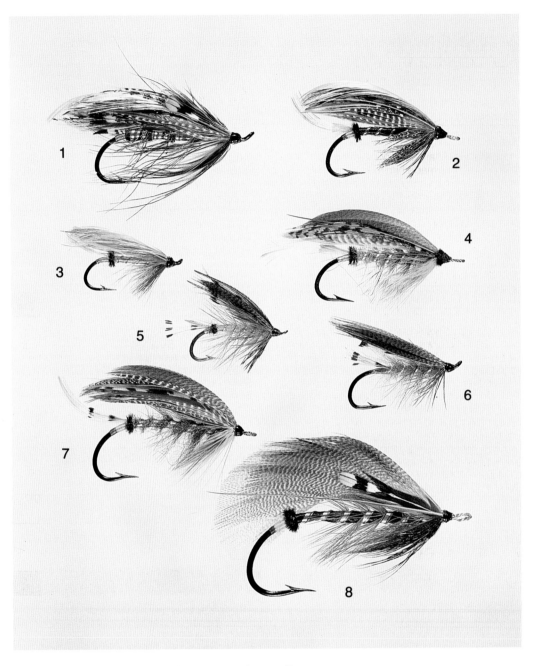

1 Nicholson   **2** Sir Richard   **3** Goldfinch   **4** Lemon Grey
5 McGildowney   **6** Golden Olive   **7** Lee Blue   **8** Thunder & Lightning

3 Goldfinch

COMMENT

This pattern is a fairly faithful following of Rogan's original dressing. Variations of detail do, however, abound: some have jay throats, some wings entirely of toppings; a gold tinsel body is also sometimes found. Cornelius O'Gorman's dressing had the toppings of the wing facing inwards so that the tips cross.

This dressing and the following flies on this plate all originate in Ireland.

DRESSING

Tag: Silver twist and yellow floss.
Tail: Topping.
Butt: Black herl.
Body: Yellow floss.
Rib: Oval silver.
Hackle: Pale yellow.
Throat: Claret.
Wings: Vertical strips of yellow swan, and two or three toppings (or entirely of toppings).
Cheeks: Chatterer, or kingfisher.
Horns: Red macaw.

4 Lemon Grey

COMMENT

A hunt through all the usual compilers of Irish flies has come up with no consistent dressing. Malone offers three alternatives, Kelson and Hale are in reasonable accord, but Pryce-Tannatt has differences. There was always a feeling that the Irish tyers put in variations to please their customers, and in any case each locality had a slightly different tying of a standard. It was Sidney Spencer's favourite for misty conditions. He felt that low-lying mist kept down fish like no other condition. He discovered the fly in Donegal in the early 1930s.

DRESSING

Tag: Silver twist and yellow floss.
Tail: Topping.
Butt: Black herl.
Body: Silver monkey, or seal fur, or donkey.
Rib: Silver.
Hackle: Irish grey.
Throat: Yellow (or claret under yellow, according to Kelson's father's notes).
Wing: Tippet strands, teal, guinea-fowl; mallard; (optional) topping.

5 McGildowney

COMMENT

When we were invited to go to fish the River Bush in County Antrim, we wondered which would be suitable flies. Francis Francis's book came to our help with the four patterns he quoted. The originals were made for him by Wm Doherty and Son, fly tyers of Bushmill. Unfortunately, the way Francis recorded his patterns is often ambiguous. The fly illustrated is therefore a reasoned interpretation. On the complex tyings Francis becomes almost unintelligible, and this is why we tend not to refer to him for early authentic dressings.

DRESSING

Tag: Silver twist and light-orange floss.
Tail: Strands of tippet and blue macaw.
Butt: Peacock herl.
Body: Two turns of light-orange floss and yellow mohair.
Hackle: Dirty medium-brick-dust red over the mohair.
Throat: Jay.
Wing: Mixed bustard, mallard, tippet and peacock (tied in the order: tippet, bustard, peacock, with mallard over).

6 Golden Olive

COMMENT

Irish flies can be confusing. There are *eight* dressings of this name in Malone, including one also known as the Violet Olive and another also known as the Butterman. What's more, in *Sport in Ireland* by S. B. Wilkinson (1931 and 1987) a Golden Olive is the name given to a fair measure of a home-made ginger and whiskey liqueur to be taken on cold fishing days in that country.

The main variations are found in the winging – how many and how bright the fibres beneath the mallard overwinging. Normally Irish flies of this character do not have a topping over the wing; nowadays a topping *is* thought worth including.

DRESSING

Tag: Silver wire and orange floss.
Tail: Topping and tippet.
Body: Golden-olive seal fur.
Rib: Oval silver (or gold).
Hackle: Natural blood-red cock (or natural red).
Throat (optional): Jay.
Wing: Tippet, with bronze mallard over.

7 Lee Blue

COMMENT

The Lee is a river in southern Ireland flowing into the sea at Cork Harbour. Grimble suggested the following patterns for this river: Blue & Yellow or the Lee Blue, Grey & Yellow or Yellow Anthony, Grey & Brown, Claret Palmer, and so on. He gave the dressings of the four best, which included the Lee Blue. He took his dressing from William Haynes of Patrick Street, Cork. The Lee patterns were also recommended for the Bandon, which is the next river to the south and west.

DRESSING

Tag: Silver twist and yellow floss.
Tail: Topping and tippet strands.
Butt: Black herl.
Body: Light-blue seal fur.
Hackle: Light blue (or medium blue).
Throat: Lemon yellow.
Wing: Dark mottled turkey, bustard, yellow, claret and blue swan, peacock wing; teal and mallard.

8 Thunder & Lightning

COMMENT

Francis Francis suggests Pat Hearns of Ireland for the origination, while other authors attribute it to James Wright of Sprouston. It is a simple classic which is still in use as a featherwing, though widely adapted as well to tubes, Waddingtons and other styles in modern materials. Its reputation has always stood high as the fly to use as the water is clearing and falling after a rise in water.

It suffers a usual problem; that its 'proper' winging ingredients are not long enough in the fibre for really large sizes, so dark turkey is often used. The tyer here used whole feathers.

DRESSING

Tag: Gold twist and yellow floss.
Tail: Topping and Indian crow.
Butt: Black herl.
Body: Black floss.
Rib: Fine oval gold and flat gold.
Hackle: Orange.
Throat: Jay in small sizes, dyed blue guinea-fowl in large sizes.
Wing: Bronze mallard strips set vertically (or brown turkey); topping.
Sides: Jungle cock.
Horns: Blue and yellow macaw.

Badminton Library 1

This plate and the following contain patterns from a leather and vellum wallet of flies tied according to instructions in the Badminton Library *Salmon and Trout* volume published in 1885. Major John P. Traherne was invited to write the section entitled 'Salmon Fishing with the Fly'. In turn he applied to Kelson for the dressing of the patterns and some appended notes.

The hooks are stylised. They are eyed, rather than gut-looped. They are Limerick in the bend and incorporate the Cholmondeley-Pennell design of having the shank slightly upturned at the eye so that the centre of the down-turned eye would be in line with the body, rather than below it. The set of 21 includes the Jock Scott, the Silver Grey, Childers, and the Claret Jay.

The fly wallet, under the name of Chas Farlow & Co, 191 the Strand, London, W C, was sold as 'The Badminton Fly Book containing the entire Set of Flies recommended by H. G. The Duke of Beaufort, and Major Traherne, in the Badminton Library'.

The flyleaf gives hook sizes from 7/0 to size 7.

1 Durham Ranger

COMMENT

This appears to be the earliest pattern to include jungle cock. Its birth date is traceable to 20 February, 1846, when on its first cast into Cauld Slap the line tightened into a 30½ pounder. Mr Scruton, the inventor, was one of a regular party from Durham and Leeds to the Tweed at Coldstream. A whole series of Rangers was developed by James Wright – Black, Silver, Blue, Red and Orange. The end of the jungle cock must align with the extremity of the bend, the end of the first tippets with the butt, and the end of the second tippets with the first bar of the first tippets.

DRESSING

Tag: Silver twist and yellow floss. **Tail:** Topping and Indian crow. **Butt:** Black herl. **Body:** Two turns of orange floss followed by two turns of dark-orange seal fur, with the remainder black seal fur. **Rib:** Silver lace and flat silver. **Hackle:** Orange over the seal fur (or badger dyed orange). **Throat:** Light-blue. **Wing:** Long jungle cock back to back enveloped by two tippets back to back, enveloped by another two tippets back to back, as described. **Sides (optional):** Jungle cock. **Cheeks:** Chatterer. **Horns:** B. & y. macaw.

2 Butcher

COMMENT

This is a totally different pattern from the trout fly of the same name. Kelson attributes it to John Jewhurst of Tunbridge: 'So superior in outline, in constituent materials, in style and character was this happy creation, that henceforth his built wings made a regular commotion in the angling world, besides a reputation for themselves which can never die out.' Until 1838 it was called the Moon Fly.

For the fly to look well Kelson considered that the tippet underwing should be veiled by the other winging materials; they should not be bundled in a confused mass on top.

DRESSING

Tag: Silver twist and yellow floss. **Tail:** Topping, teal and blue macaw. **Butt:** Black herl. **Body:** Quarter red, quarter blue, quarter claret and quarter blue seal fur. **Rib:** Flat silver. **Hackle:** Black over the front half of the body. **Throat:** Yellow under guinea-fowl. **Wing:** Tippet and golden pheasant breast feather, turkey, golden pheasant tail, guinea-fowl, bustard, peacock wing, parrot, yellow swan, macaw. **Cheeks:** Chatterer. **Horns:** B. & y. macaw.

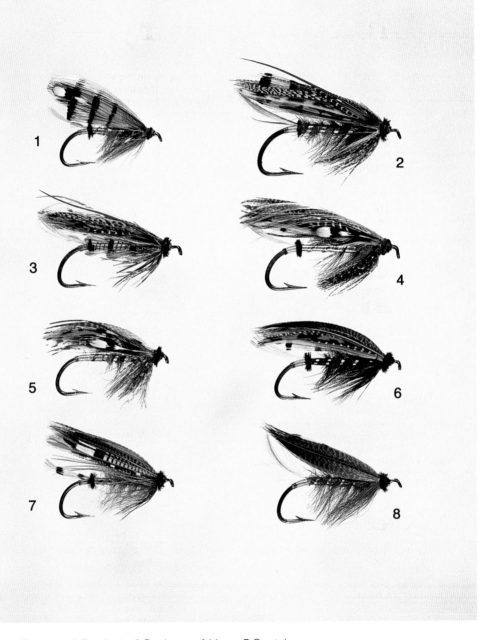

1 Durham Ranger **2** Butcher **3** Popham **4** Lion **5** Captain
6 Black Jay **7** Dirty Orange **8** Fiery Brown

3 Popham

COMMENT

This may be famous as a classic pattern but it has failings: the cost and difficulty of veiling it with Indian crow, the complexity of tying it (which made it unpopular with Francis Francis, though he gave credit to its killing properties 'on two or three rivers in the North, Ness and Brora and occasionally elsewhere') and its lack of balance in having such a weak throat hackle under so full a wing. Kelson attributed it to F. L. Popham and considered it 'a very useful old standard pattern'.

DRESSING

Tag: Silver twist. **Tail:** Topping and Indian crow. **Butt:** Black herl. **Body:** Rear ⅓ orange, middle ⅓ lemon yellow and front ⅓ pale-blue floss, butted with black herl and veiled above and below with Indian crow. **Rib:** Fine oval gold over the rear ⅔; fine oval silver over the front ⅓. **Throat:** Jay. **Wing:** Tippet in strands, bustard, florican, peacock wing, scarlet, blue, orange and yellow swan, golden pheasant tail; two or three toppings. **Sides (optional):** Summer duck (in Pryce-Tannatt). **Cheeks:** Chatterer. **Horns:** B. & y. macaw.

4 Lion

COMMENT

As the Dunkeld salmon fly is to the Dunkeld trout fly, so is the Lion to the Peter Ross, the silver and red being very similar, and the wing being much augmented. Among some fishermen it was a pattern on a par with the Silver Grey, possibly being even more attractive when the water was a little stained. 'In the event, however, of one or two downright refusals, the jungle . . . should be snipped off,' said Kelson. Hale's pattern is similar, but Pryce-Tannatt omits it. With bright jungle cock it was recommended for the Tay, Tweed, Lyon, Spey, and Lochy; with dull jungle cock for the Usk, Findhorn and Erne.

DRESSING

Tag: Silver twist and yellow silk. **Tail:** Topping. **Butt:** Black herl. **Body:** Rear ⅘ flat silver; front ⅕, scarlet seal fur. **Rib:** Oval silver. **Hackle:** Natural black from three parts down the body. **Throat:** Guinea-fowl. **Wing:** Strands of tippet, golden pheasant sword and peacock herl; yellow and red macaw, bustard, golden pheasant tail, teal, guinea-fowl; mallard; topping. **Sides:** Jungle cock. **Horns:** B. & y. macaw.

5 Captain

COMMENT

This fly is known under any of these names: Captain, Captain Poynder, or Poynder (or Poinder). Kelson considers it one of his own patterns introduced by Bernard to Scotland, where it is erroneously called the Poynder. He recommends it as a good general pattern – an alternative for the Durham Ranger. It can be tied very small for lakes and shallow streams. Hale lists it as the Captain, and Pryce-Tannatt omits it.

Only two examples were left in the wallet; sadly, the one illustrated, the better of the two, has had its tail ravaged by a moth.

DRESSING

Tag: Silver twist and light-blue floss. **Tail:** Topping and chatterer. **Butt:** None. **Body:** Two turns of light-orange floss; two turns of dark-orange, two turns of dark-red-claret, and the remainder dark-blue seal fur. **Rib:** Flat silver. **Hackle:** Badger dyed light-red-claret over the seal fur. **Throat:** Blue hackle under guinea-fowl. **Wing:** Pintail, teal, guinea-fowl, peacock wing, Amherst pheasant, bustard and golden pheasant tail; light-orange, dark-orange, dark claret and dark-blue swan; mallard; topping. **Sides:** Jungle cock. **Horns:** B. & y. macaw.

6 Black Jay

COMMENT

'Unlike the rest of the Jays it will be found most useful in dark water. Introduced for me by Farlow' – thus Kelson. His Claret Jay shares the body style, but in claret, and has sides of ibis married to yellow macaw. Topping is added in the large sizes, as are jungle cock sides.

DRESSING

Tag: Silver twist and dark-yellow floss.
Tail: Topping.
Butt: Black herl.
Body: Two turns of black floss, with the remainder black seal fur.
Rib: Flat silver (with lace in large patterns).
Hackle: Natural black over the black fur.
Throat: Jay.
Wing: Strands of tippet, ibis and guinea-fowl; bustard, golden pheasant tail, black cockatoo tail, green and yellow swan; mallard. **Horns:** B. & y. macaw.

7 Dirty Orange

COMMENT

A quietly dressed and well-established Jay. Kelson claimed in 1895 that it was introduced for him by Farlow 'many years since'. Hale's pattern is faithful to Kelson's.

DRESSING

Tag: Gold twist and light-blue floss.
Tail: Topping and tippet. **Butt:** Black herl.
Body: Two turns of light-orange floss, the remainder light dirty orange seal fur.
Rib: Flat gold. **Hackle:** Light dirty orange over the seal fur. **Throat:** Jay.
Wing: Ginger turkey, guinea-fowl and strands of golden pheasant breast feather; bustard, peacock herl, golden pheasant tail, white-tipped black turkey, red macaw, dirty orange and dark blue swan; mallard over.
Sides: Summer duck. **Horns:** Blue macaw.

8 Fiery Brown

COMMENT

There are wonderful stories about trying to find the 'real' fiery brown which has a reputation for being the most taking of colours. It is a sort of search for the Holy Grail. It should have a vivid flame to it. The Irish have always had a name for dying seal fur in the most lustrous shades, with the Rogans of Ballyshannon being considered the masters of the art. The firm still exists and still has this high reputation.

Malone has three tyings under this name. Hale has this simple tying.

DRESSING

Tag: Gold twist and light-orange floss.
Tail: Topping.
Butt: None.
Body: Fiery brown seal fur.
Hackle: Fiery brown.
Throat: Fiery brown.
Wing: Tippet strands under broad bronze mallard.
Horns: Blue and yellow macaw.

Badminton Library 2

Who was the Major Traherne who was entrusted with the salmon section? Cholmondeley-Pennell, who edited the Badminton Library fishing volumes, introduces him: 'A safer pilot through the shoals and quicksands of the art than Major Traherne, or a more experienced and practical exponent of its mysteries, cannot be found within the "three seas that girth Britain".'

Traherne claimed thirty years' experience in 1885, in England, Scotland, Ireland and Norway. Footnotes refer to his visits to Canada – to the Natasquam and the Restigouche. He wrote *The Habits of the Salmon* in 1889.

Like Kelson, he mentioned how to mend a line to slow the pace of the fly, but fishermen seem to have waited for A. H. E. Wood before the significance of mending dawned on them.

The choice of flies for the Badminton Library is fairly conservative, though Traherne was in fact an inventor of extremely bright and gaudy patterns with the most exotic of components – Gitana, Quinchat, Juno, Black Prince, Bluebell, Blue Boyne, Chatterer, Fra Diavolo, and others.

His relationship with his contemporary Kelson seems mixed; sometimes he was praised; sometimes Kelson was a severe critic.

1 Spring Grub

COMMENT

Originally wingless flies like caterpillars, the grubs developed into the shrimp and prawn patterns, and other dressings are included in that section. This fly is included in most of the compilers, with the only marked variation coming in the choice of material for the centre hackle, either natural blue or the blue hackle from the vulturine guinea-fowl, which is a bright cerulean blue.

DRESSING

Tag: Silver twist and light-blue floss.
Tail: Ibis and blue macaw.
Tail hackle: Furnace hackle dyed orange.
Body: Yellow floss ribbed with black chenille, followed by a natural blue (or blue vulturine hackle); front half, black floss ribbed with oval silver.
Head hackles: Natural coch-y-bonddu under guinea-fowl dyed orange.

2 Beaufort Moth

COMMENT

The Dukes of Beaufort have long been extensive landowners, with stretches of the Severn and Wye in their domains. Little wonder that many of them have been keen fishermen. The eighth Duke had six recommendations to add to the list. His Moth he considered very taking during the last hours of daylight 'if the fish are shy'; it was put to wide use on rivers in England, Scotland, Wales, Canada and Labrador.

The pattern looks much like an enlarged Coachman for trout.

DRESSING

Tag: Flat gold.
Tail: Topping.
Body: Bronze peacock herl.
Rib: Flat gold.
Throat: Natural red hackle.
Wing: Two small white hen feathers.

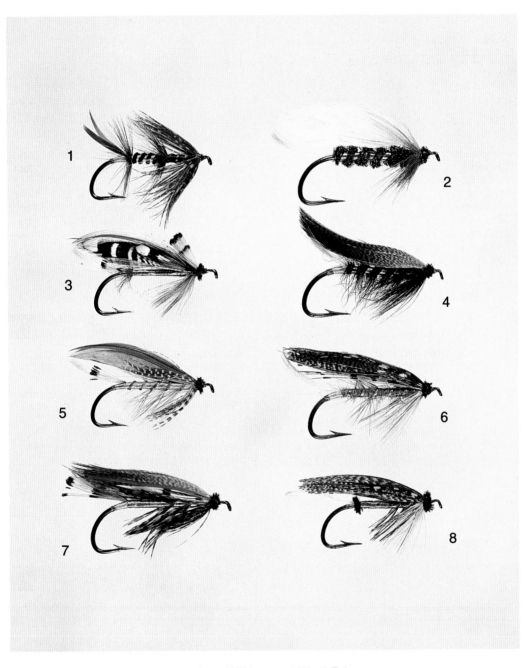

1 Spring Grub **2** Beaufort Moth **3** Silver Wilkinson **4** Black Fairy
5 Critchley's Fancy **6** Lemon-Tipped Grey Monkey **7** Green Grouse
8 Blue Jay

3 Silver Wilkinson

COMMENT

To the conservatives used to Turkeys and strip wings this was a 'gaudy Irish' fly. It was formerly called the Silver Belle, then rechristened after its inventor, the Rev. P. S. Wilkinson, who was a regular visitor to the Tweed at Coldstream and patronised James Wright. Its history is outlined in Henderson's *My Life As an Angler* (1876); it was certainly one of the earliest all-tinsel-bodied flies.

We give the dressing as illustrated, which is rendered accurately by Hale, and in brackets we give the wing for the Wilkinson, which is often listed separately.

DRESSING

Tag: Flat silver.
Tail: Topping and short tippet strands.
Butt: Scarlet wool. **Body:** Flat silver.
Throat: Blue under magenta (Herbert Maxwell disapproved of the blue).
Wing: Two jungle cock, back to back, veiled with summer duck and red swan; topping; small tippet over topping. (Tippet, teal, peacock wing, golden pheasant tail, red, yellow and blue swan, mallard; topping).
Sides: Jungle cock.
Cheeks: Chatterer. **Horns:** B. & y. macaw.

4 Black Fairy

COMMENT

The Eighth Duke commented: 'I prefer it on a dark day; other people fancy it on a bright one' – which is a delightful expression of how subjective the choice of a fly might be.

It is an extremely simple pattern, but it does show a style feature: the wings are vertical strips of mallard which sweep upwards at the extremity of the fibres. This is correct for the Irish patterns and similar flies, but not correct for Spey flies, which have their wings curving downwards. This difference in style is merely a matter of using fibres from the right or the left side of the feather to achieve the sweep wanted.

DRESSING

Tag: Gold twist and yellow floss.
Tail: Topping.
Body: Black wool (or seal fur).
Rib: Flat gold.
Throat: Black cock hackle.
Wing: Vertical strips of bronze mallard.

5 Critchley's Fancy

COMMENT

In our own experience, which is supported by a reasonably wide search through salmon fishing literature, there do seem to be times when a particular pattern or colour is exclusively successful. One fisherman seems to be taking all the fish; when he lends his fly the borrower is the only one taking fish – until the fly is lost or worn out. The Duke was given this pattern by Mr Critchley, who alone succeeded on the Restigouche in Canada in June and July 1879.

DRESSING

Tag: Silver twist and pale-blue floss.
Tail: Topping and tippet fibres.
Butt: None.
Body: Light-orange floss.
Rib: Silver lace.
Hackle: Reddish orange.
Throat: Teal.
Wing: Vertical strips of cinnamon turkey with teal and red macaw each side.
Horns: Blue and yellow macaw.

6 Lemon-Tipped Grey Monkey

COMMENT

The Duke found it 'a very useful fly. When there is not sun enough to make the Silver Grey sparkle, this pattern is often very killing.' It is very much in the Irish mould, with fur body and strands under a mallard wing, typically without a topping. Equally typically, there is little constancy in the dressings given by the various writers.

DRESSING

Tag: Silver twist and yellow floss.
Tail: Topping.
Body: Grey monkey fur.
Rib: Oval silver.
Hackle: Green olive.
Throat: Yellow.
Wing: Mallard, tippet, golden pheasant tail, bustard, guinea-fowl and green parrot.
Horns: Blue and yellow macaw.

7 Green Grouse

COMMENT

Hale and the Badminton Library are in agreement on this one; Pryce-Tannatt gives a more involved wing with golden pheasant tail and florican added. Francis Francis uses grey mallard and not the more usual brown. A style note comes from 'Hi-Regan' (J. J. Dunne) in his editions of *How and Where to fish in Ireland*: 'the grouse fibres should be trimmed beneath the shank: without this peculiarity these (there) universal flies fail.'

The Badminton Library note is: 'one of the best flies for the Blackwater, Cy Cork, Ireland'.

DRESSING

Tag: Silver twist and medium-orange floss.
Tail: Tippet with fibres of magenta and blue swan.
Body: Light-green floss.
Rib: Flat silver.
Hackle: Grouse.
Throat: Jay.
Wing: Silver pheasant, brown mallard, red macaw, tippet.

8 Blue Jay

COMMENT

Some of the Irish patterns were *bona fide* Jays, like the Blue, the Black and the Claret. Other patterns had jay included either as a body hackle or as an extra or substitute throat. We therefore meet an occasional Jay Butcher or Jay Wilkinson, or even a Jay Jock Scott. Flies with jay in them were strongly recommended for the rivers in the south of Southern Ireland.

DRESSING

Tag: Flat silver.
Tail: Topping.
Butt: Black herl.
Body: Medium-blue floss.
Rib: Flat silver.
Hackle: Jay over the front half of the body.
Throat: Yellow.
Wing: Bustard, tippet, green parrot, purple swan, guinea-fowl.

Doctors

The Doctors are some of the best-known and most widely successful of the complicated featherwing classics. There seems no clear date for the invention of the first, which was the Blue Doctor, but it can be traced in embryo to the early part of the last century; the others followed, the Silver no doubt because the success of similar patterns such as the Silver Grey and the Silver Wilkinson was so apparent. James Wright is said to have had a hand in the development of the Black Doctor fly as well.

For some writers Doctors were gaudy Irish flies and newfangled. Stoddart only gave the one Doctor, as did Francis Francis, and they agreed in giving the body as blue floss.

Donald Overfield gives the Kelson dressing in his chapter on James Wright, yet he illustrates a tying with jungle!

The flies in the plate illustrate the changes that were to overtake the classic flies. Their rigid stylistic format was modified first to encompass developments like greased-line fishing, and then after 1950, and in a rapidly accelerating surge, they were converted to the hairwing style, most certainly quicker and easier and cheaper to tie, and thought to be far better takers of fish.

1 Silver Doctor

COMMENT

This pattern is now well and truly universal both as a salmon fly and for other game fish. It is tied simplified for trout wet flies, and strong and heavy for steelhead; it is also tied dry for trout and sea trout. Some tyings suggest a blue body hackle; this is a defect, since the teeth of the fish play havoc with it. The tendency now is to put the blue hackle in as the first of the two throat hackles. We feel that light materials should be chosen as this is lightest in tone of the three most regular patterns.

DRESSING

Tag: Silver twist and yellow floss.
Tail: Topping and chatterer.
Butt: Scarlet wool.
Body: Flat silver.
Rib: Oval silver.
Hackle: None.
Throat: Pale-blue under wigeon.
Wing: Tippet, summer duck, pintail, golden pheasant tail, light-yellow and light-blue swan, bustard; mallard and topping.
Horns: Blue and yellow macaw.
Head: Red.

2 Hairwing Silver Doctor

COMMENT

There are no established hairwing variations on the classics. Modern books suggest suitable dressings, usually having acquainted the reader with a featherwing tying.

We might use oval instead of flat tinsel for the body (the effect is little different, but it is easier to tie oval, and oval is stronger) and replace all the wing materials with hair equivalents. But we have grounds for believing that a topping possesses a valuable quality, so we might keep a topping over even a hairwing.

DRESSING

Tag: Silver twist and yellow floss.
Tail: Topping and strands of blue hackle.
Butt: Red wool.
Body: Oval silver.
Rib: Oval silver.
Throat: Pale-blue under wigeon.
Wing: A small amount each of yellow, scarlet, and blue plain dyed hair, with grey squirrel or silver baboon over, and a topping over that.
Head: Red.

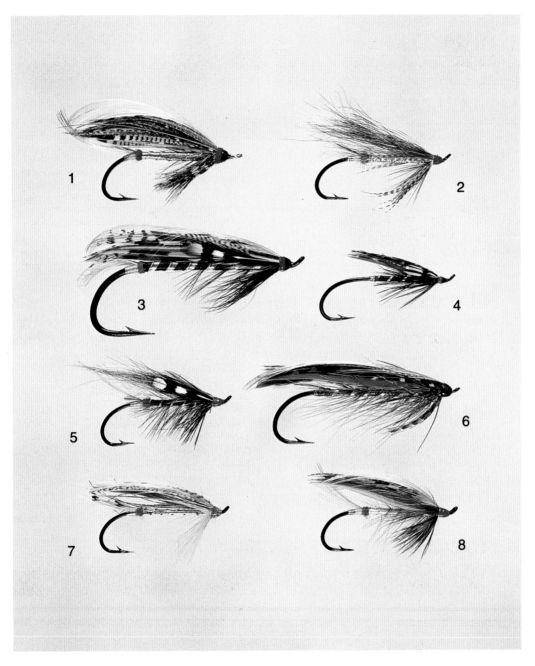

1 Silver Doctor **2** Hairwing Silver Doctor **3** Black Doctor
4 Low-Water Black Doctor **5** Hairwing Black Doctor **6** Blue Doctor
7 Helmsdale Doctor **8** White Doctor

3 Black Doctor

COMMENT

Read your way through Hardy and Farlow catalogues of before the Second World War and you will hardly find a salmon-fishing country for which this fly is not recommended. Dark flies are good, red is good, blue is good – this fly has a bit of everything, so it must be good.

None of the early Doctors included sides of jungle cock. Kelson did not specify it, nor did Pryce-Tannatt, though Hale did in 1919. As we know, this compilation was 'borrowed' from Hardy's, so it may have been that firm which brought in the distinctive sides.

DRESSING

Tag: Silver twist and yellow floss. **Tail:** Topping and Indian crow. **Butt:** Scarlet wool. **Body:** Black floss. **Rib:** Oval silver. **Hackle:** Black (Kelson specifies blue). **Throat:** Jay (dyed blue guinea-fowl in large sizes). **Wing:** Tippet in strands, pintail, dark mottled turkey, blue and yellow swan, red macaw, guinea fowl, golden pheasant tail; bronze mallard; topping. **Sides (optional):** Jungle cock. **Cheeks:** Chatterer. **Horns:** B. & y. macaw. **Head:** Red.

4 Low-Water Black Doctor

COMMENT

Greased-line fishing and the style of flies which were tied to suit it are considered in detail in the section on 'Development'. Since the river on which it all started was the Dee, initially all the known Dee flies which already had a good reputation as summer flies were used. But there was no reason to exclude all the old fully dressed favourites, if they could be tied sufficiently slimly. This tying has most of the characteristics of the Black Doctor, yet is a more lively and slender creation, and dressed short in accord with the requirements of the fishing style.

DRESSING

Hook: Light-wire, long-shank. **Tag:** Silver twist. **Tail (optional):** Topping. **Butt:** Red wool. **Body:** Black floss. **Rib:** Oval silver. **Hackle:** Black, over the front half of the body. **Throat:** Tied as a beard (or omitted), strands of jay or dyed blue guinea-fowl. **Wing:** Red and blue swan, bustard, dark turkey, bronze mallard topping (a single strand of each of the feathers with its pair for the far wing); topping. **Sides:** Jungle cock. **Head:** Red.

5 Hairwing Black Doctor

COMMENT

The fly-tying suppliers have varied and interesting stocks of suitable hairs for winging. Grey squirrel, natural or dyed so that the barring is still evident, is extremely useful and, in terms of the conservation of wild life, sensible to use. It is also available plain-dyed, which means that the barring has been bleached out before dying. Since the Black Doctor is the darkest of the three major patterns, we have looked to make the wing quite dark.

DRESSING

Tag: Silver twist and yellow floss. **Tail:** Topping and Indian crow (or substitute). **Butt:** Red wool. **Body:** Black floss. **Rib:** Oval silver. **Hackle:** Black. **Throat:** Jay (dyed blue guinea-fowl in larger sizes). **Wing:** Small amount of yellow, red and blue plain-dyed hair, a small amount of barred grey squirrel, red squirrel; topping. **Sides:** Jungle cock. **Head:** Red.

6 Blue Doctor

COMMENT

Hale and Kelson give a similar dressing, the latter suggesting it as one of the early fancy patterns on the Tweed, and well-known on all rivers. On the Helmsdale it was thought no use at all, according to Grimble, though he wrote well of it for the Inver, the Awe (with variation), the Shin, the Lyon and of course the Tweed.

DRESSING

Tag: Silver twist and yellow floss.
Tail: Topping and chatterer.
Butt: Scarlet wool.
Body: Pale-blue floss. **Rib:** Oval silver.
Hackle: Pale-blue.
Throat: Jay (or dyed blue guinea-fowl).
Wing: Tippet strands, guinea-fowl, golden pheasant tail, light mottled turkey, pintail, yellow and light blue swan, ibis, mallard; topping.
Cheeks: Chatterer. **Horns:** B. & y. macaw.
Head: Red.

7 Helmsdale Doctor

COMMENT

The Helmsdale has quite a number of yellow patterns, particularly the Torrish and the Pale Torrish (also known as the Salscraggie). Both seem better balanced flies, with their central joint, than this dressing.

Pryce-Tannatt breaks away from his tradition of giving all his Doctors the same wing. Hale has a Helmsdale which has a floss and seal-fur body. Kelson lists an Improved Helmsdale (to be had of Nicol McNicol, Reay, Thurso, he wrote), which has much the same basis, but sides and cheeks of Indian crow.

DRESSING

Tag: Flat silver.
Tail: Topping and strands of tippet.
Butt: Scarlet wool.
Body: Flat silver.
Rib: Oval silver.
Throat: Lemon.
Wing: Strands of peacock herl, scarlet, blue, orange, yellow and white swan, cinnamon and light mottled grey turkey, speckled bustard; topping.
Head: Red wool.

8 White Doctor

COMMENT

Hale and Poul Jorgensen largely agree on this pattern. Although it was listed fairly regularly in the major catalogues, the fly has nothing like the fame of the other Doctors, but it is worth including as it is a relatively rare white-bodied fly.

White does have its supporters under some conditions – where contrast is needed, or as the day darkens into the evening.

DRESSING

Tag: Silver twist and yellow floss.
Tail: Topping.
Butt: Scarlet wool.
Body: White floss.
Rib: Oval silver.
Hackle: Pale-blue.
Throat: Dyed blue guinea-fowl.
Wing: Two golden pheasant breast feathers back to back, yellow, green, red and blue swan, golden pheasant tail and peacock wing; brown mallard; topping.
Cheeks: Chatterer. **Head:** Red wool.

LOCAL STYLES

Strip Wings

Royal Deeside has possibly the finest scenery of any of the major salmon rivers. Mountain, heather, Scots pine, birch and gorse – and the magnificent river winding its way to the sea – make an irresistible attraction. But it can be bitter cold in Aberdeenshire. Rafts of ice float down the river and grue, which is the water freezing on the bed of the river and then rising to the surface, can spoil the spring fisherman's day. The Dee has always had a good run of early fish, and in cold conditions a fly which cuts through the surface and rapidly starts to work at the depth at which the fish lie is the aim of the best Dee designs. The style is known widely as the '**Dee strip wing**', and there are many traditional patterns in this style, though from about 1890 it appears that more modern flies with vertical wings of mixed construction were ousting old favourites. Another reason for the decline of the old patterns was that the components for the wings were becoming less available – the turkeys were no longer part of the farmyard rag-tag of poultry, and the other bird whose feathers were so highly prized, the glead (gleed or gled), more usually known as the red kite, a bird of prey, was becoming extinct on Deeside.

The distinctive characteristic of faithfully tied Dee flies is first of all the style and set of the wings. Fairly narrow strips of matching fibres are taken from the appropriate feather, for example cinnamon turkey, and they are laid on the top of the wing horizontally, one at a time, reversing the wind of the tying silk to secure the farther wing. The result should be two long mobile strands which, when worked in the water, have a scissor action. Too much material in the wing will stifle this tendency. The next point is the relative length of the body. Extra-long-shanked hooks are used, keeping the weight of the iron as low as practical, and the length of shank to width of gape would be normally considered disproportionate. The final main identifying feature is the slenderness of the body and the extreme mobility of the hackling materials. Nearly all have the lightest of spun seal fur (or equivalent pig's wool or mohair) for the basis of the body, with pronounced tinsel ribbing over. Grey or black heron hackles are used to hackle the body up to and including the throat. For some traditionalists there should be an 'over

throat' of teal or wigeon. When jungle cock is applied to these patterns it has an intermediate length between that of normal 'sides' and 'cheeks'. It should be tied at about 30° *below* the line of the hook shank – a feature not usual elsewhere.

Strip wings were not confined to the Aberdeenshire Dee. Many early patterns used turkey tied in horizontal strips. Tying instructions in a number of instances indicate whether simple wings should be tied horizontally or vertically. Several Tweed flies were strip wing – White Wing (page 39), Dunwing, Drake Wing, Double White Tip and Grey Drake. Tyers on the Usk favoured black turkey with white points, Earn fishers chose flies with mandarin wings, and Pryce-Tannatt instructs that his Claret Alder should have its wings set horizontally.

Major J. W. Hills was a regular fisher of the Cumbrian Eden from 1889 to 1902, and in that time saw the decline of the sombre 'home-grown' turkey flies in favour of the gaudy patterns. It took thirty or so years for the Silver Greys and Doctors to infiltrate the Eden, and the design of the Bulldog, by Strong of Carlisle, probably started the slide. In 1889 a fisherman might well put a Grey Turkey over the pool first; in coloured water he might choose a Dun Turkey, but by 1902 the change was complete. R. C. Bridgett, noted for his writings about trout and sea trout, continued to use the Grey Turkey well into the new century – as we see from his adventures on the Border Esk and other rivers recounted in *Tight Lines: Angling Sketches* (1926).

The Eagles   This group has many of the characteristics of the Dee strip-wing patterns. However, the Eagles have an impression of bulk which is in fact an illusion: the fluffy fibres composing the body and under-throat hackles sleek and pulse most attractively in the water, not obscuring the slender silhouette of the body, which is usually of seal fur or tinsel. There is a singular lack of consistency in the dressings. Obviously the trade had their own belief in their own tyings. Equally, in early days, no doubt much depended on what materials were readily to hand. The fluffy hackle really is eagle feather, taken from the thighs of the golden eagle (*Aquila chrysaëtus*), which used to have a wide range throughout Scotland. This range is nowadays much reduced, and the bird is given maximum protection under the law. Obviously we need to turn elsewhere for suitable feathers. Fortunately, poultry can provide them in the thigh feathers of the white turkey. This is sold nowadays as marabou. In smaller sizes the thigh feathers of the hen pheasant may be used – suitably dyed – though no doubt an albino cock pheasant would be worth investigating. Hen pheasant as a substitute was mentioned by Kelson, so it does have 'authority', and it predates 1895, the date of his book, because it is mentioned against the Purple Emperor in his coloured cards accompanying *Land and Water*, an earlier sequence of published patterns.

David Collyer is a rare modern author in suggesting a tube-fly Eagle, derived from the original dressing. It is to be found in *Fly Dressing II* (1981).

Grimble compiled a valuable reference for fishing historians in his three books on the *Salmon Rivers of Scotland, Ireland, England* and *Wales*, for it can be seen from the date of the second edition (1913) which patterns had gained currency in which rivers. For some reason the Eagles rapidly found their way to the salmon rivers of the south of England, where they gained considerable popularity. Yellow is said to be a good colour in cold water, and rivers like the Hampshire Avon had a run of early fish.

Spey Flies   Those who have fished the Spey in May and June will have indelible memories of this magnificent Highland river: of its untamed scenery and rich wildlife – the busy oyster-catchers and sandpipers, plaintive curlews, swooping gulls excited by the insect catches, and the grand brown trout.

Happiness may fairly be described as a grateful spring fish in the pools which one's fly is searching, and a whisky distillery nearby on the river bank.

There is the satisfaction of honest physical work – needed when body wading in the strong flow – a satisfaction echoed in smooth and effortless Spey-casting wherever the banks or trees hazard the back cast. An essential on this as on all other big rivers is an ability to reach out with a controlled fly – twenty-five yards regularly may not be enough – thirty-five yards or more can well be needed.

From Grantown, forty or so miles from the mouth, the heart quickens and the spirit burns with optimism all the way to the sea, with delectable beats such as Castle Grant, Tulchan, Pitcroy, Knockando, Carron and Laggan, Arndilly and others like Delfur and Orton spreading before one.

Nowadays, the traditional patterns, as given in examples in the following pages, are part of the past. The modern Spey patterns are universal, but J.A.J. Munro's shop at Aberlour offers a range of local tyings: modern Spey tyings which may charm visiting fishermen as much as the fish of the Spey and its major tributary the A'an (Avon).

There is a fine roll call of old patterns. In *Autumns on the Spey* (1872) A. E. Knox hints forcibly that these were '*old* Spey flies' – Gold Speal, Silver Speal, Gold Reeach, Silver Reeach, Gold-green Reeach, Silver-green Reeach, Gold-green fly, Silver-green fly, Green King, Purple King, Black King, Gold Purple Fly (Gold Purpy), Culdrain Fly, Gold Heron, Black Heron and Carron Fly. He adds that 'several varieties have of late years been added, which though modest and unassuming compared with the gaudy exotics . . . must still be considered innovations, partaking as they do, more or less, of the plumage of the Golden Pheasant'. Knox suggests that these 'simple and unassuming flies, both in composition and appearance,' are more effective in taking newly-run fish in the lower waters than the most brilliant exotics, and that fly is really a misnomer; there is much resemblance to shrimp or prawn, and the special cock hackles which are taken from near the tail of the Speyside poultry give the impression of the many legs of these small crustaceans. We outline the characteristics of the style on page 70.

Dee and Other Strip Wings

As our first fly we have chosen the Akroyd. It is only 4 inches long. Just once have we seen an example fully 6 inches long, and that in William Blair's workshop at Kincardine O'Neil on Deeside (Blair of the Blair spoon). His bore the second set of wings sprouting from the joint between the body sections, which is the tying practice when available winging material is too short to cover the full length of the shank. Blair claimed it had caught fish. Certainly no fish would have escaped the anchor hawser of tripled gut which was still knotted to its eye.

This pattern epitomises the qualities of the Dee flies and, simplified, remains very much a favourite with us, in its cinnamon-turkey-winged guise as well. It is interesting that the Badminton Library mentions neither Dee nor Spey patterns, and there are none of the Turkeys or other strip wings of long standing. The Lonsdale Library, however, has a fine illustration of the Onset and is very informative on both styles. Jock O'Dee, Moonlight, Tartar, and Gledwing are other Dee patterns.

1 Akroyd

COMMENT

Variously and inaccurately spelt Ackroyd, this fly is the invention of Charles Akroyd of Brora in 1875. He is said to have nicknamed it the 'poor man's Jock Scott'. Megan Boyd, tyer on the Brora, records that the original was tied with a centre butt. There is also a suggestion that the over-throat of wigeon or teal was omitted, but since so many early gut-eyed flies include this feature it is fair to consider it sufficiently authentic.

The Pryce-Tannatt dressing is given, with Kelson's differences in brackets. Hale follows Kelson.

DRESSING

Tag: Silver (gold).
Tail: Topping and tippet.
Butt: None.
Body: Rear half, light-orange (yellow) seal fur; front half, black silk (seal fur).
Rib: Oval silver over seal fur, flat over silk (gold throughout).
Hackle: Lemon over seal fur, black heron (or black) over floss.
Throat: Teal (black heron).
Wings: Cinnamon turkey strips, or white.
Sides: Jungle cock, drooping.

2 Glentana

COMMENT

Hale includes the Gled Wing under this name. Glentana is a beat running down to Aboyne in the Middle Dee, full of fine streamy pools. Generally the Dee runs clear, with peat stain only after spates. Nowadays much of the spring fishing is bait rather than fly, until the water starts to warm in mid-April. From then on to the end of the season small flies, of which there are so many Dee patterns, have their turn.

DRESSING

Tag: Silver.
Tail: Golden pheasant red breast feather.
Body: Rear third, light-orange seal fur; front two-thirds, light-claret seal fur.
Rib: Silver lace and flat silver.
Hackle: Black heron.
Throat: Wigeon.
Wings: Cinnamon turkey with light points.

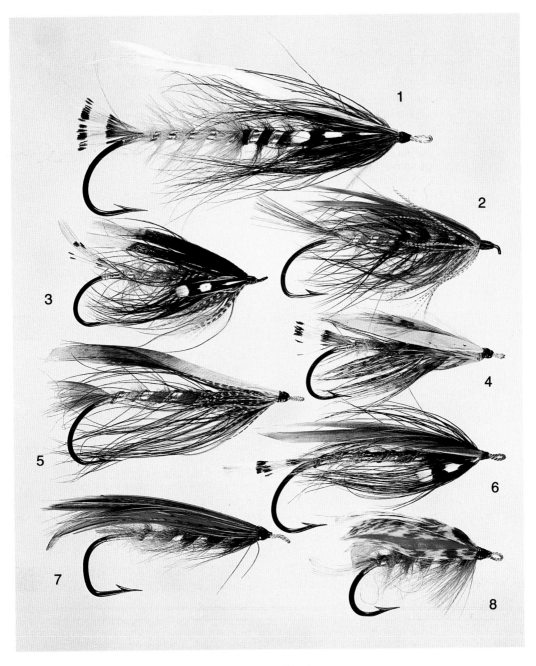

1 Akroyd   **2** Glentana   **3** Dunt   **4** Lady Grace   **5** Tricolour
6 Gardener   **7** Turkey Jackson   **8** Grey Turkey

63

Local Styles

3 Dunt

COMMENT

We have given Hale's pattern; Kelson's is the same. Pryce-Tannatt had differences – tail: topping, and small jungle cock back to back; body: one-third yellow, one-third orange, one-third fiery brown seal fur. Kelson attributes the pattern to William Murdoch, who writes: 'There is not a better all-round fly of the plain sort than the Dunt put upon the Dee in spring or autumn.'

DRESSING

Tag: Silver and light-blue floss.
Tail: Topping and tippet.
Body: One-third yellow, one-third orange, and one-third red-claret seal fur.
Rib: Silver lace and flat silver.
Hackle: Black heron.
Throat: Teal.
Wings: Plain brown turkey with black bars and white tips.
Sides: Jungle cock, drooping.

4 Lady Grace

COMMENT

Our elderly example shows variations in having a tail of strands of tippet and a body of yellow, light-orange, claret, and blue segments. Kelson attributes it to Garden's and considers it a famous low-water fly on the Dee.

DRESSING

Tag: Silver twist.
Tail: Point of golden pheasant red breast feather.
Body: Quarter light-orange, quarter red-orange, quarter claret and quarter blue seal fur.
Rib: Flat silver.
Hackle: Dyed yellow guinea-fowl over claret and blue.
Throat: Light-orange.
Wing: Two strips of swan dyed yellow.

5 Tricolour

COMMENT

Variations exist, as may be expected. For instance, the order of the body colours may be yellow, light-blue, and red. Some tyers used grey heron hackle in place of the black. Kelson mentions a variation: 'when dressed with a red breast hackle of the golden pheasant and with white wings, it is known by the name of "The Killer".'

It is considered a general standard and dates from long before Kelson's influence.

DRESSING

Tag: Silver thread.
Tail: Tip of a golden pheasant red breast feather.
Body: Rear quarter yellow seal fur, followed by equal sections of red and light-blue seal fur.
Rib: Silver lace and flat silver.
Hackle: Black heron.
Throat: Teal.
Wing: Cinnamon turkey.

64

6 Gardener

COMMENT

From the well-known tackle firm of Garden. All the compilers seem in reasonable accord on this pattern, though examples with bodies of floss silk have been current.

Flies of this quality justify our turning to collections to demonstrate how they *should* appear, rather than how we might imagine from reading a dressing instruction with no guiding illustration.

DRESSING

Tag: Gold and cinnamon floss.
Tail: Topping and tippet.
Body: One-third yellow, one-third green, one-third dark-blue seal fur.
Rib: Silver lace and flat silver.
Hackle: Topping.
Throat: Black heron.
Wing: Cinnamon turkey.
Sides: Jungle cock, drooping.

7 Turkey Jackson

COMMENT

For sheer ugliness this hook style takes some beating. Even the Lonsdale Library plates illustrate nothing quite so outlandish. However, the pattern is a fine example of the traditional fly of simple wing becoming more complicated to keep up with and reflect the new fashions in salmon flies. Hardy's catalogues in the 1930s listed plain and simple Turkeys, their Group 1 priced more cheaply than their Group 2 Turkeys (fancy). The prices? For a size 1: plain, one shilling and tenpence (9p); fancy, two shillings and fourpence (11½p).

DRESSING

Tag: Flat silver.
Tail: Topping and Indian crow.
Body: One-third yellow, one-third claret, one-third black seal fur.
Rib: Oval silver and flat silver.
Hackle: Natural black.
Wing: Cinnamon turkey tied flat, red swan, topping over.

8 Grey Turkey

COMMENT

A real old-stager with wide currency about the Borders and beyond, particularly on the Cumbrian Eden. Much variation is to be found in body and hackle, with some tyings having a body of silk rather than seal fur.

Balfour-Kinnear in his enlarged 2nd edition of *Flying Salmon* (1947) was still recommending a Grey Turkey.

DRESSING

Tag: Flat silver.
Tail: Topping and Indian crow.
Body: Rear sixth yellow, one-third red, remainder blue seal fur.
Rib: Silver lace and flat silver.
Hackle: Natural blue.
Throat: Natural blue.
Wing: Grey mottled turkey, strands of red swan, topping.

Eagles

It is difficult to determine who was the first user of these patterns, or what inspired him to choose what at first sight must have appeared unlikely fly-tying material. Francis Francis listed them in his *Book on Angling* (1867). Then came a surge in interest in which the body and hackling style were retained but progress was made to a complex wing instead of the strips of turkey, swan or bustard. It is intriguing to note that Dee flies enjoyed considerable popularity because they were cheap, as Pryce-Tannatt points out: 'This is by no means a subordinate consideration, as anyone who has fished in a blustering spring gale can fully testify.' Then came their demise – fashion as well as lack of availability of the prime material bearing their equal portion of the blame, no doubt.

1 Grey Eagle

COMMENT

The example shows excellently the apparent bulk at the base of each body hackle fibre, tapering to a fine mobile point. The body in Pryce-Tannatt is light-orange, deep-orange, scarlet and pale-blue seal fur, in that order. Hale gives the sequence illustrated, but with brown mottled turkey wings.

DRESSING

Tag: Oval silver.
Tail: Tip of a golden pheasant breast feather.
Body: Lemon-yellow, pale-blue and scarlet seal fur.
Rib: Flat silver.
Hackle: Grey eagle.
Throat: Wigeon or teal.
Wing: Grey mottled turkey, set flat.

2 Yellow Eagle (Hale)

COMMENT

Grimble records the following Eagles for the named rivers: Test, Yellow Eagle; Avon, Yellow and Grey Eagles; Stour, Yellow and Grey Eagles; Frome, Yellow and Grey Eagles; Exe, Eagles; Borgie, Yellow Eagle; Naver, Yellow and Grey Eagles; Dee, Eagles; Lochy, Silver Eagle; Tummel, White Eagle. They do not seem to have reached Ireland in his time.

DRESSING

Tag: Flat silver.
Tail: Golden pheasant breast feather.
Body: Yellow, scarlet and light-blue seal fur.
Rib: Flat silver and (optional) lace.
Hackle: Eagle dyed yellow.
Throat: Wigeon or teal.
Wing: Two strips of grey turkey.

1 Grey Eagle   **2** Yellow Eagle (Hale)   **3** Yellow Eagle (Francis Francis)
4 Yellow Eagle (variation)   **5** Floodtide   **6** Black Eagle
7 Hallidale Eagle   **8** White Avon Eagle (variation)

3 Yellow Eagle (Francis Francis)

COMMENT

Francis Francis allows two Eagles, the Yellow and the Grey. 'I believe in the evening, the "yalley aigle" is the favourite, and is the most effective of the two.' He then speaks of 'a claret body and hackle, with mixed wings of long brown turkey, argus and bustard feathers, with a gold pheasant sword feather in the midst, does well also, as does the black body and silver tinsel, with gallina shoulder and mixed wing'.

DRESSING

Tag: Oval silver.
Tail: Topping.
Body: Flat silver.
Throat: Yellow eagle under teal.
Wing: Strips of bustard.

4 Yellow Eagle (variation)

COMMENT

To our eyes this is probably the best of the patterns shown: a long and extremely elegant hook – with all the leverage problems imaginable! – modest application of eagle feather, and characteristic strip wing. The darker hackle points mar it slightly, but that is the way of many of the feathers. We know, because we have collected them when grouse shooting and stalking.

DRESSING

Tag: Flat silver.
Tail: Tippet feather.
Body: Yellow, orange, scarlet and light-blue seal fur.
Rib: Flat silver.
Hackle: Yellow cock.
Throat: Wigeon or teal.
Wing: Brown turkey with black bar and white tip.

5 Floodtide

COMMENT

Golden pheasant swords are stiff feathers each side of the main tail feathers. For more flexibility and translucency it is worth substituting with dyed cock hackles.

DRESSING

Tag: Flat silver and crimson floss.
Tail: Topping and summer duck.
Butt: Black herl.
Body: Canary, yellow, dark-orange and crimson seal fur. **Rib:** Flat silver and silver lace. **Hackle:** Yellow eagle over the dark-orange and crimson fur. **Throat:** Two turns of dyed crimson guinea-fowl.
Wing: Two jungle cock enveloped by two golden pheasant swords; bustard, Amherst tail, yellow and crimson swan; topping.
Sides: Jungle cock. **Cheeks:** Jungle points.

6 Black Eagle

COMMENT

Paul Jorgenson lists this pattern, and Collyer gives a tube example of an Eagle, but he chooses to tie the marabou (eagle) feather as a beard.

DRESSING

Tag: Flat silver.
Tail: Topping and Indian crow.
Body: Black seal fur.
Rib: Flat and oval silver.
Hackle: Black marabou, from third turn.
Wing: Strips white-tipped black turkey.

7 Hallidale Eagle

COMMENT

This, and Floodtide above, have moved towards complex modernity with their involved wings. Patterns with jungle cock seem datable post 1846.

DRESSING

Tag: Flat or oval silver and yellow floss.
Tail: Tippet and wigeon.
Butt: Black herl.
Body: Rear three-fifths, light-yellow; front two-fifths, light-orange seal fur.
Rib: Double oval silver.
Hackle: Golden eagle dyed yellow.
Throat: Guinea-fowl.
Wing: Two tippets; red and yellow swan; golden pheasant tail with golden mohair over; topping over.
Sides: Double jungle cock.

8 White Avon Eagle (variation)

COMMENT

This example has a throat hackle of eagle feather, rather than a body palmer hackle. Marabou, the substitute, is often tied beard-style as well.

DRESSING

Tag: Fine oval gold.
Tail: Topping and wigeon strands.
Body: Flat silver.
Rib: Oval silver.
Throat: White eagle under wigeon or teal.
Wing: Golden pheasant sword feathers back to back; topping.
Sides: Jungle cock.

Spey Flies

The Lady Caroline seems to be the only Spey pattern genuinely to have survived: the rest, for their history and odd appearance, continue to be quoted. Jorgensen lists Black Heron, Gray Heron, Brown Heron, Carron, Gold Riach, Lady Caroline, Orange Heron and Purple King. He emphasises the need for long-shank fine-wire hooks, and he also points out that the bronze mallard strips for the wings should be lighter in the root to keep faithful to the pattern style. The body hackles are tied in butt-end first, giving longer fibres at the tail and resulting in a scuttering shrimp-like appearance. They are wound in the opposite spiral to, and are bound down by, the rib. While the hackle is long and flowing, the wing is short – only as long as the body (if as long as that) – and the swathes of mallard (or other prescribed winging material) are broader than Dee strip-wing fibres, but tied in in much the same way. The result is a neatly 'roofed' fly like the underside of a keel-less racing boat, with a hump-backed appearance which looks rather wicked.

1 Red King

COMMENT

Most of the examples shown in the plate come from Jess Miller's fly collection. Some are of undoubted antiquity, those with the woollen heads probably being the oldest. Several of the patterns he showed us have this feature.

As with the Dee strip-wing flies and the Eagles, the hooks should be longer in the shank than standard, and of reasonably fine wire to cut down the weight of the large sizes.

DRESSING

Tag: None.
Tail: None.
Body: Red Berlin wool (brick-coloured).
Rib: Gold and silver.
Hackle: Red spey, contra-rotating.
Throat: Teal – one turn.
Wing: Mallard with light roots, pent style.

2 Purple King

COMMENT

'For general work, this is the best of the Kings' – so said Kelson. Our research leads us to agree with earlier writers who comment that no two tyers ever have the same pattern for the same name – though each is 'authentic'.

DRESSING

Tag: None.
Tail: None.
Body: One part of blue and two parts of red Berlin wool, mixed, or purple wool.
Rib: Gold and silver.
Hackle: Red spey, contra-rotating.
Throat: Teal – one turn.
Wing: Mallard with light roots, pent style.

70

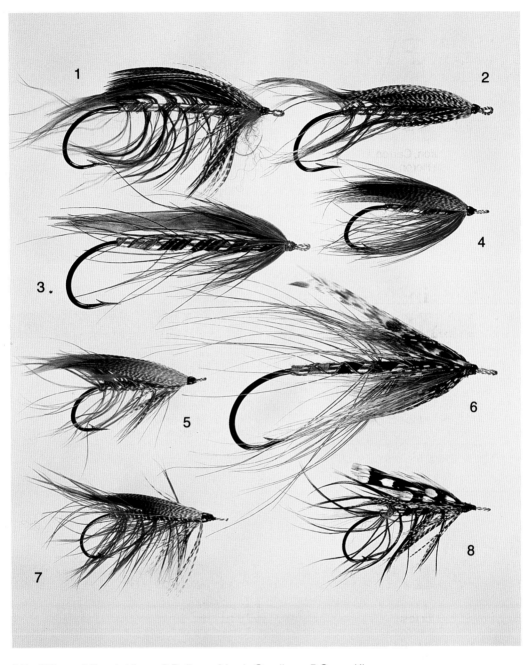

1 Red King   **2** Purple King   **3** Dallas   **4** Lady Caroline   **5** Green King
6 Grey Heron   **7** Gold Reeach (Riach)   **8** Glen Grant

71

Local Styles

3 Dallas

COMMENT

Kelson says: 'This capital fly on the Spey was christened by Mr Little Gilmore . . . the description given is from a pattern forwarded by Mr C. M. Burn's fisherman at Pitcroy; and proved to be correct by one being sent to me by John Dallas (the inventor) himself.'

DRESSING

Tag: None.
Tail: None.
Body: Rear sixth, yellow Berlin wool; front five-sixths, black Berlin wool.
Rib: Flat silver, oval silver, red strand, blue strand – equally spaced.
Hackle: Black spey, contra-rotating.
Throat: Golden pheasant breast.
Wing: Plain cinnamon turkey strips.
Head: (optional): Orange wool, picked out.

4 Lady Caroline

COMMENT

This is the only 'standard' Spey pattern still current, and one of the few earlier Spey standards to have a tail. Hardy's have listed it consistently, though, with the impetus Wood gave to it as one of his greased-line patterns, mostly as a low-water dressing. It was named after Lady Caroline Gordon-Lennox, daughter of the then Duke of Richmond and Gordon at Gordon Castle. Grimble gives a further Spey 'Lady' fly: Lady Florence. He includes Lord March and Miss Elinor as well.

DRESSING

Tag: None.
Tail: The tip out of a golden pheasant breast feather.
Body: Brown and olive-green Berlin wool mixed 2 parts to 1.
Rib: Flat gold and oval silver and gold.
Hackle: Grey heron.
Throat: Golden pheasant breast feather.
Wing: Bronze mallard with light roots, pent style.

5 Green King

COMMENT

Kelson's rib is more complicated: gold tinsel (narrow), silver tinsel (narrow), and light-olive-green thread. The tinsels are wound on equally spaced apart. The hackle is then wound in and the green thread is tied crossing over the hackle stem. This pattern was said to be particularly effective as a representation of the stonefly (known locally as the Green King) at about the end of April, and was thus a true imitative pattern.

DRESSING

Tag: None.
Tail: None.
Body: A mixture of light- and dark-green, brown and yellow Berlin wools, or green wool.
Rib: Flat silver and oval gold.
Hackle: Red spey, tied contra-rotating.
Throat: Teal – two turns.
Wing: Bronze mallard with light roots, pent style.

6 Grey Heron

COMMENT

On smaller patterns expect the usual bronze mallard with light roots. Note the way that the ribs are tied: first, flat silver; then contra-rotating oval silver with the hackle; last, the lace, wound the usual way.

DRESSING

Tag: None.
Tail: None.
Body: Two or three turns of yellow wool, the rest black wool.
Rib: Flat silver, gold lace, oval silver.
Hackle: Grey heron.
Throat: Guinea-fowl.
Wing: Grey mottled turkey.

7 Gold Reeach (Riach)

COMMENT

Kelson noted that the Gold*en* Riach killed best in spring and autumn. The pattern was 'high fly' in a five-year comparison of flies from 1 August to 15 October at Wester Elchies. According to Knox, the Silver Riach has an all-black body, grey spey-cock hackle, and emphasis on silver in the ribbing.

DRESSING

Tag: None.
Tail: None.
Body: Three turns of orange Berlin wool, the rest black wool.
Rib: Flat narrow gold, gold twist and silver twist, from different starting points, tied contra-rotating.
Hackle: Red spey, contra-rotating.
Throat: Teal – two turns.
Wing: Bronze mallard with light roots.

8 Glen Grant

COMMENT

Kelson calls this 'an old standard'. Knox does not list it, and he reached into history for the patterns he gave. Jungle cock was introduced on the Tweed in 1846, it appears, so this is obviously a 'modern' old standard.

The Spey Valley is a Grant stronghold, with Gran(t)town and Castle Grant at the topmost regular beats.

DRESSING

Tail: Golden pheasant yellow rump centre.
Body: Three turns of yellow wool, the rest black wool.
Rib: Silver lace and silver tinsel.
Hackle: Black spey, tied contra-rotating.
Throat: Teal.
Wing: Two long jungle cock, two medium jungle cock, and two short jungle cock, and teal.
Head: Yellow wool.

THE DEVELOPMENT OF PATTERNS AND STYLES

Introduction

The turn of the century was the heyday of the ornate fly: the following years saw both development of styles of fishing and, leading from that, a change in the style of flies. It would be a mistake to conclude that small flies were never used before about 1900: Kelson commented on 'small doubles' for the Dee. We understand this size to be about that of the Blue Charm illustrated on page 85, and we deliberately include the pattern fully dressed to give a comparison with the 'small' patterns which followed, and which surround it in our illustrations. We therefore take a look at some examples of flies from 1900 to about 1940, with an outline of the four major personages: Chaytor, Crosfield, Pryce-Tannatt and Wood.

Chaytor is not so important as a style-setter for small flies: his strength was common sense and simplified tyings. Crosfield fished not necessarily very small but fished fast. Of Pryce-Tannatt there is not too much about how he fished, but he wrote what was then and remains the definitive book on the dressing of salmon flies. Wood of Cairnton saw salmon taking natural insects from the surface in 1903, and was able to turn his observations, and style of fishing close to the surface, into the predominant style for summer fishing up to the present day.

Chaytor chose to avoid a multiplicity of patterns – he disliked overdressed, costly shop flies and suggested some simple patterns. The three best-known of these are the White & Silver, Claret Fly and Gipps. Close study of his book *Letters to a Salmon Fisher's Sons* (1910) reveals more patterns, some of which he espoused and one more which he designed.

The Tees fly which he mentions, predating 1820, is quite some pattern: 'The body is a huge caterpillar of coarse red wool as thick as a lead pencil, with a fibre of gold tinsel from an old epaulette twisted round it. There is a stubby tail made of a few barred strands from a jay's wing and the fly is winged with two tail feathers of the wren, tied so as to lie almost flat along the body like the wings of a stone-fly.' The next fly mentioned is found in a section about working a sea-trout fly or a big March Brown on a light line and thin gut into the current and upstream along the side. In September 1904 he records using a small green Heckham Peckham to take three fish and he lost a fourth. He has a slight criticism of the Earl Hodgson model collection of 72 patterns, but when Chaytor wants to offer a large fly in stained or muddy water he uses a Jock Scott or a sort of Silver Wilkinson. He refers to the use of a Jock Scott, large and small, as well as a flaming Yellow Turkey. The dropper fly which took him a fish on the last day of the season is given on page 143. He then speaks of a 'dull brown little fly with a dun turkey wing'. We also have the earliest Medicine – predating Horsley's and Falkus's – a silver body with a pale blue hackle and a plain dark mallard wing.

His tying instructions are straightforward: rather than gut for the loop use fiddle strings. Use oval tinsel, taper the body smoothly up from the tail, and then smaller again at the shoulder. Put on a thin throat hackle, stripped on one side if need be – 'no fly has more than six legs'. Do not wax the tying silk for tying in the wing, the regular dub of varnish will hold well enough. The whole aim in tying a fly is to get a lively motion in the water and also neatness. Double hooks he was against: 'There are some who even think that success is to be had only with double hooks, or with some spinning head or some fanciful "short-rising" hook of monstrous shape. (Illustrations of all three are given – an Aaro spinner Mar Lodge and the Bickerdyke 'Salmo Irritans' March Brown.) He asserts: 'In the repeated trials that I have given to double hooks I have lost an enormous number of fish upon them.' He liked eyed hooks for small flies, so our examples of his tyings are tied according to his preference. If Chaytor applied his mind to the essentials in salmon flies, and banished tags and tails as superfluous, it is interesting to note that he did not discard jungle cock sides. Modern thinking seems to class them as an extravagance: unless you breed jungle cock, the feathers are becoming difficult to acquire, and this now has an influence on their popularity.

The first edition of the Lonsdale Library *Salmon Fishing* by Eric Taverner (1931) is certainly one of the most informative salmon fishing books ever written. Its discussion of the salmon fly and illustrations give the clearest idea of the development of this style of fishing to that date. The editor is not alone in mentioning the name of Ernest Crosfield with some awe. He is placed as one of the finest amateur fly tyers of all time, and was an incomparable catcher of salmon – in his own style. Crosfield gave us no book. He produced an article or two – in Farlow's catalogue, in *Fisherman's Pie*, by W. A. Hunter (1926), and in magazines. That he was quite a fisherman became evident as we started to find material about him. He fished widely – on a lower beat of the Wye, as an early British visitor to Iceland, on the Dee, the Helmsdale, the Shannon, the Spey, the Tay, the Shin and other rivers. His Iceland catches are mentioned in the book *Ellidaár* by Ásgeir Ingólfsson (1987), found for us by Ron Coleby. It is the documentation of one Icelandic salmon river from early days of rod fishing through a disastrous phase of over-netting to its re-establishment as a rod fishery of note. Obviously the fish have never been of large average weight, but at the time when Ernest Crosfield fished it with his brother, Shetney, there were plenty of fish; and, apart from some Canadian records, Crosfield's were some of the highest numbers caught in a day, to a single rod, *ever*. From these visits he devised the Crosfield fly, now one of the Icelandic standards. His own, and best known, invention is the Black Silk. It is sad that we cannot show his tying of it, but we have Pryce-Tannatt's, which is a happy alternative. However, we can show his tying of the Akroyd, and the Brockweir, the name of the bridge on one of the lowest beats of the Wye, of which he was a regular tenant.

His preoccupation seems to have been summer salmon fishing, and the need for suitable flies. He was not a greased-line man to start with but, like Wood, he wanted his flies to fish close to the surface, so he fished rather fast to keep them from sinking. Though the examples we have are of single hooks, there was a range of Farlow's patterns of special doubles in the 1930s – Lady Caroline, Lee Blue, Bengie, Cound, Black Silk, Fiery Brown, Claret Rogan, Mystery, Claret Jay, Blue Charm, Joe Brady, Lemon Grey, Gold Ranger, Logie and Sherbrook – which obviously had his seal of approval.

He preferred metal-eyed hooks to gut-eyed because they allowed a much slenderer tying. He was an advocate of flies which were thin and translucent, rather than opaque, when held up to the light. Though he kept claiming that his flies were simplicity itself – or others claimed it on his

behalf – he was slightly tarred with the traditional brush, though with the difference (which equates with Rogan's style in Ireland) that he tied in his wing components in series rather than as one opaque lump. Each wing material would have its place to shine and glow. To achieve the slimness that he wanted in his flies he omitted tying silk until he came to the wing and hackle. His technique is outlined in the Lonsdale Library. Heads were neat and strong. In *The Art of the Atlantic Salmon Fly* Bates sums up his tying virtues as an economy of material, intentional translucence in the wings, and slimness of dressing.

Crosfield and Wood corresponded. Jock Scott devotes some pages in *Greased Line Fishing* to their discussions – on the difficulty of hooking fish on the doubles, about striking, and about the slow control with the greased line over the just-subsurface fly. Crosfield is mentioned regularly in other books, such as Hartman's *About Fishing* (1935): 'Compare it . . . and note how sleek and neat and thoroughbred this Crosfield fly appears. The small tapering head; the flat arch of the slender wing meeting the upward curve of the tail, the sinuous sweeping hackles and the well-proportioned body. . . . Such a fly would dance among the waters, responding to every twist and turn in the current . . . showing off its pretty colours and positively inviting the fish to make further enquiries.' We feel that he should be included in our book for his influence in our thinking about salmon flies. Do we not nowadays look in our modern and hairwing patterns for those three attributes which Bates summed up for us?

Throughout this book many are the references to Pryce-Tannatt. To students of the salmon fly he above all others gave the clearest instructions on how flies should be dressed, and provided the best illustrations. In 1914, the date of the first edition of *How to Dress Salmon Flies*, chromolithography had just given way to process printing. The plates in his book were not stylisations, as are those in Kelson's *The Salmon Fly*, or woodcuts as seen in the Badminton Library. They allowed the reader to see how Pryce-Tannatt tied the flies about which he wrote. As such, they are witness to his ability and they freeze in time the fashion and style of the day as he interpreted the dressings. It is the best possible reason for including in this book contemporary examples of patterns rather than tying new ones. Pryce-Tannatt was a singularly able amateur; we would hate our praise of his

The Development of Patterns and Styles

flies to overshadow the undoubted ability of the trade tyers, male and female, who at their benches and in their homes tied fly after fly of immaculate style and consistency. However, the tyers for Farlow's, Hardy's, Malloch's or Fosters of Ashbourne never had their abilities recorded in a book as Pryce-Tannatt's are.

In this book we are able to show some flies tied on hooks of his design – his Rational Irons – and some flies from his own hand. Their provenance is the same as the Crosfield flies: both men were guests of J. A. Hutton on his celebrated beat on the Wye. So also was my father (FJB's); and Woolliams, the keeper, gave him a parcel of flies, some of which we use to illustrate patterns, or the great men's interpretation of them. To confirm what we already consider we know, we have closely studied Plate 5 in Moc Morgan's *Fly Patterns for the Rivers and Lakes of Wales* (1984), which gives examples of Pryce-Tannatt's tying. The hook and the head style, as well as the dressing style, are in unmistakable accord.

The literature on greased-line fishing deserves close study. From Wood's formulation of his technique until 'plastic' lines became of common use, it was adopted as the correct way to fish for salmon in low-water summer conditions. Many of the more straightforward principles continue, with floating lines and small flies – fish slowly and fish the fly near the water surface. He liked handlining in, then shooting line.

Wood was a considerable correspondent, but he allowed others to explain in books his techniques and theories. He was very systematic, which was not necessarily a trait of all fishermen. His fishing cards demanded quite a lot of filling in: size of hook (to be measured against printed graduations), caught, lost, pulled/rose, kelts, pool, weight, fly, time landed. His compiled records, being full of detail, afforded him a chance of drawing conclusions. It seems that he did not have much interest in the cold and cloudy days of spring, but did best in the hot and low conditions which to older anglers would have seemed hopeless. In general terms his predilection for short rods – for he disliked two-handed casting – may have told against his totals of fish. He probably made up for this in some part with his extraordinarily detailed knowledge of his water, and huge distance was not necessary in the low-water conditions in which he excelled.

His thoughts on hooks were not entirely new –

see example 4 on page 85 – but he did popularise what we now call low-water dressings, with no part of the dressing extending beyond the point of the hook. He liked the dressing to be as thin, transparent and misty as possible: 'the older and thinner the fly becomes through wear, the better the fish seem to like it, provided the weather is hot and the water clear'. In patterns he liked the Blue Charm for its darkness and the Silver Blue for its lightness – giving him a choice. He thought flies for greased-line work should not have hard feathers in the dressing; any extra water resistance would cause the fly to skate on the surface. Hardy tied his low-water flies – and their Logie is the all-claret-body type. The Bumbee, the Green Peacock and the Sailor seem to have fallen out of popular use now, though the rest – Blue Charm, Logie, Jockie, Jeannie, Silver Blue, March Brown and Lady Caroline – live on, though possibly adapted to hairwing.

He fished the Redshanks and the Blueshanks – flies with no dressing but merely a coat of enamel on the shank – and is said to have caught fish on them in 1933, which allows us to wonder if the body should be considered as of equal importance with the wing in fly designs, and to conclude with Lee Wulff that the motion of a fly through the water at the end of a rod and line is an attractive motion with a concept of life in its own right.

Mending the line to control the fly is treated in Jock Scott's book as if it was an invention of Wood's. Kelson wrote on it twenty years earlier, but Wood impresses it on students of his technique so convincingly that we believe Jock Scott. In general, until Wood, salmon fishers struck or at least tightened on their fish and this is a good current opinion, upheld by both authors. His style was to have a sharp hook of fine wire and allow the fish to swim through the fly, letting the downstream pull of the line draw the fly into the fish's scissors and thus take a good grip (Crosfield tried this on kelts and hooked them well.) The history of the idea springs from some dibbling he did in 1903, which brought his attention to the attraction of a fly on or very near to the surface. He did try inducing the fly to float awash – which presages Lee Wulff with his Surface Stonefly (page 235).

It must not be considered that he only fished small flies with the floating line: he would fish big flies in the spring, and fish them with all the control of speed a well-mended floating line can offer; and he would strip in big flies under the surface in the summer with success. He would dibble – which is an element of his fishing which is not widely mentioned. Arthur Hutton, from his experience of the Wye, always looked to water *height* as critical in his fishing; Wood established for us another criterion of extreme importance – water *temperature*. For as soon as the water temperature exceeds 48 °F a small fly fished just subsurface is, for reasons known alone to the fish, more effective than deeper sunk flies.

A point worth pondering about low-water hooks is this: a small dressing on a light iron – effectively an iron one or two sizes larger than the fly dressing – will put the hooking element of the fly further rearwards of the dressing, and the gape of the hook will be a little wider than it would have been if the hook and dressing had been the same size. Low-water flies are small: size 6 is quite a large dressing, and 12s are spoken of freely. Those who claim that low-water hooks offer unwarranted leverage, and thus have a poor hold on the fish's mouth during a long struggle, seem to overlook how little greater the hook shank is than the standard equal sizes of dressing and fly, and how small the hooks are in general concept. With fine leaders it is possible to fish sharp fine wire hooks with no danger of the hook being the weakest link. Fine wire penetrates more readily than thick heavy wire, and Terence Horsley is not alone in advocating fine wire even in the larger sizes of spring hooks. Nowadays we have control of the depth at which the fly fishes by choosing a line of different density, rather than relying on the weight of the hook itself.

Dee Summer Patterns   The last two plates in this section show flies grouped together because between them they represent an epoch – that of fishing small flies in the summer. Most of the patterns were chosen for the greased-line style, and were dressed very short on fine-wire long-shank hooks. Since the Dee was the river on which A. H. E. Wood conducted his experiments, traditional Dee and Don patterns were adapted to his style. Although the Hairy Mary would rightly be categorised as a hairwing, it also falls definitively into this group. Equally, a pattern like the Musker's Fancy No. 1 should be included. Its hair wing is composed of the fur of Nellie, a Cairn Terrier, who caught for her master, Sir James Roberts of Strathallan Castle on the Earn, more than 500 fish. His flies were tied at George Smith's of Ballater, and the patterns – Jeannie, JDR, and so on – were all adapted.

Frederick Hill, author of *Salmon Fishing – the Greased Line on Dee, Don and Earn* (1948), was gillie at Strathallan, and his patterns, and variations of the standards, are good examples of how flies were thought of at this period.

The greased line period ran from 1913 to 1960; Wood had the Cairnton Beat, and formed his theories, between 1913 and 1934.

The ideal low-water fly is dressed only about halfway down the shank and the wing should be short and spare and no longer than the body. There is no need for much hackle in small flies. The Minto Wilson brand of hook is highly regarded for lightness of wire and thus slenderness of body.

Chaytor, Crosfield and Pryce-Tannatt

Chaytor is the first tyer on show here. Examples of his own tying are to be seen in the colour plates in the Lonsdale Library. They are on gut loops, or more likely fiddle-string loops, as Chaytor considered them more flexible than gut. We produce copies on eyed hooks, which he countenanced for smaller sizes.

Crosfield died in 1925, many years before Pryce-Tannatt, so his patterns are given next. An engaging note of his abilities as an all-rounder is given by Jock Scott in *Game Fish Records*. As a trout fisher, salmon fisher, stalker and big-game shot he was unequalled. He was also quite a footballer and cricketer, the latter interest incidentally shared with Kelson. Interestingly, despite all his natural talent, he does not seem to have killed a huge number of fish – 1,500 or so by the end of 1919, according to Jock Scott, which is not very significant compared with M. G. F. McCorquodale's total of over 8,000 from the Spey alone. Kelson is thought to have killed about 4,000.

Notes on Pryce-Tannatt's dressings are to be found throughout this book.

1 Claret

COMMENT

Chaytor offers an alternative dressing: a smooth body of port-wine silk with a 'pigeon's blood' hackle and wings of brown or dun turkey. The Lonsdale Library shows a broad silver rib, which despite Chaytor's saying in his book that he omits tags, is given a couple of turns at the end of the body. There seems to be some flexibility about Chaytor's patterns, since the plate captions the flies as 'original'!

DRESSING

Tag: None.
Tail: None.
Body: Rough claret wool.
Throat: Claret.
Wing: Mallard.

2 Gipps

COMMENT

Chaytor calls this a 'sober little fly'. The casual eye detects great similarity to a simplified Akroyd, or to a Black Maria. Approximately contemporary illustrations show a rib, though this is not apparent from Chaytor's book. This fly and a green Heckham Peckham were his choice for low and clear conditions.

DRESSING

Tag: None.
Tail: None.
Body: Rear half orange brown, front half black – roughly tied.
Rib (optional): Fine tinsel.
Throat (optional): Black.
Wing: Dun turkey.

80

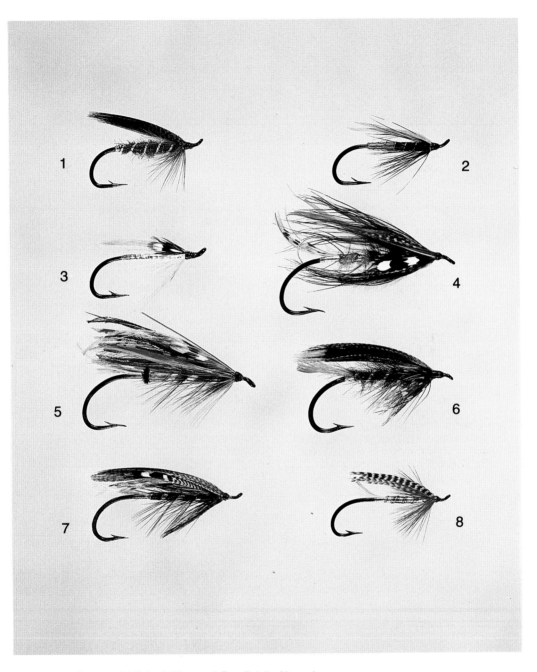

1 Claret   **2** Gipps   **3** White & Silver   **4** Crosfield's Akroyd
5 Crosfield's Gordon   **6** Crosfield's Brockweir   **7** Crosfield's Black Silk
8 Silver Blue

3 White & Silver

COMMENT

This is the fly which Chaytor describes as rather like a little Silver Wilkinson. When tied with an optional variation, a light-blue throat hackle, the resemblance is more marked. It is known also as Silver & White, or Silver Body. Bates (*Art*) gives the wing as dark turkey; the Lonsdale Library plate shows dun turkey, though the text repeats dark turkey, and the cheeks are about one-third the length of the wing.

DRESSING

Body: Silver tinsel.
Throat: Rather long white.
Wing: Dark turkey.
Cheeks: Jungle cock.

4 Crosfield's Akroyd

COMMENT

His dressing starts closer to the eye than expected for a pattern specified as best tied on long-shanked lightish-wire hooks. He has omitted the expected yellow palmer hackle over the yellow body segment, but retained the essential sleek mobility, though much of the black body segment is masked by the jungle cock.

DRESSING

Tag: Flat silver.
Tail: Topping and separated strands of tippet.
Body: Rear half, golden yellow seal fur; front half, black seal fur.
Rib: Silver twist and flat silver.
Hackle: Black heron over the black seal fur.
Throat: Teal.
Wing: Cinnamon turkey, tied in traditional Dee style.
Sides: Jungle cock, slightly drooping.

5 Crosfield's Gordon

COMMENT

Kelson considered this pattern, originating from the Dee and apparently designed in the 1890s by Cosmo Gordon of Maryculter Lodge, near Aberdeen, as one of the most difficult to establish as an original dressing. He eventually listed two dressings! Crosfield again starts the dressing very short and keeps the turns of broad tinsel few. As usual the hallmark of a neat head is his clear signature. It should be noted that his three flies are not on loop-eyed hooks, but the tapered eye is neatly brazed closed to the shank, so there is less thickness of metal in this small area.

DRESSING

Tag: Flat silver.
Tail: Topping and slender Indian crow.
Butt: Black ostrich herl.
Body: Rear quarter, orange floss; front three-quarters, ruby floss. **Rib:** Silver twist and flat silver. **Hackle:** Light-claret over the ruby floss. **Throat:** Light-blue.
Wing: Underwing of two dark-magenta cock hackles: yellow, red and blue swan; golden pheasant tail; strands of bronze peacock herl; topping over.
Sides: Jungle cock. **Horns:** B. & y. macaw.

6 Crosfield's Brockweir

COMMENT

Fly-tying, Principles and Practice (1940), by Major Sir Gerald Burrard Bt, gives this note and the dressing below: 'a useful fly in coloured water, particularly on the Wye. 1¾–1 inch irons'. The Brockweir is named after the last stretch of the Wye which is not fully tidal. The book, which appears otherwise fairly undistinguished despite its many printings, includes the dressing of the Brockweir though the pattern seems fairly obscure. The lack of distinction which may be accorded the book stems partly from the fact that it lists the dressings of only *nine* salmon flies.

DRESSING

Tag: Fine round silver.
Tail: Two small jungle cock feathers back to back with topping between.
Body: Dubbed claret seal fur.
Rib: Round silver twist.
Throat: Guinea-fowl.
Wings: Strips of black and white turkey with bronze mallard strips over.
Cheeks: Jungle cock.
(Crosfield has used Indian crow for the tail, adds a claret hackle palmered on the body and omits the jungle cock.)

7 Crosfield's Black Silk

COMMENT

J. A. Hutton says: 'Pryce-Tannatt and Ernest Crosfield are the two best amateur fly tyers I have met, and I am glad to say both of them put very little feather in the wings of their flies' (*Rod-Fishing for Salmon on the Wye*, (1919). In *Salmon Fishing* (Lonsdale Library, 1931) Taverner noted that Crosfield used the body material (floss silk) to tie in all materials until it needed tying off. Tan tying silk was used. This original by Pryce-Tannatt shows the following variations: a flat tinsel tag; a rib of twist and flat tinsel; summer duck, not Amherst in the wing.

DRESSING

Tag: Silver twist and yellow floss.
Tail: Topping and a few strands of tippet.
Body: Black floss.
Rib: Oval silver. **Hackle:** Bright claret.
Underwing: Tippet strands, the point of a golden pheasant breast feather and one or two toppings.
Throat: Blue jay.
Overwing: Six strands of golden pheasant tail and two of Lady Amherst tail to be tied on each side; two narrow strips of bronze mallard.

8 Silver Blue

COMMENT

A variation on this pattern is Hugh Falkus's Medicine, with a slim, smooth body of flat tinsel or even silver paint, wings of teal or mallard, and a red head (*Sea Trout Fishing*, 1981). Earlier Terence Horsley, in *Fishing for Trout and Salmon* (The Sports and Pastimes Library, 1944), shows his example of a lightly dressed Silver Blue: 'a light dressing on a low-water iron. The shank of the fly is painted with silver nail varnish.' Incidentally, Horsley liked irons of the finest possible wire throughout the range of flies he fished. Chaytor had a similar pattern, with a mallard wing.

DRESSING

Tag: Flat gold or silver.
Tail: Topping.
Body: Flat silver.
Rib: Silver thread.
Throat: Blue.
Wing: Pintail or teal.
Head: Red.
(This is an original tied by Pryce-Tannatt.)

Low-Water Flies 1

Wood went to Hardy's for his flies, so we do not expect to have examples of his own tying to illustrate the patterns. We do, however, have his style notes, which should be borne in mind by those purporting to tie the sort of low-water flies which he would have used, for he outlined how he considered the flies should look. (The Toys and Redshank and Blueshank may be overlooked as an overdiminution of dressing.) The wing should be low and flat against the top of the shank and the dressing can hardly be too light.

It would be wrong to think that no fishermen used small flies until Wood presented his greased-line technique. Kelson lists plenty of patterns, to which he appends notes like 'a good fly in summer on the Dee: it is usually dressed on small summer hooks'. The inventors and dates of invention of some of the small standards, so easily adapted to the low-water style, are not easily found. Kelson is unreliable or occasionally distorts the truth, claiming many patterns as his own or his father's, while all he did was formularise the dressing.

1 Jimmie

COMMENT

The colours are stronger than the Jeannie's. The fly is not so generally well-known, though inclusion in Pryce-Tannatt (1914) gives it some authority. Kelson does not list it, Hardy's do not list it in their 1907 catalogue, and Hale's second edition of 1919 omits it.

This is another pattern for which a hairwing may be substituted.

DRESSING

Tag: Silver.
Tail: Topping.
Body: Rear half bright orange floss, front half black floss.
Rib: Oval silver.
Throat: Natural black.
Wing: Mottled brown turkey.
Sides: Jungle cock.

2 Bumbee

COMMENT

Kelson says it is a good fly on the Dee; it is usually dressed on small double hooks. He attributes its design to W. Garden. Similar in many ways to the Jimmie, its wool tail bespeaks an older parentage. It is still listed and fished in North America. Pryce-Tannatt gives it a red wool tail and sets the wing horizontally.

DRESSING

Tag: Silver twist.
Tail: Tuft of orange wool, short.
Body: Rear third orange wool, front two-thirds black seal fur.
Rib: Silver oval.
Throat: Coch-y-bonddu.
Wing: Mallard.

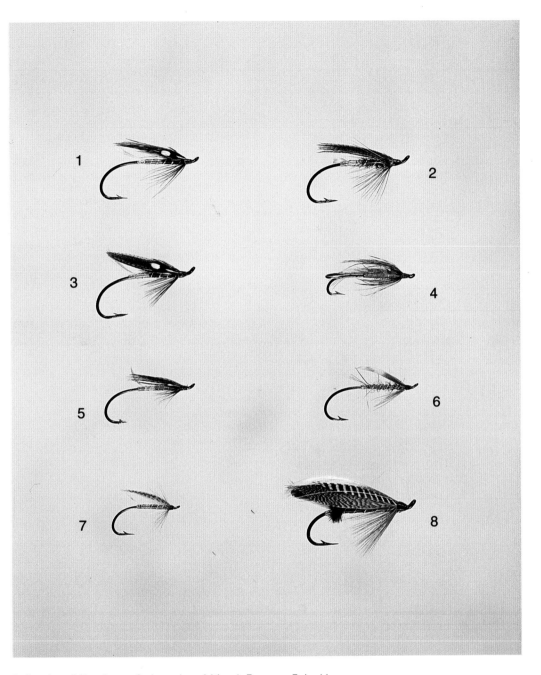

1 Jimmie **2** Bumbee **3** Jeannie **4** March Brown **5** Jockie
6 March Brown Variation **7** Logie **8** Blue Charm

3 Jeannie

COMMENT

One of the very many yellow and black patterns, this has quite a length of history. It is attributed by Kelson to W. Brown, but is not found in Sir Herbert Maxwell or in Francis Francis's list. Easily adapted to hairwings, it remains a standard summer fly of considerable popularity.

DRESSING

Tag: Silver twist.
Tail: Topping.
Body: Rear third yellow floss, front two-thirds black floss.
Rib: Silver.
Throat: Natural black hackle.
Wing: Mallard.
Sides: Jungle cock.

4 March Brown

COMMENT

Here is an example devised for '*Salmo irritans*', the short-rising fish which might be hooked by an extra-long slender double, a design by John Bickerdyke, the pen name of Charles Henry Cook. It seems to anticipate the extended-shank style of A. H. E. Wood by some years. A Jock Scott in this style is to be found illustrated in Viscount Grey of Falloden's *Fly-Fishing* (Haddon Hall Library, 1920), and figures, tied as a Jock Scott, in the Farlow's advertisement in Maxwell's *Salmon and Sea-Trout* (1898). The extremely narrow gape and long shank would not endear them to those sensitive to long levers.

DRESSING

Tag: Gold twist.
Tail: Topping.
Body: Finely dubbed hare's ear.
Rib: Oval gold.
Hackle: Picked out body dubbing.
Throat: English partridge.
Wing: Hen pheasant tail.

5 Jockie

COMMENT

This is perhaps John's favourite of the low-water summer patterns, and his first salmon, from the Don, came to this fly. The example is tied on the Minto Wilson lightweight low-water hook. Hackle fibres may be tied to give a slightly different winging treatment, and the jungle cock sides may be omitted.

DRESSING

Tag: Gold twist.
Tail: Topping.
Body: Rear third yellow silk, front two-thirds claret silk.
Rib: Oval gold.
Throat: Coch-y-bonddu.
Wings: Mallard.
Sides: Jungle cock.

6 March Brown Variation

COMMENT

To give a little more life to a drab pattern, fluorescent floss has been added to the tail and included as a secondary rib. Experiments such as this were recommended shortly after fluorescent materials became widely available. The march brown natural is worth imitating in a salmon fly pattern; so many instances are recorded of salmon seen eating the insects that captures have ensued almost instantly on the presentation of a good fly pattern. The standard pattern often has a body of one-third golden-yellow seal fur or wool and two-thirds hare's ear.

DRESSING

Tag: Silver tinsel.
Tail: Strands of fluorescent floss.
Body: Dubbed hare's fur.
Rib: First, silver; second, a thin strand of fluorescent red floss.
Throat: English partridge.
Wing: Hen pheasant tail.

7 Logie

COMMENT

This is another of the classic summer Dee flies. Tied with the standard mallard wing, the maximum size it can be dressed is about 1½ inches, but when brown mottled turkey is substituted larger sizes are possible. In the smaller sizes it is a classic for variation: shiny yellow hackle fibres for the underwing, or yellow hair under the mallard, or a complete hairwing, with yellow hair and dark brown squirrel or equivalent. Body variation in the classic patterns is common – from an all-claret body with jungle cock sides to a body of one-third yellow floss and two-thirds claret floss.

DRESSING

Tag: Silver thread.
Tail: Topping.
Body: Rear third yellow floss, front two-thirds claret floss.
Rib: Oval silver.
Throat: Blue.
Wing: Yellow swan with mallard strips over. (Crossley (*see* below) emphatically disliked jungle cock on this pattern, and omitted the yellow underwing.)

8 Blue Charm

COMMENT

This pattern is a long-standing favourite, its fame coming from its regular use in smaller sizes in summer conditions. Both winging materials are relatively short in the fibre, which precludes its being tied in large sizes. Kelson lists it, Crossley recommends it, but probably Wood's use of it in the course of his greased-line technique has given an impetus to its popularity. The example is, on purpose, in the style of what Kelson would have described as a small summer fly. It is for contrast.

DRESSING

Tag: Silver twist (Pryce-Tannatt adds golden-yellow floss).
Tail: Topping.
Body: Black silk (Kelson had claret silk).
Rib: Oval silver. **Throat:** Blue hackle.
Wing: Broad strips of mallard with a narrow covering of teal topping over.
(Hill gives a surprising modification for sunny days: tail, topping; body, pale-blue silk; rib, flat or embossed; throat, blue-green; wing, capercaillie cock, a back body feather with topping over.)

Low-Water Flies 2

The Badger, the Clark, the Cluny, the Fairy, the Lizzie, the Rival and the Sailor – all according to Kelson were low-water patterns to be tied on small doubles for the summer, but either they proved less efficient or tyers looked to other inspiration for their patterns. In modern terms any of these dressings can be adapted to a hairwing. In fact there could be an advantage in checking some of the nearly anonymous hairwing patterns against the old dressing instructions to establish some recognisable naming system.

It is interesting that fishermen at this time could see reason in and benefit from changing the standard patterns. Will a teal wing kill when a mallard wing will not? Will a dark-green floss body prove more effective than a black body? Will a red tail prove more attractive than the more usual topping tail? We can only suppose that confidence was engendered by the change.

Low-water flies like these seem to have become unfashionable, to the advantage of doubles and long-shank trebles. Contrast this with Gary Anderson's observation (writing of North American conditions) in *Atlantic Salmon and the Fly Fisherman*: 'for some reason I cannot explain the low water patterns outfish smaller regular wet flies in periods of low water'.

1 Green Charm

COMMENT

In June or July, Frederick Hill would sometimes use a Green Charm. He would from time to time choose this as a dropper, the use of which he favoured, preferably as doubles. The pattern has crossed the Atlantic: Fulsher and Krom list it as a hairwing style.

DRESSING

Tag: Silver.
Tail: Topping.
Body: Dark-green silk.
Rib: Flat silver.
Throat: Pale-green.
Wing: Teal.

2 Green Peacock

COMMENT

Murdoch is noted by Kelson as writing: 'On blazing bright hot days during June and July, there is no fly so fatal on the Dee, taking the river all over, as the Green Peacock dressed on Nos 7, 8 and 9 *double hooks*. Brown of George Street and Garden of Union Street always dress it true to pattern.'

William Murdoch in *More Light on the Salmon. What a Dee Salmon Sees, Hears and Does on its Journey from the Grey North Sea to the Mountain Pool in the Cairngorms* (ND, 1925?) has the 'hero' (the salmon) take a Green Peacock.

DRESSING

Tag: Silver tinsel or yellow floss.
Tail: Topping.
Body: Pale-blue floss.
Rib: Oval silver. **Throat:** Pale-blue.
Wing: Peacock sword in strands.
(It appears in Kelson, Hale and Pryce-Tannatt, and is very close to the Sir Charles in Frederick Hill: tag, gold tinsel; tail, topping; body, olive-green silk; rib, embossed gold; throat, pale navy blue; wing, teal with peacock.)

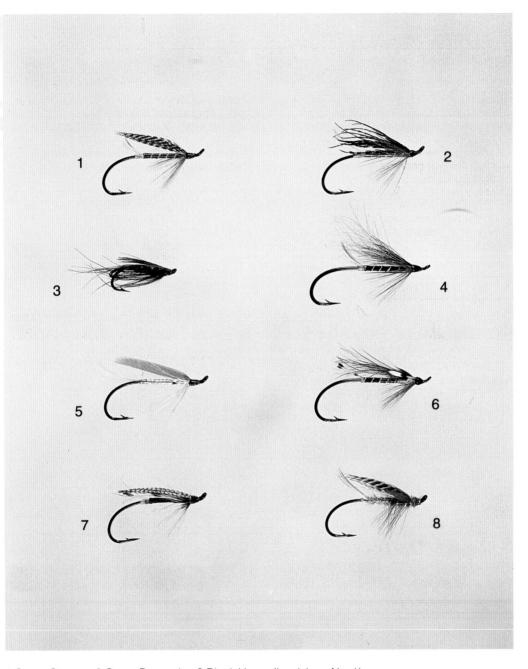

1 Green Charm   **2** Green Peacock   **3** Black Heron (Lewisham No. 1)
4 Hairy Mary   **5** Lewisham No. 2   **6** Musker's Fancy No. 1
7 Little Inky Boy   **8** Sailor

3 Black Heron (Lewisham No. 1)

COMMENT

This fly is an 'original' tied by Crossley and was given to John's father as an example of the pattern: 'I do not mind heron hackle protruding beyond the hook as the hairs are so incredibly fine.' In his book *The Floating Line for Salmon and Sea Trout*, Crossley gives the dressing which follows. Bates offers a teal wing for this pattern, probably drawing on Frederick Hill's version in *Salmon Fishing: the Greased Line on Dee, Don and Earn*. Hill adds the alternative tail of red ibis, and a turn or so of yellow silk at the tail of the body.

DRESSING

Body: Black.
Hackle: Heron hackle.
Wing: A little mallard.
(The rib in the example illustrated is flat silver and the tail is topping, though neither is mentioned in the dressing detailed in Crossley's book.)

4 Hairy Mary

COMMENT

This fly is in context in this plate since it rapidly became a low-water reliable. However, it might have been appropriate to include it under hairwing flies, as it was one of the early hairwings leading to their growth, development and popularity in replacing featherwing patterns. In larger sizes, the thickness and stiffness of the hair needs to be increased; in smaller sizes, the more mobile hairs are needed.

DRESSING

Tag: Silver or gold.
Tail: Topping.
Butt: Black (or none).
Body: Black silk.
Rib: Silver or gold.
Throat: Blue.
Wing: Brown hair (squirrel, bucktail, or the like).

5 Lewisham No. 2

COMMENT

As a definitive author on the greased-line style, Crossley and his patterns deserve mention, if only to mark an epoch of our salmon fishing history. He included Blue Charm, Logie, Jeannie, March Brown and Silver Blue in his selection.

His singular feat of catching a dead woman from the Aberdeenshire Dee was, however, accomplished with a Black Doctor. We once fished with his gillie, who was delighted to be remembered as having played a part in this saga.

DRESSING

Tail: Topping.
Body: Silver tinsel.
Throat: Buff.
Wing: Buff turkey.

6 Musker's Fancy No. 1

COMMENT

Frederick Hill was keeper/gillie on the Carlogie beat of the Aberdeenshire Dee for Captain H. T. Musker, who said: 'It is easily the best greased-line fly for low water I have ever used. It is made to represent the Logie, Blue Charm and Silver Blue.' Hill's slim book on his experiences on this river and the Earn and Don is required reading for students of the greased-line technique.

The example given is from Sir James Roberts, his subsequent employer on the Earn, and the owner's variation on the pattern was to include 'Nellie' fur, from a Cairn terrier, which caught its master over 500 fish!

DRESSING

Tag: Silver tinsel.
Tail: Topping.
Body: One-third black silk, one-third red silk, one-third silver tinsel.
Rib: Silver.
Throat: Blue.
Wing: Teal and mallard mixed.
Sides: Jungle cock.

7 Little Inky Boy

COMMENT

We have returned to Kelson for this pattern to continue the tradition of small summer flies. 'Several nondescripts of mine take the character of the Little Inky Boy, the gut being dyed in different colours. These patterns are best made with thin bodies and light wings.' This is quite a departure in body style, yet Kelson gives few notes about it, omitting it in his discussions of body materials and subsequent text.

DRESSING

Tag: Silver twist and a turn of crimson Berlin wool.
Tail: Topping.
Body: Fine trout gut dyed black, closely coiled.
Throat: Three turns of coch-y-bonddu dyed yellow.
Wing: A few tippet strands, two narrow strips of unbarred summer duck, with topping over.

8 Sailor

COMMENT

Kelson and Hale give the same dressing, and Kelson adds his expected notes – that it is excellent on the Dee in summer dressed on small double hooks. It remained regularly in the trade catalogues and then, despite Wood's use of it, retired into obscurity. It is easy enough to convert to a hairwing dressing using grey squirrel tail, or silver baboon.

DRESSING

Tag: Silver.
Tail: Topping.
Body: Rear half yellow, front half blue seal fur.
Rib: Silver.
Hackle: Blue over blue.
Wing: Strips of teal, and topping.
Cheek: Chatterer.
Head: Blue wool.

NORTH AMERICA
AND HAIRWINGS

Introduction

Nowadays we find that salmon flies are mostly tied with hair in the dressing, whether as singles, doubles, long-shank trebles, tubes or Waddingtons.

Hair has a long and quite complicated history in fly tying. From writers like Morgan we know that hair, squirrel tail, spaniel tail, or cat's whiskers were being used in Britain in 1770. In *Angling in All its Branches* (1800) Samuel Taylor writes that a salmon fly 'may be forked, if thought proper, with two or three hairs of a squirrel'. It is unlikely at this period that there was much thought beyond some concept of insect imitation. There was probably no search for more brilliancy or mobility than which feathers could offer. Just one or two hair oddities did exist, such as maned flies of the Owenmore type, and one or two other Irish patterns like the Nora Criena or Mohair Canary, and indeed the Garry Dog. But for the most part at that time they were not influential. So there was a period in which salmon flies became bright and attractive – attractors in every sense to the fish – which could only be achieved by the most exotic and eye-catching of bird plumages, a time when Kelson pontificated and Pryce-Tannatt tied with exquisite neatness and style. When eventually Wood promulgated his low-water style of fishing with the greased line, it began to dawn on the fishing public that many of the complexities in their flies really were superfluous. By the 1950s Great Britain was ripe to receive influence – which would endure – from elsewhere.

The 'elsewhere' was North America, which in early days had relied on British patterns and fly dressing thought for its flies. But hair in tyings was a part of its history as well – had not Robert Roosevelt in 1869 referred to a 'choicest caribou fly'? And the Rat patterns were in use before the First World War. These early hair patterns may have had two origins: steelhead patterns, which demanded tough construction; and the principle make-do-and-mend when standard feathered patterns were used up and unobtainable. Once the substitute materials proved themselves, design could start with a clean slate, free of too many preconceptions. The wide variety of hairs available gave rise to limitless combinations of ideas and patterns.

With fauna as diverse as that found in North America the opportunities for exploiting the different materials were evident. Straight hair, crinkly hair, shiny hair, matt hair, and buoyant hair – barred, flecked, brindled, plain, and dyed. Pattern after pattern could be formulated easily, each with the potential of being *the* killing pattern. There was another point: the classic fully tied featherwing salmon flies are expensive to make in terms of materials and of time. Any simpler and more cost-effective style of tying is always welcomed, and much of the present popularity of hairwing flies stems from this, perhaps as much as claims for any increased efficiency in attracting salmon. Suddenly in the 1950s patterns like the Hairy Mary were being used in Britain instead of the very similar featherwing Blue Charm. Stoat's Tail tubes were being tried as alternatives to Jeannies and Logies; the tentative ripples of experiment became a flood-tide of change in fashion. The classics were adapted and new patterns were invented by the score, for hairwings were well within the scope of the amateur tyer.

How is hair used, and which hair is chosen? The main duties will be to provide a wing, a tail or a hackle, or a combination of them. The wing for a wet fly might be in the classical mould, extending over the top of the hook shank in the usual proportion to the throat hackle, or it may be far longer in the American bucktail or streamer style. For a dry fly it will be in a single tuft or separated tufts, pointing back over the shank, vertical, or sloping forwards. For hackling a wet fly hair might be applied at joints, evenly distributed all round, or at the head, as a beard or evenly distributed. Hair can be used in tails either as a substitute for wool, floss or feather or in new styles – long and sinuous, perhaps. In contrast, hair dry-fly tails are usually stiffer than feather to help make the fly cock and float well. Sometimes hair will be used for shellback tyings, such as a prawn or shrimp, and deerhair may be used as a body material.

A fur – rabbit's – may occasionally be used in the role of hair. Patterns like the Muddler Minnow include deerhair in a dual role, and derivations of the Muddler style use rabbit fur.

What the hair is wanted for will help to determine which is chosen. Read a first-class modern fly-tying book like Darrel Martin's for detail and depth. Choices include fox and coyote; stoat, mink, badger and weasel; squirrel, chipmunk and the like; bear – black, brown and polar; skunk; goat; monkey; calf tail; and, among the deer, caribou, moose (elk), fallow, red and roe, antelope and bucktail. Some dogs produce suitable hair, but human hair is straight and does not taper to a point, which makes it less favoured. The different hairs offer a wide variety of length, texture and stiffness, and in the proper place these properties have their virtues.

On the whole we can assume that featherwing patterns are no longer being tied for regular use; hair is now ubiquitous in wings, hackles and tails. From now on, nearly all patterns will be based on hair.

The vast range of patterns in common use is unlikely to diminish as long as salmon occasionally seem to display amazing fussiness. Earl Hodgson recalled a day when the only fly to attract fish was a Dusty Miller (silver/orange body). When the hook broke other flies were tried with no success, but when the defective Dusty Miller was knotted on again the fish renewed their attack. Sidney Spencer was also a great fan of the Dusty Miller, provided the front half of the body had the true pinky flame. He swore by the Lemon Grey for conditions of low mist. Neil Graesser reports occasions when one colour and one only was particularly effective. Once, when he was a guest on the Laxford in north-west Scotland, trials with Shrimps and other patterns failed entirely; what the fish wanted and what they would have was his maroon Usk Grub. He also states that when the smelt run on the Cassley, the Mar Lodge with a body of silver, black and silver, a good fly at any time, is particularly effective. He mentions an occasion in Wales when a Halsam was *the* killer, while the Mar Lodge, Silver Grey and Silver Wilkinson – of similar tone – were not attractive at all. Crawford Little reports that a copper-bodied fly did all the slaughter on a day on the Downie Beat on the Beauly in Inverness-shire. When the successful fisherman lent it to his companion that fisher at last started to take fish. In due course the fly was lost, and that was the end of all sport. There are many, many similar accounts.

Although modern hairwing patterns are classified, their invention is often loosely attributed and variations are rife. There seem to be many more black patterns than of any other colour – black in wing or body or both. They certainly give a good silhouette and their success seems to accord with a theory about

the salmon's eyesight. It is that the fishes' tissues waste during their migratory fast, which leads to a vitamin deficiency, making their eyesight progressively less acute to the brighter colours. The seasonal sequence of fly colour is yellow through orange, red and claret to black. Then, right at the end of the season when flies are sunk because the water is cold, flies of brighter colours are used again, to be sure that the fly is noticed by the fish. It could just be that the smaller the fly, the less the pattern is important; generally it will be seen as a silhouette. Theories about eyesight and eye chemistry may be totally irrelevant, but this one is found not just in English and American literature but also in France, so it does have wide currency.

The next most popular 'colour' is silver. Watch a minnow or small bait-fish turn and dart in the current – its silver flash might well betray its presence. In the same way many salmon and sea-trout flies represent small fish, and there are plenty of patterns which are silvery. It seems that there are two ways of considering the reflectivity of a silver body: it may mirror the surroundings and thus make the fly *less* outstanding, or it may catch the light and make it *more* outstanding. Probably there are elements of both in the fly's traverse across the salmon lies – though it may be difficult for the fisherman to know which aspect of the fly, the introvert or the extrovert, has attracted a fish to take.

Plain flat tinsel is fairly vulnerable to tearing by the fish's teeth. An overlay of a rib of oval is usually added, which produces its own contribution of glitter and reflectivity. Embossed tinsels are standard on some patterns, and among the more modern materials 'flectolite' impressions on metallic-finished plastics give a prismatic shimmer of rainbow colour. The old-fashioned tinsels need a good polishing before they are applied, but over the years they do tarnish and re-establishing their brightness when they are already incorporated in a fly is difficult. The modern plastics do not tarnish, but have not had time to prove their longevity. In early days tinsel was not that widely used; perhaps it was difficult to obtain. Then recommendations were to obtain it from epaulettes or even 'from the hatbands of liveried servants' (1838). Subsequently it has been sold on cards or small drums, and is easily available.

Under the heading of tinsel are: wire, thread or twist, oval, flat, and very occasionally the now-obsolete lace. *Wire* is solid and round in cross-section. It is more commonly used in trout patterns, but is sometimes used in suitable diameters in tags and in very light low-water salmon flies. *Thread* is also round in cross-section but is a winding of fine tinsel round a cotton or silk core. It is thus minutely faceted and its core material makes it strong and unlikely to break as it is being tied in. *Oval* is like thread, but with an oval cross-section: both thread and oval are available in many gauges, and a broad oval is often an improvement over vulnerable *flat* tinsel, which is a thin metallic ribbon in a range of widths. Since it lies proud of the body material, thread or oval offers some protection to body.or palmer hackles. In the Spey patterns, as we have seen, it may be wound in the opposite spiral over the hackle, criss-crossing it at intervals and thus giving the hackle extra security from unravelling. Some patterns call for both flat and oval ribbing material; modern practice, except in the larger sizes of fly, is to use oval wherever practical. *Lace* is a compound, a combination of several strands of thread. Its place was to augment a spiral of flat tinsel rib. Oval has filled this role in recent years.

Bodies may be made entirely of tinsel – usually flat, with a rib. Any hackle tied over tinsel is vulnerable, so it is often tied in at a joint, like some Snow Fly patterns. Some flies have the body separated into sections with one or more of tinsel – the Lion is mostly silver, with just a small red section under the throat. The rear half of the body of the Bulldog is silver, and the type of tinsel to dress it properly is oval. In general the lighter body section or tone comes nearest the tail; very few end up with tinsel or a paler section at the throat.

Gold patterns are less acutely bright. Comparatively few all-gold bodies are tied, though Sir Herbert Maxwell did want to confound his Tweed gillies by not using a silver-bodied Wilkinson and devised the Sir Herbert, for immediate successful use on the Tweed. The Dunkeld is another traditional pattern, and among the modern tyings there gold versions within the Rat and the Cosseboom series.

Kelson was specific about the times for gold or silver tinsel – silver early in the year: 'in summer and particularly in autumn, all patterns, even silver bodies, are more effectual when dressed with ribs of gold tinsel. . . . Where there is a preponderance of yellow tones on the body, I prefer silver early in the day, the rays of gold being singularly eclipsed by the materials it embraces; and gold in the afternoons.'

Even more muted is copper. It seems to be unpopular, probably more because it is less easily obtainable as a fly-tying material than because it is less effective than the other tinsels. There are certainly enough reports of a copper-bodied fly being *the* fly to the exclusion of other patterns for us to list some copper dressings.

At this stage it is worth thinking about how a salmon may see a fly. In *Salmon Taking Times* Reg Righyni propounded the theory that flies can be classified, and each category will have its place in certain conditions. His headings were: *Translucent illusion* – Yellow Torrish, Silver Grey, Dusty Miller; *Translucent illusion/normal image* – Lady Caroline, Dunkeld, Lemon Grey, Green Highlander; *Flashing illusion* – Silver Doctor, Silver Wilkinson, Mar Lodge, Bloody Butcher; *Silhouette* – Black Doctor, Stoat's Tail, Blue Charm; *Normal image/silhouette* – Thunder & Lightning, Jock Scott, Akroyd; *Normal image* – Creel Fly, March Brown, Logie and Kate.

It is extremely difficult to prove anything about salmon fishing, but there probably is something in the concept that some rivers fish better with particular colours of fly. If a number of generations of gillies are prepared to insist that some colours are better on their river, they may feel that there is foundation of fact for their assertion. Most writers on Iceland suggest that flies with blue in them are to be chosen in preference to those without. Francis Francis and Kelson intimated that rivers should be considered in terms of their 'colour'. Graeme Harris wrote in *Trout and Salmon* about changing the colour of a fly – not the size nor the style – to try to induce visible fish to take. Because he could see how the fish reacted he could draw conclusions, and a major colour change could produce fish for him while repeated hammering with a fly of the same colour only seemed to induce boredom. This does not contradict the idea that rivers are 'coloured', because what he is saying is that when even the best of choices fail it is worth trying something different.

John's preference, all year round and irrespective of river, is for some yellow in a fly, and a pattern which includes yellow and mobility and translucency, and which both he and the fish can see, is an Akroyd in some tying style or another. Since there is plenty of black in it as well, most of the other considerations mentioned above are met too. Arthur's choice would be for black or brown, with some red about the fly.

A note on tying in the hair for hairwinged patterns. Prepare a wet varnished base of even turns of tying silk, lay on some hair, take two turns of tying silk, varnish, add more hair, and so on. Then trim the waste ends, whip finish and varnish. In this way the fibres are held positively against the body beneath and with the wraps of tying silk around them.

If a large bunch is tied in at one time too much reliance has to be placed on the friction between the fibres and any varnish or glue which has seeped in. If the hairs start to loosen, the wing comes apart. However, when the winging is very sparse, is it probably simplest to apply it in a single bunch, particularly when a neat head is required.

A very secure, but less neat, method is as follows: tie the hair pointing forwards, trim the waste ends, sweep the hair back over the shank in the expected way, bind down and whip finish, varnishing liberally.

For dry flies the winging hair should be applied early in the construction, as the waste ends may then be trimmed smoothly into a suitable underlay for the body.

Most of the good modern fly-tying instruction books explain how to handle hair, but one which we favour is the enlarged edition of *Hair and Fur in Flydressing* by Thomas Clegg. The first edition came out in 1957; by 1969 he was able to add much new material, and a new section on reservoir trout flies. Since the booklet gives over 40 patterns of wet salmon flies, a good choice of wet sea-trout flies, and about 30 dry-fly styles and patterns we thoroughly recommend it. Another advocate of hair in the place of feather is W. H. Lawrie with *All-Fur Flies and How to Dress Them* published in 1967.

Rats

Once New England's rivers were generously populated with salmon, whose only major predators were native Indians with their traditional nets and weirs. But even in colonial times the fish started to encounter problems – their spawning runs were obstructed by dams built – without fish passes – to harness water power. With increasing pollution as well, salmon became extinct in many of the rivers. By 1870 there were only seven rivers in Maine with anything like regular runs of salmon. In the late 1950s the salmon was declared an endangered species by the Secretary of the Interior.

In 1966 Federal funds became available to start a restoration programme, with the Penobscot proving the most willing patient, and at last offering fishing on a practical level again.

Canada had never suffered anything like this trauma. Once the runs of salmon were so dense that it was possible to cross the rivers on their backs, and they could be pitchforked onto the banks to be used as fertiliser. Those days are long past; the pressures of expanding population have taken a toll, mining exploitation has seriously polluted the salmon rivers, and recovery has not yet been achieved after disastrous forestry spraying against spruce bud worm.

1 Grey Rat

COMMENT

This series originated in 1911, being the combined efforts of Roy Angus Thomson, whose initials give the patterns their name, Colonel Monell and Herbert L. Howard. It is open to doubt whether the Grey Rat or the Rat (Black Rat) was the first. Bates suggests that all the early patterns included the jungle cock, and that only later has it been considered optional. Fulsher and Krom give a wing of black and white hair mixed, and this is standard in their list of dressings for the series.

DRESSING

Tag: Flat gold, or oval gold for double hooks.
Tail: Topping.
Body: Underfur of grey fox.
Rib: Flat gold.
Wing: Guard hair of grey fox.
Collar: Grizzle.
Sides (optional): Jungle cock.
Head: Red.

2 Silver Rat

COMMENT

Shirley Woods considers the Silver Rat 'a truly universal fly' and an excellent change of pace from the Blue Charm. It is a favourite of his in 'roily' water. The pattern is said to be a great killer on the Matapedia, and has its keen devotees in Iceland. Bates puts the Silver Rat near the top of his list for periods of discoloured water in the Restigouche–Matapedia area of Quebec.

DRESSING

Tag: Fine oval gold.
Tail: Topping, short.
Body: Flat silver.
Rib: Oval gold.
Wing: Guard hair of grey fox.
Collar: grizzle.
Head: Red.

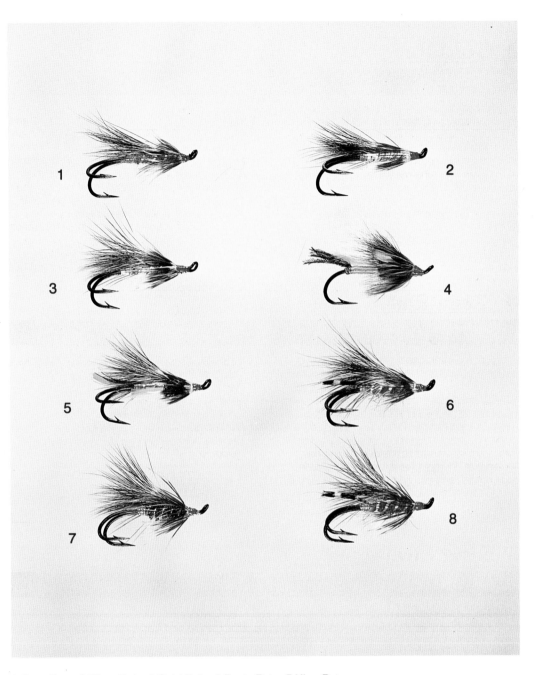

1 Grey Rat **2** Silver Rat **3** Gold Rat **4** Rusty Rat **5** King Rat
6 Red Rat **7** Black Rat **8** Brown Rat

3 Gold Rat

COMMENT

Jungle cock sides are optional. This is about the fourth of the Rats to be designed, in the autumn of 1911. If the original winging material is not available, Bates suggests silver African monkey, racoon, or mixed black and white Monga monkey. Curly, kinked hairs such as antelope and calf tail are not recommended.

DRESSING

Tag: Flat silver.
Tail: Topping dyed red (Amherst topping).
Body: Flat gold.
Rib: Oval silver.
Wing: Guard hair of grey fox.
Collar: Grizzle.
Head: Red.

4 Rusty Rat

COMMENT

Possibly the best of all this series, and not even originated by Thomson, Bates attributing it to Dr Orrin Summers. The pale half of the body is subject to variation, so Bates's formula is given, with Fulsher and Krom's alternative in brackets. Plain orange is sometimes used: jungle cock is optional. They add a Wagstaff Special as a further pattern which is similar; its wing has brown hair. Gary Anderson recommends the pattern for the River Gold and the Margaree as well as the North-West and South-West Miramichi. He says that in sizes 2 and 4 it is good on the Sainte Anne.

DRESSING

Tag: Oval gold.
Tail: Two or three peacock sword herls tied short.
Body: Rear half, bright yellow floss, veiled above with a strand of yellow floss (fluorescent orange floss, veiled above with strand of fluorescent orange floss); front half, bronze peacock herl.
Wing: Guard hair of grey fox.
Collar: Grizzle.
Head: Red.

5 King Rat

COMMENT

This is a combination pattern from Fulsher and Krom, with elements of Black, Silver and Rusty Rats. Originally it was recorded as the Father, Son and Holy Ghost, but was soon renamed as this was an unacceptable religious reference.

DRESSING

Tag: Oval silver.
Tail: Peacock herl over yellow floss of the same length.
Body: Rear half, flat silver, veiled top and bottom with yellow floss, front half, bronze peacock herl.
Rib: Oval gold and flat silver.
Wing: Guard hair of grey fox.
Collar: Grizzle.
Head: Red.

6 Red Rat

COMMENT

Bates does not list this one, so we turn to Fulsher and Krom for their dressing. The variations are: jungle cock optional, tag of embossed silver, tail of fluorescent red wool, body half embossed gold, half fluorescent red wool, the wool ribbed with embossed gold.

DRESSING

Tag: Oval silver.
Tail: Two strips of barred wood duck, back to back.
Body: Red seal fur.
Rib: Flat gold.
Wing: Guard hair of grey fox.
Collar: Grizzle.
Head: Red.

7 Black Rat

COMMENT

Bates lists the Rat and the Black Rat as very similar. Elsewhere we have found the original black floss or wool replaced by bronze peacock herl for its extra shimmer, for instance among some of the Black Bear and their look-alike patterns. A tail is not always included in this tying.

DRESSING

Tag: Flat or oval silver or gold.
Tail: Topping.
Body: Bronze peacock herl or black seal fur.
Rib: Silver (or none).
Wing: Guard hair of grey fox.
Collar: Grizzle.
Head: Red.

8 Brown Rat

COMMENT

This is the last Rat we show here, though the Blue Rat is included in the section on Scandinavia and Iceland. The Copper Rat has a copper tag and a flat copper tinsel body. Gary Anderson mentions a White Rat. Debatably the series has some resemblance in shape to the natural stonefly which is prevalent at times in the rivers where the flies originated. There is no doubting the series' importance in North America; it is also widely accepted abroad, particularly in Scandinavia. In a way they are a modern update on a Rover series by Hardy's in Silver, Blue, Red, Gold, Black and Grey.

DRESSING

Tag: Oval or flat silver.
Tail: Two short sections of barred wood duck.
Body: Fiery-brown seal fur.
Rib: Flat gold.
Wing: Guard hair of grey fox.
Collar: Grizzle.
Head: Red.

Cossebooms

More on Canada. It is not a total tale of despondency. The fishing is some of the finest available and the salmon fishing is now treated as a truly valued resource. Our trip to Canada was in 1964, the first expedition from our base at Presque Isle, Maine, being after the 'black fish' or kelts immediately the ice broke up. Then, on hearing that the grilse were starting to run, we made a very successful trip to the S.W. Miramichi, similar to a Scottish salmon river in many ways. Each year, however, the pools can alter fundamentally, depending on how the ice came down and gouged new channels or shifted gravel banks. The hottest spots we found were where the fish chose just one of three new cuts through a gravel bar. It was perfect for single-handed casting from the bank. We could see the fish, and the memories of them tilting up to the fly remain indelible, an aesthetic peak in salmon fishing. Shad ran the river, porcupines made their stately way along the riverside paths, skunks we treated with circumspection, the sun shone and we caught fish. The 'bright fish' season opens much later than on Scottish rivers such as the Tay, so we used typical light summer gear – floating lines and low-water-style flies in singles and doubles.

1 Cosseboom

COMMENT

The originator was John C. Cosseboom, who was a poet, a newspaper writer, and a champion fly caster. He had various theories about salmon flies, one being his preference for a red head, which he thought gave a focal point for the fish. The Cosseboom, also known as the Cosseboom Special, is considered the best of the patterns. It started as a streamer on the Margaree in about 1922, and a year later was adapted, and slightly simplified, to Atlantic salmon fly style.

It has also been adapted to dry-fly style, and as such we also show it in the dry-fly section.

DRESSING

Tag: Silver, embossed or flat.
Tail: Olive-green floss.
Body: Olive-green floss.
Rib: Silver, embossed or flat.
Wing: Grey squirrel.
Collar: Lemon.
Sides (optional): Jungle cock.
Head: Red.

2 Gold Cosseboom

COMMENT

Apparently over thirty Cosseboom variations were devised. Bates records the Gold's origination as being on the Margaree in 1923, and then used later that year on Anticosti Island. It is said to be particularly effective in clear water. Gary Anderson also recommends it for the Nova Scotian River Gold.

DRESSING

Tag: Silver, embossed or flat.
Tail: Topping.
Body: Embossed gold.
Rib: Oval silver.
Wing: Grey squirrel with a few strands of green herl over.
Collar: Light-blue.
Sides (optional): Jungle cock.
Head: Red.

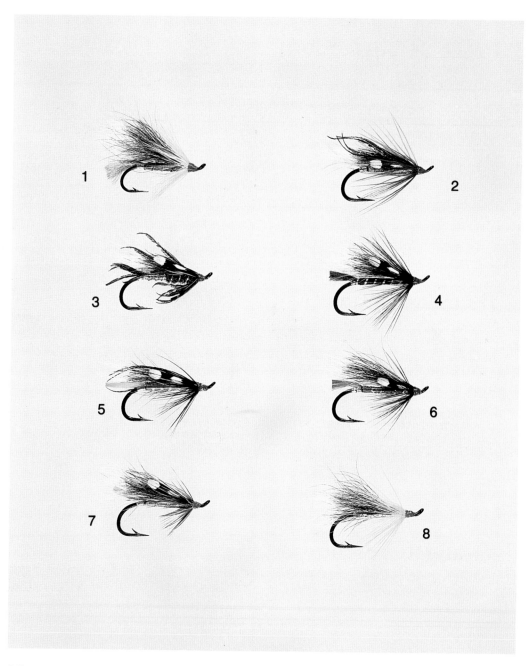

1 Cosseboom   2 Gold Cosseboom   3 Peacock Cosseboom
4 Black Cosseboom   5 Orange Cosseboom   6 Red Cosseboom
7 Yellow Cosseboom   8 Silver Cosseboom

3 Peacock Cosseboom

COMMENT

None of the authorities has any notes on this one of the series, so we don't have much to say either, though it does look very much as if the Rat concept of a herl half-body is being copied. Jorgensen does list it.

DRESSING

Tag: Embossed silver.
Tail: Four or five green herls.
Body: Rear half embossed gold, front half bronze peacock herl.
Rib: Oval silver over both sections.
Wing: Grey squirrel tail with a few herl strands over.
Throat: Green herl strands about half as long as the body.
Sides (optional): Jungle cock.
Head: Red.

4 Black Cosseboom

COMMENT

Embossed silver is sometimes used. Two turns of the collar hackle may be taken under the wing in any of the Cossebooms to make it stand out more. It can be tied with a tail of topping and a body of black ostrich herl.

Gary Anderson mentions this as a good pattern for the Lower Humber and the Cains River.

DRESSING

Tag: Flat silver.
Tail: Black floss cut short.
Body: Black floss.
Rib: Flat silver.
Wing: Grey squirrel.
Collar: Black.
Sides (optional): Jungle cock.
Head: Red.

5 Orange Cosseboom

COMMENT

Bates records that this is the only one of the series to have a black head. An essential on all these patterns is to keep the tail short, so that the fly is not nipped without gaining a hook-hold.

DRESSING

Tag: Flat gold.
Tail: Orange floss or wool.
Body: Orange floss or seal fur or wool.
Rib: Flat gold.
Wing: Grey squirrel with a few strands of green herl over.
Collar: Black.
Sides (optional): Jungle cock.
Head: Black.

6 Red Cosseboom

COMMENT

For those who believe in this style of fly, and who believe that colour really matters, every colour is available. We have few notes on the extra efficiency of this tying over the others. Again, Jorgensen sees it as important enough to include.

DRESSING

Tag: Embossed gold.
Tail: Red floss or wool, cut short.
Body: Red floss or wool or seal fur.
Rib: Embossed gold.
Wing: Grey squirrel tail.
Collar: Black.
Sides (optional): Jungle cock.
Head: Red.

7 Yellow Cosseboom

COMMENT

The formula below is that given by Bates. Fulsher and Krom have a Nova Scotian pattern which differs: tag, flat silver; tail, topping; butt, red chenille; body, forest-green wool; rib, oval silver; throat, bright yellow; wing, yellow calf tail; head, red.

DRESSING

Tag: Embossed silver.
Tail: Yellow floss or wool.
Body: Yellow floss or wool.
Rib: Embossed silver.
Wing: Grey squirrel tail.
Collar: Grizzle.
Sides (optional): Jungle cock.
Head: Red.

8 Silver Cosseboom

COMMENT

We found this dressing in Fulsher and Krom, but not in Bates, nor in Jorgensen. It seems like a later design, with no specifications for tag and tail.

DRESSING

Body: Flat silver.
Rib: Oval silver.
Wing: Grey squirrel tail.
Collar: Yellow.
Head: Red.

Hairwings 1

Our North American experiences were perforce limited; we saw a Lee Wulff fishing documentary on TV – those on salmon fishing in Labrador were the most mouth-watering. There were rivers swarming with fish, and it seemed to be just a matter of choosing the fish to present a fly to, and making sure it was a heavy one. The further north the fisherman goes, the less spoilt and the more impressive the fishing.

Other modern writers on the North American scene are Shirley Woods and Gary Anderson. All discuss rivers – where to go, and how to fish them, with some historical background. For a prospective visitor it would be negligent not to read them. Joseph Bates' two books on the Atlantic salmon fly omit little for the student of American salmon flies. Add to the library Fulsher and Krom's paperback on the hairwing patterns and the fish will hardly have a chance. We have drawn from all three sources for our representative selection of North American patterns. We have already mentioned that the British classic patterns may simply be converted to the hairwing style, and other British hairwings will be found in the sections that follow.

Here are some black and some white tyings.

1 Black Dose

COMMENT

Among the variations the simplest resemble simple Black Doctors. This is the Canadian featherwing dressing from Jorgensen: tag, fine oval silver and yellow floss; tail, topping; butt, none; body, black floss (or black seal fur); rib, oval silver; hackle, none, or black; throat, black; wing, two strips of black turkey under red, yellow and blue swan and golden pheasant tail, veiled with grey mallard, with bronze mallard over and topping; sides, jungle cock. Sometimes there is a claret throat and usually a couple of turns of blue at the tail end of the body.

DRESSING

Tag: Oval silver and orange floss.
Tail: Topping.
Body: Rear quarter, fluorescent blue floss; front three-quarters, black wool.
Rib: Oval silver.
Hackle: Black.
Throat: None.
Wing: Two strands each of orange-red and green fluorescent floss under red phase squirrel tail or black squirrel tail.
Head: Black.

2 Night Hawk

COMMENT

A Canadian pattern listed regularly in the UK tackle catalogues. The hairwing dressing hardly simplifies the pattern, being merely a substitute for a black winging feather. Bates in *The Art* . . . shows splendid wry humour in his note of its origination. A Mr White was the inventor, but was shot to death in 1906 for having dinner with his assailant's wife. 'Fortunately these two events occurred in an order favourable to anglers.'

DRESSING

Tag: Flat silver and yellow floss.
Tail: Topping and (optional) kingfisher.
Butt: Red wool.
Body: Flat silver.
Rib: Oval silver.
Throat: Black.
Wing: Black squirrel tail (or black swan, or crow, or goose), with topping over.
Sides: Jungle cock.
Cheeks: Kingfisher.
Head: Red and black.

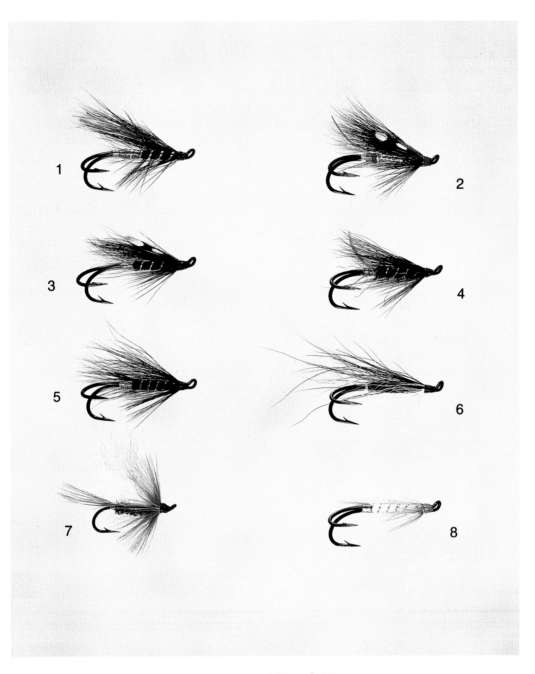

1 Black Dose **2** Night Hawk **3** Black Bomber **4** Black Coltrin
5 Black Conrad **6** Black Wulff **7** Ingalls' Butterfly **8** The Priest

3 Black Bomber

COMMENT

The Silver Grey Bomber was the favourite of Joe
Aucoin, the inventor. They were first used on the
Margaree River, and still have a reputation in
Nova Scotia. Neither the Black (which can also
have a fluorescent tip) or Brown Bomber
(similar, with brown body and brown wing)
should be confused with British trout flies or
North American dry flies of similar name.

    The Bomber name was inspired by *the* boxer
of the time . . .

DRESSING

Tag: Oval silver and yellow floss.
Tail: Topping.
Body: Black wool.
Rib: Oval silver.
Throat: Black.
Wing: Black squirrel, topping.
Sides: Jungle cock.

4 Black Coltrin

COMMENT

This was used extensively by Shirley Woods as
his 'dark' choice of fly, which he favoured often
in high and somewhat murky water conditions. It
is very close to a Black Dose variant. His tinsel
body alternative is the Silver Rat, and the
Roger's Fancy is his 'bright' pattern, of the three
main standbys. His tying illustrated in his book
has a very noticeable yellow floss element in the
tag.

DRESSING

Tag: Oval silver and yellow floss.
Tail: Topping.
Body: Black seal fur or mohair.
Rib: Oval silver.
Throat: Black.
Wing: Black hair.
Sides: Jungle cock or barred summer duck.

5 Black Conrad

COMMENT

There are many black patterns barely
distinguishable from each other. The Black Bear
is a standard, with the minor variations earning
themselves different names. Sometimes the
Black Bear is tied with a red head to give a focal
spot of colour. Similar are All Black, Black
Spider, Belfast Killer and, in Britain, the
Stoat's Tail.

DRESSING

Tag: Oval silver.
Butt: Fluorescent red, green, orange or blue
floss or wool.
Tail: Black hackle fibres.
Body: Black wool.
Rib: Oval silver.
Throat: Black.
Wing: Black bear.

6 Black Wulff

COMMENT

What originally was designed and tied as a
salmon and trout dry fly has been adapted to
wet-fly style with considerable success in
Newfoundland. Tied dry as an alternative to the
Grey and White Wulffs, the dressing is: tail,
black hair (generous); body, black or red floss
or wool; throat, natural red; wing, black hair;
collar, black.

DRESSING

Tag: Turn of flat silver.
Tail: Short topping.
Body: Black floss.
Throat: White moose hair.
Wing: Black moose hair.

7 Ingalls' Butterfly

COMMENT

One of the best of the Miramichi patterns,
devised by Maurice Ingalls in 1956. The original
pattern seems to be the best. The fly is similar to
the Beaufort Moth and the Coachman trout fly,
but the action comes from the split wings, which
pulsate in the water. It is also known as Ingalls'
Splay-wing Coachman.
  Father Mercer's adaptation, often the only fly
to take fish on the Miramichi under warm-water
conditions, has a slim unribbed black body and
– for the hottest part of the summer – a bright-
orange wing and yellow hackle.

DRESSING

Tag: Flat gold or oval silver.
Tail: Bright-red hackle fibres.
Body: Peacock herl.
Rib: None.
Wing: White calf tail, polar bear, bucktail or
goat divided flat at 30 degrees.
Collar: Hot ginger.

8 The Priest

COMMENT

Originated by the Reverend Elmer J. Smith of
Doaktown, New Brunswick. 'It is killing in cold
water pools, also effective in slow water if
movement is imparted.' The White Miller has a
non-fluorescent body, red hackle fibre tail and
throat, and is otherwise similar. Defeo's Evening
Fly (tag, oval gold; tail, brown hackle fibres;
body, fluorescent white wool; rib, oval gold;
throat, natural red; wing, sparse white calf tail),
the White Doctor and White Wings are other
'white' patterns.

DRESSING

Tag: Oval silver.
Tail: Light-blue dun hackle fibres.
Body: White fluorescent wool.
Rib: Oval silver.
Throat: Light-blue dun, wound.
Wing: White calf tail.
Head: White.

Hairwings 2

The principles of tying hairwings do not differ much on either side of the Atlantic, but there may be elements of local style. The Miramichi is the birth river of many tying innovations and much thought. Their wet flies in the standard mould seem to have more and closer turns of tinsel than might be used in Britain. Bodies in North America seem to be tied in more of a tapered cigar form than in Britain, where they are normally tied parallel and as slim as possible. The hairwings themselves are tied very flat and short and sleek for the most part in North America, yet there is a growing tendency to keep them sparse in Britain, but longer than the hook shank, perhaps twice or even three times as long.

In this style the special qualities of the hair chosen will certainly be evident; in the short, flat wing, however, the material barely has a chance to show to the fish as it is largely masked by the body – which leads us back to A. H. E. Wood. He proved regularly that he caught fish on flies which were just bodies, with no need for mobility or translucency or colour from the wing, *because there wasn't one*. This raises again the question of the relative importance of colour and shape in body and wing. Silver and gold predominate in the bodies of this group of flies.

1 Echo Beach

COMMENT

A pattern redolent of a trip to the South-West Miramichi at Red Bank. The last of the salmon were showing, and the first of the grilse entering the pools. A classic time of canoeing white water rapids, adventures with a drunken guide, arrest by wardens and a few fish. They were lovely bright fish, salmon of about eleven pounds and grilse of about four pounds.

DRESSING

Tag: Silver lurex.
Tail: Topping.
Butt: Fluorescent orange floss and fluorescent red wool.
Body: Embossed silver.
Rib: Oval silver.
Throat: Brown.
Wing: Yellow calf tail under black calf tail under white calf tail.

2 Silver Downeaster

COMMENT

For the Down East, the body is grey, and the throat is tied collar-style. For the Downeaster the dressing is: tag, oval silver and fluorescent red floss; tail, topping; butt, black herl; body, grey floss; rib, silver oval; throat, orange; wing, black bear.

DRESSING

Tag: Oval silver.
Tail: Topping.
Butt: Black herl.
Body: Flat silver.
Rib: Oval silver.
Throat: Orange.
Wing: Black squirrel.

110

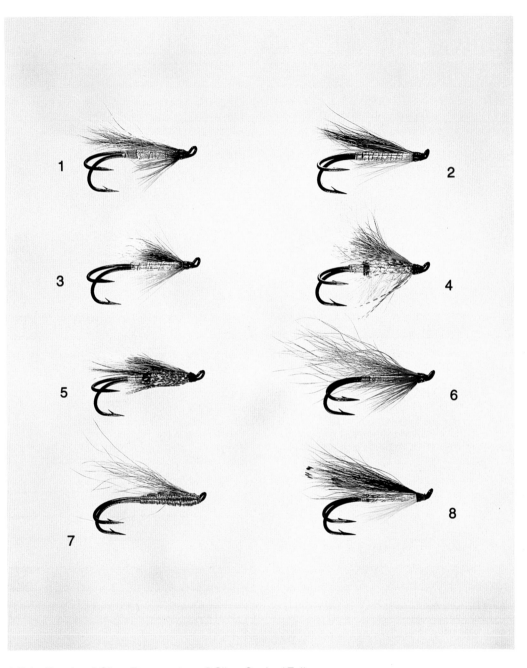

1 Echo Beach   **2** Silver Downeaster   **3** Silver Squirrel Tail
4 Lady Amherst   **5** Gold Fever   **6** Bucktail & Gold   **7** Gold High River
8 Gold Kenny's Killer

3 Silver Squirrel Tail

COMMENT

This simple pattern, which falls into line with Medicines, but is more muted in the throat, could be made even simpler by the use of 'metallic' silver nail varnish (lacquer) for the body. The Gold Squirrel Tail is the same dressing with a gold body.

DRESSING

Tag: None.
Tail: None.
Body: Flat silver.
Rib: Oval silver.
Throat: Natural medium-blue dun.
Wing: Grey squirrel.

4 Lady Amherst

COMMENT

The classic pattern – with a complicated wing of jungle cock veiled by Amherst tippet, in turn veiled by shorter Amherst, with sides of jungle cock and cheeks of chatterer – has been much simplified. Ubiquitous grey squirrel makes the wing. The fully dressed pattern is a true American classic, devised in 1925 by George Bonbright. On the Cascapedia it dominated all other choice of fly. It was widely listed in British catalogues.

DRESSING

Tag: Oval silver and yellow floss.
Tail: Topping.
Butt: Black herl.
Body: Flat silver.
Rib: Oval silver.
Hackle: Badger.
Throat: Teal or grizzle or wigeon.
Wing: Grey squirrel – generous.
Cheeks: Fans of fluorescent blue floss.

5 Gold Fever

COMMENT

The use of embossed tinsel for the body is a reversion to early traditional practice – like the earliest tying of the Dunkeld or the Dusty Miller. Very often oval is substituted, or, in the larger sizes, Mylar tubing.

DRESSING

Tag: Flat gold and yellow floss.
Tail: Black hackle fibres.
Butt: Black wool.
Body: Embossed gold.
Rib: Oval gold.
Throat: Guinea-fowl.
Wing: Grey squirrel over yellow-dyed grey squirrel.

6 Bucktail & Gold

COMMENT

This is a reminder of the streamer or bucktail style which has been abbreviated to orthodox low-water style salmon tyings. A look into Bates's *Streamers and Bucktails* will open horizons on proven patterns which might be reduced.

DRESSING

Tag: Round or oval gold.
Tail: Topping.
Body: Flat gold.
Rib: Oval gold.
Throat: Medium-blue tied extra-long.
Wing: Brown bucktail with a blue bucktail bunch tied in each side – extending to the end of the tail.

7 Gold High River

COMMENT

This style of tying has something in common with Sawyer's Pheasant Tail Nymph, in that the tying 'silk' is the body material. In this case silver or gold tinsel is used, though copper wire would be an alternative. The result of this pattern is a quite different shape. The butt ends of a slim bundle of bucktail are tied pointing towards the fly head, the tip ends are then folded forwards and the hair is folded forwards and backwards in turn as the body is built up. At the appropriate place for the wing, the tips are folded back for the last time, and the head is formed of the turns of tinsel which tie everything down.

DRESSING

Body: Bucktail and tying tinsel.
Wing: Tips of the bucktail.
Head: Final turns of the tying tinsel.

8 Gold Kenny's Killer

COMMENT

This is a pattern from Britain – Ken Burns was the inventor of the Silver Kenny's Killer. Crawford Little made the variation in order to differ from Bourrach, his choice of silver-bodied long-winged flies. He reports that the silver version is excellent in the smaller sizes for summer salmon and grilse in bright weather and low, clear water.

DRESSING

Tag (optional): Oval gold.
Tail: Tippet strands – long.
Body: Flat gold.
Rib: Oval gold.
Throat: Yellow cock.
Wing: Black squirrel tail.

Hairwings 3

In North America there is a style of fishing called 'the Patent'. It was an invention of Colonel Lewis S. Thompson, who fished the Restigouche at Kedgwick Lodge. He was an early user of hair-winged flies, for in the 1890s he had used some A. S. Trude trout flies. These he had tied larger for salmon, then 'one day in 1928, while fishing Jimmie's Hole on the Rogers water . . . the Colonel while resting the pool cast his large 5/0 hair fly (Red Abbey) upstream, let it float down on a loose line like a large mouse and saw it grabbed by a large salmon which had withstood all assaults. To an experienced and able fisherman such as Colonel Thompson that experience was not merely a hint, but an education, and from then until his death in 1936, he not only practised but developed fishing "The Patent".' This was reported by Walter C. Teagle and Bayard W. Read in *The Anglers Club of New York Bulletin*, October 1945. The fly fishes with no drag from the line, and the water pressures alone make the hair fibres flutter and pulsate. The fish should be tightened on, as they rise.

Copper, blue and grey feature in the dressings of this group of flies.

1 Cains Copper

COMMENT

The Cains is one of the tributaries of the Miramichi. Accordingly it is the source of several patterns – this one, the Cains River special and numerous streamer patterns which were originally designed to catch 'black fish' (kelts) at the opening of the season. Bates lists 21 of these patterns designed by Fred N. Peet, an angler from Chicago. For those with an interest in history, the dressings can be found in Bates's *Streamers and Bucktails*.

DRESSING

Tag: Fine oval copper tinsel or wire.
Tail: Fluorescent red hackle fibres.
Butt: Black chenille.
Body: Flat copper tinsel.
Rib: Oval copper or wire.
Wing: Grey squirrel over orange-dyed hair.
Collar: Black cock.

2 Copper Killer

COMMENT

There are several alternatives for the tail – brown partridge hackle fibres or golden pheasant tippet. Wire may be used instead of oval copper tinsel, which is difficult to acquire.

DRESSING

Tag: Oval copper and fluorescent yellow floss, or pale green floss.
Tail: Strands of red squirrel tail.
Butt: Fluorescent red floss or fluorescent orange wool.
Body: Flat copper.
Rib: Oval copper.
Throat: Bright-orange.
Wing: Red squirrel tail.
Head: (optional): Red.

114

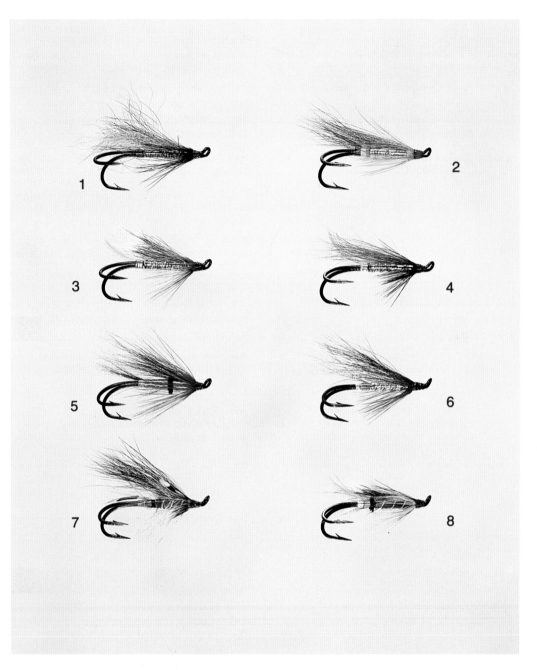

1 Cains Copper **2** Copper Killer **3** Pot Scrubber **4** Tarnished Silver
5 Blue Colburn **6** Icy Blue **7** Nipisiguit Grey **8** Lemon Grey

3 Pot Scrubber

COMMENT

A British pattern with the original having its body made from the abrasive domestic scouring pad used for cleaning dishes – hence the name. A North American equivalent is the Copper Rat – tag, oval copper; tail, peacock sword fibres; body, flat copper; rib, oval copper; wing, black and white hair mixed; collar, grizzle; head, red.

DRESSING

Hook: Double.
Tag: Oval silver.
Tail: Topping.
Body: Copper lurex or flat copper.
Rib: Oval silver.
Throat: Brown.
Wing: Grey squirrel tail.

4 Tarnished Silver

COMMENT

A pattern for those who really believe in copper, rather than just silver or gold. There is a distinct advantage in polishing copper extremely well before tying with it, and then varnishing it.

DRESSING

Tag: Flat silver.
Tail: Topping.
Body: Rear half flat copper, front half flat silver.
Rib: Oval gold.
Throat: Black.
Wing: Red squirrel tail.

5 Blue Colburn

COMMENT

There is a series of Colburns – Colburn Special, Claret Colburn, Orange Colburn – each taking its name from the body colour. Bates in *The Art of the Atlantic Salmon Fly* illustrates the Green Colburn, dressed with a fluorescent green body. None has a rib.

DRESSING

Tag: Oval silver.
Tail: Blue-dyed grey squirrel tail.
Body: Medium-blue floss in a thick cigar shape, with a butt of black herl in the centre.
Wing: Blue-dyed grey squirrel.
Collar: Light-blue or black hackle.

6 Icy Blue

COMMENT

As expected, blue hairwing variations of the standards are tied. This is similar to the Silver Blue, the Blue Charm is tied with a grey squirrel wing, and so on. The Silver Doctor and Blue Doctor adaptations are given wings of red squirrel over grey squirrel over strands of red, blue and yellow floss. The Black & Blue has a black hair wing.

DRESSING

Tag: Flat silver.
Butt: Fluorescent blue floss.
Tail: Topping.
Body: Flat silver.
Rib: Oval silver.
Throat: Blue.
Wing: Blue-dyed grey squirrel over white hair.

7 Nipisiguit Grey

COMMENT

This was one of the North American classics and all the winging has been replaced by hair. The original featherwing dressing is given in brackets. It dates from 1927. Sometimes black cock takes the place of the grizzle throat hackle. The Nipisiguit Green is: tag, gold wire; tail, fluorescent-yellow-dyed hackle fibres; butt, fluorescent orange floss; body, fine black chenille; rib, oval gold; throat, bright orange; wing, dyed bright-green squirrel tail.

DRESSING

Tag: Fine oval gold and yellow floss. **Tail:** Topping (and summer duck). **Butt:** Black wool (peacock herl). **Body:** Grey fox underfur (grey muskrat underfur). **Rib:** Oval silver (gold). **Hackle:** Pale grizzle over the front three-fifths of body (none). **Throat:** Pale grizzle. **Wing:** Black bear hair (tippet strands and brown mottled turkey tail under blue swan, Amherst pheasant tail, teal and brown mottled turkey, veiled with summer duck, with bronze mallard over and topping). **Sides:** Jungle cock.

8 Lemon Grey

COMMENT

This is another of the grey-bodied flies used in North America, which include Black Deceiver, Texas Jack, Whalin Galen, and Parson (a conversion from a trout pattern).

DRESSING

Tag: Flat silver and yellow floss.
Tail: Topping.
Butt: Black herl.
Body: Grey fur.
Rib: Oval silver.
Throat: Blue dun and yellow mixed.
Wing: Yellow-dyed hair over grey squirrel tail.

Hairwings 4

It seems very much that there are 'coloured' rivers in North America in the same way as in Britain. Sometimes it may be that the natural and available fly-tying materials dictate what patterns of flies are fished in a river, or trial and error has dictated the menu. The Nipisiguit patterns, particularly the Nipisiguit Grey, were the flies for that river until the Rat patterns, to which they are very similar, took over.

Shirley Woods is most interesting in his observations on green flies. The Sainte Anne, he feels, is very much a 'green' river. With his Cullman's Choice Lee Wulff devised a green pattern different enough from what was normally shown to the fish rather than use a pattern of a completely different colour.

Gary Anderson quotes the Gaspésie rivers as being silver-fly rivers; Newfoundland fish favour Thunder & Lightnings; on the Cascapedia a Yellow Canary does well; the Cosseboom is successful in most parts of Nova Scotia and New Brunswick. What becomes clear is that reliance on a good guide is worthwhile. Not all areas make it obligatory to have a guide, but the visitor might well end up on unproductive water without professional advice.

Flies in this section include orange, red, green and yellow.

1 Orange Blossom

COMMENT

A Variation includes a body in two equal sections, the rear of embossed silver and the front of yellow seal fur, a rib of oral silver and a wing of mixed brown and white hair. Shirley Woods chooses this pattern for when the river is somewhat dirty. Fulsher and Krom give a body hackle of yellow cock, and add jungle cock at the shoulder.

DRESSING

Tag: Fine oval silver and yellow or orange floss.
Tail: Topping and (optional) Indian crow,
Butt: Black herl.
Body: Embossed silver.
Rib: None.
Wing: Palest natural brown bucktail.
Collar: Bright orange.
Head: Black.

2 Orange Puppy

COMMENT

Recommended by Gary Anderson for the Lower Humber in his list of flies for Newfoundland and Labrador. The Orange Charm, with black floss body and woodchuck guard hair or eastern pine squirrel wing, is not widely different.

DRESSING

Tag: Embossed silver.
Tail: Orange hackle fibres.
Body: Black chenille.
Hackle: Orange (alternatively tied as throat).
Wing: Grey squirrel tail.
Head: Black with a previous turn of orange chenille.

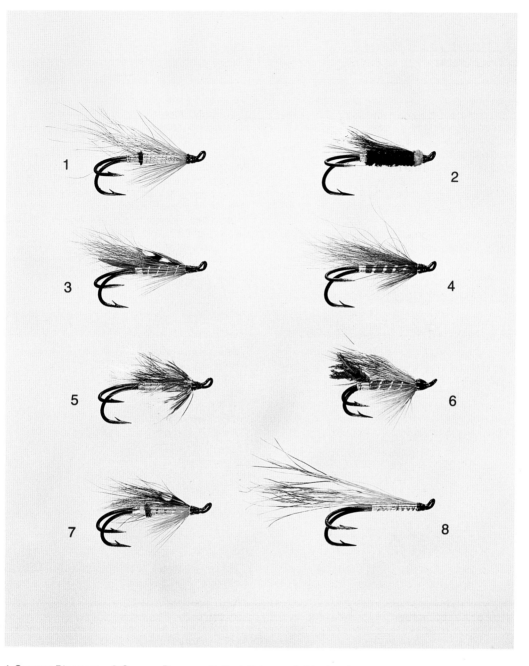

1 Orange Blossom **2** Orange Puppy **3** Red Abbey **4** Montreal
5 Grizzly King **6** Roger's Fancy **7** Warden Watcher **8** Yellow Badger

3 Red Abbey

COMMENT

Fulsher and Krom give a variant pattern of Jorgensen's. The brackets beside the dressing give their dressing. It is included as a reliable standard by Al McClane in his monumental *International New Standard Fishing Encyclopaedia*.

DRESSING

Tag: Fine oval tinsel.
Tail: Red goose fibres (red ibis).
Body: Red floss or wool (seal fur).
Rib: Oval silver (flat).
Throat: Brown hackle fibres as a beard (as a collar).
Wing: Fox squirrel tail or brown bucktail (red phase squirrel tail).
Sides: Jungle cock (none).
Head: Black.

4 Montreal

COMMENT

A great number of standard trout patterns have been adapted to the low-water salmon fly style, and some of their feather components have been replaced by hair. If grey squirrel is used for the wing, the pattern is called the White-tipped Montreal. The Yellow Montreal has a wing of yellow-dyed calf tail and a collar of yellow hackle.

DRESSING

Tag: Flat gold.
Tail: Dyed yellow hackle fibres.
Body: Claret floss.
Rib: Flat gold.
Throat: Claret.
Wing: Red squirrel tail (originally brown turkey).

5 Grizzly King

COMMENT

This was a standard trout and steelhead pattern. It has also been regularly tied as a streamer. Other green patterns which are regularly shown are the Green Charm Hairwing, which has a wing green-dyed greyish monkey hair, and the Deer Lake Special, which Gary Anderson notes is favoured for the Upper Humber, where other patterns with a moose-hair wing are popular.

DRESSING

Tag: Oval gold.
Tail: Red-dyed topping.
Body: Fluorescent green wool (originally green wool).
Rib: Oval gold.
Wing: Grey squirrel tail (originally grey mallard).
Collar: Grizzle.

6 Roger's Fancy

COMMENT

Designed by Shirley Woods 'some years ago' for his fishing companion Major-General Roger Rowley, it has proved itself on a good number of Canadian and Icelandic rivers. He wrote about it in 1974 in *Trout and Salmon* and Bates considers it to be 'an important pattern'.

The fly shown is of Woods' own tying.

DRESSING

Tag: Fine oval silver and fluorescent yellow floss wound over white floss and lacquered.
Tail: Three or four peacock sword herls.
Body: Bright-green wool or seal fur.
Rib: Oval silver.
Throat: Bright-yellow under bright-green.
Wing: Grey fox guard hair.
Sides: Short jungle cock or barred wood duck.

7 Warden Watcher

COMMENT

In style this is a contrast with the following fly. Other yellow patterns in brief are the Yellow Bucktail (silver body, orange throat, and wing of yellow-dyed grey squirrel with orange topping over and jungle cock) and the Yellow Duce (yellow floss body, yellow throat, and wing of yellow-dyed grey squirrel over a strand of fluorescent green floss).

DRESSING

Tag: Flat gold and fluorescent yellow floss.
Tail: Topping.
Butt: Peacock herl.
Body: Yellow floss.
Rib: Flat gold.
Hackle: Orange.
Wing: Black bear.
Cheek: Jungle cock.

8 Yellow Badger

COMMENT

In 1985 one of the British hairwings went to Canada. Derek Knowles planned a dry-fly trip to Wilson's Camp on the Miramichi. He opened his innings with a grilse on his Yellow Badger wet fly, and continued to do well with this pattern of his. We include it because as a style it clearly works well in North American waters, and because it is a very different style of hairwing from theirs.

DRESSING

Tag: None.
Tail: None.
Body: Flat silver.
Wing: Strands yellow-dyed badger, very sparse and twice the shank length.

TUBES AND
WADDINGTONS

Introduction

Tubes At first it was just a trickle and then it became a wave – the small low-water flies, the use of which Wood had propounded at Cairnton, were being displaced. In the 1950s and 1960s, the Stoat's Tail tube fly was the way to take summer salmon. The leader material was threaded through a plastic tube on which a small cone of hairs was tied and knotted to a treble which was then partially concealed by the hair. Silk lines were still being fished, so the fly had little tendency to skim. The tiny hooks cut into the fishes' mouths and took a surprisingly good grip.

Development of the tube has taken place in three main ways: in size, in weight and in complexity of dressing. The early low-water examples rarely exceeded ½ inch. The dressing was either hair, hair and feather or feather, applied to the tube, all with little interest in the body. The tube might be clear plastic, black, red or yellow. The simplicity was such that the fly-tying trade could see the benefit: the price of flies would not come down but the speed of tying was much increased and the need for special ingredients was much reduced. With the current conviction that a treble hook is a better hooker than a single of large size, or even a double, the tube's future is assured. In the larger sizes for spring and autumn fishing the body is usually dressed and long strands of dyed bucktail, often just tied in at the head, create the winging. Some patterns are jointed, with winging material tied in at the tail and in the centre, but for reasons of speed and simplicity the head is usually the only area dressed with 'winging'. Weight is a function of the tube material. For lightness plastic tubes are used, aluminium tubes with plastic liners are heavier, and brass or copper tubes with liners are the heaviest.

The extension of a tube – rubber or latex over the rearmost end and over the eye and part of the shank of the treble – is no new thing. Tom Saville related with amusement how Thomas Clegg, author of *How to Tie Tube Flies* and other books, used a small moulded bicycle valve rubber from Dunlop for the purpose and christened it a mouse's French letter. Its only duty is to make sure that fly and hook stay aligned, yet it should not be so tight as to prevent the tube's being able to slide on up the leader when a fish has taken. It saves the dressing from possible damage. It also removes a long arm of leverage from the hook which might make the hook-hold less secure.

American tube flies. The style has its admirers in North America, but one of its virtues is denied their fishermen – the hooking ability of a good treble – because trebles are largely banned. Tubes are tyed, however, and either singles or doubles are used. Derek Knowles relates how badly a single on his Yellow Dolly tube hooked fish. Although authors write about 'composite' tubes (two or three threaded on at a time) making up a fly, British practice is to choose the correct pattern in the correct size. The break from this tradition only comes with the occasional application of a Muddler head when a surface riffle is wanted.

Waddingtons Richard Waddington, with great attention to detail, turned his mind to what the salmon saw in big salmon flies. He felt that the standard single-iron flies bore very little resemblance to fish – the illusion might be there but the nature of the fly design was unbalanced, with the weight of the hook dragging the body of the fly out of line with the wing. He felt that a treble hook at the tail would be more symmetrical, and a fly tied with the same profile from all sides would look more like a fish and thus be more attractive. The base would be a shank with an eye at the head and an eye for the treble at the tail end. Alex Martin Ltd were invited to tie the early patterns, and Waddington's endeavours with his prototypes proved more successful in rising and retaining their hold on fish than did single irons. These early patterns were fairly fully dressed: the trebles sported tags and butts, and the bodies were tied with palmer hackles and highly mobile feather winging, obviously derived from standards like the Wilkinson and Thunder & Lightning. Subsequent development has been towards simplicity – substitution of dyed bucktail for heron hackles, and unadorned trebles. Incorporation of nylon strand into the tying of both shank and treble to ensure that they align during fishing is a fiddly business. A sleeve of rubber tubing, like that used on tubes, is far quicker and permits a change of treble when needed.

Black-japanned, bronze or silver trebles are all available. There is little evidence to support preferences in hook colour, though silver in the small sizes might have a strong place in some fishermen's affections. Weight is adjustable only in so far as lead or wire can be included in the preparation of the shank during the fly-tying operation. Most amateurs have their own code to identify their weighted patterns – for instance, brown head varnish on their trout flies, and on their salmon flies dark-blue varnish rather than the more usual black. Crawford Little, in a recent article in *Trout and Salmon*, explains how he likes to see extra weight incorporated in a Waddington – added at the head end of the fly (beneath the wing dressing), both to counterbalance the weight of the treble at the tail end, and to counterpoise the pull of a line which fishes more shallowly than the fly. His suggestions are either a spiral of lead wire or a brass collar. Another method is the lead from a wine-bottle seal, which is cut into a narrow ribbon. Bound over with tying silk it makes a smooth, firm and weighty foundation. (The same principle may be applied to big tube flies for those who prefer to fish deep but with floating lines.)

Those who are spinning enthusiasts – threadliners – may remember that Alexander Wanless advocated the use of light spinning lines cast by 'balanced' light rods (he had his made by Hardy's). By adding a 'governor' he could throw as light a weight as a fly; the governor would have either 'intermediate' or 'floating' qualities, and would exercise some control on how the fly (or bait) fished. In his illustrations he shows a treble-hooked shanked fly of exactly this basis of construction. However, the dressing was in the normal style of a salmon fly – wing on top and throat hackle below, and so on. He did not have the idea that the fly might appear much the same from all sides and angles. So it is fair to say that this style of construction may fairly be dated to the 1930s or earlier.

Brora flies – the style , not the fully dressed classic pattern – are referred to by some authors. They are a development by Rob Wilson of the tackle shop in Brora. Rather than using the Waddington shanks obtainable from Partridge, hookmakers of Redditch, he fashioned his own. The principles remain the same.

Our last example in the Waddington section is a Cebrit hook, included because it is articulated rather than a true Waddington. There are times and places when single hooks in large sizes have some advantages over doubles and trebles, particularly in autumn when leaves flood the river, yet a large single iron is considered to exert undue leverage.

Tube Flies

Tube flies may have originated with Mrs Winnie Morawski, working with Playfair of Aberdeen in the 1950s. She took a section of quill, to which she added the dressing, and threaded the leader through it to tie on the treble. But Ronald Coleby remembered an illustration of 'very rum salmon flies' in a copy of Wanless' *The Angler and the Thread Line* of 1932. Two plates show an indisputable tube and a precursor to a Waddington. Wanless enjoyed using a proper fly rod but also enjoyed 'spinning' with flies, being suspicious of revolving lures. He required weight (so a fly could be cast), yet fine enough hooks to suit the 'thread line'. He wrote: 'the

lures are of three types – one has a hole through the centre of it so that it slips up the line when a fish is being played. That is to prevent the small hook from being levered out of the fish's mouth by the "body" of the fly.' He tied the standard patterns on the lead tube – mixed wing and palmered body – fully dressed.

The first six patterns are on tubes designed by Ted Hunter of Melrose – anodised black, shrink-wrapped to preserve the dressing, and recessed to take the trace olive (a plastic bead with an extension tube each side of it, normally part of a Devon minnow) which aligns the treble.

1 White Wing

COMMENT

The White Wing is a Tweed pattern, of which the origin seems lost in antiquity. However, by 1880 or so there was an approximate standard: body of seal fur of various colours, a throat hackle of blue and pure white wings from swan or goose. The tube or Waddington dressing, as exemplified here, lifts the body and hackle colouring to the wing, so the red and blue are added to the white in a sparse and mobile fibre. Red trace olive.

DRESSING

Body: Black floss.
Rib: Silver.
Wing: Segments of white, blue and red hair.
Head: Black.

2 Garry Dog

COMMENT

The Garry Dog was one of the first hairwings, certainly it was a fairly early established pattern, and comes from the tying bench of James Wright of Sprouston, on the Tweed. The standard pattern easily transfers to the modern idiom.
Red trace olive.

DRESSING

Body: Black floss.
Rib: Flat silver.
Wing: Top and bottom, one-third red, two-thirds yellow hair.
Cheeks: Tufts of blue fibres, at sides.
Head: Black.

126

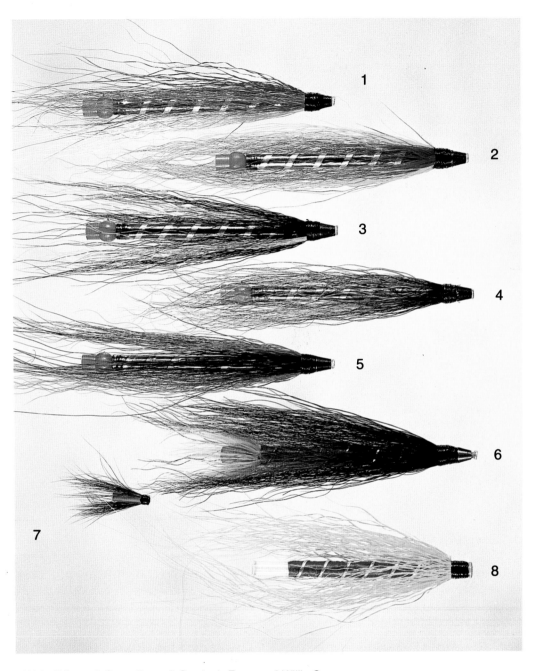

1 White Wing   **2** Garry Dog   **3** Gordon's Fancy   **4** Willie Gunn
5 Thunder   **6** Comet   **7** Stoat's Tail Tube   **8** Yellow Dog

3 Gordon's Fancy

COMMENT

Also known as the Black & Yellow, on Tweed it bears the name given here since Gordon Lessinger particularly fancies it on the Junction Pool at Kelso, where Tweed and Teviot join. Red trace olive.

DRESSING

Body: Black floss.
Rib: Silver.
Wing: Top and bottom, black hair; sides, (less) yellow hair.
Head: Black.

4 Willie Gunn

COMMENT

Named after the Sutherland Estate's head keeper on the Brora, this is a Highlands fly of modern origin – W. G. retired about 10 years ago. It has become accepted as a mixed wing, wherein the three colours are pirled together, rather than tied in as separate colour units. Bill Currie, author and regular fishing correspondent, has almost forsaken all other patterns for this, in many sizes and weights. Red trace olive.

DRESSING

Body: Black floss.
Rib: Silver.
Wing: Yellow, orange/red and black hair evenly mixed.
Head: Black.

5 Thunder

COMMENT

The well-known Thunder & Lightning (possibly of Irish origination) is universally successful – particularly, it is said, in falling water after a spate – and is easily translated to hair-winging, tubes and Waddingtons. In the form shown, it is often called Black & Orange. If blue fibre, either as wound hackle or blue hair tied short at the head, is added, then the fly is fairly referred to as Thunder & Lightning. Red trace olive.

DRESSING

Body: Black floss.
Rib: Silver.
Wing: Top and bottom, black hair; sides, orange hair.
Head: Black.

6 Comet

COMMENT

This dressing is a little more complex: the ends of the yellow fibres should align with the bend of the treble; the ends of the fibres of the red centre 'hackle' (of hair) should reach to the same point; and the overwing of hair at the head should overlap both the others.
Red trace olive.

DRESSING

Tail 'hackle': Yellow (or hair may be used).
Body: Rear half ruby red, front half black floss.
Rib: Medium-fine oval gold.
Centre hackle: Ruby red hair.
Wing: Black hair.
Head: Black.

7 Stoat's Tail Tube

COMMENT

We cannot really believe that the winging material is all that important in a fly of this size, but there must be something about the shape and silhouette which makes tiny tube flies attractive in extreme summer conditions of bright light and low water. Certainly some old-stagers in the pools will look at small dark tubes when they otherwise disdain equally small regular low-water tyings. Back in the 1950s a fly box containing a wide range of Stoat's Tails was considered indispensable on the Dee and the Don in Aberdeenshire.

DRESSING

Body: Plastic tube – red, black or translucent.
Wing: Top and bottom, black hair from a stoat's tail.
(In the early days the hair really was stoat's tail, not dyed or natural black squirrel hair. Every gamekeeper in the neighbourhood was generously encouraged to keep tails. Our greatest find was an ermine cape, with tails still attached. They are not now.)

8 Yellow Dog

COMMENT

Ted Hunter's fly tying has certainly been put to the test over the past three summers. We could not complain when one fly survived *twenty-three* fish before it turned into a bare shank! That fly was used both as a deep-sunk pattern on a Wet-Cel II as well as a near-surface fly on a floating line in high summer, drawn across the noses of running fish. It then was given extra movement by handlining on an intermediate line in late September for autumn newly-run and resident fish.

DRESSING

Body: Red floss.
Rib: Oval silver.
Wing: Evenly distributed yellow bucktail.

Waddingtons

The principle of a Waddington is a treble flexibly attached to a shank, with the shank carrying the dressing. When a fish is hooked the shank does not slide up the leader like a tube but because of the articulation where it joins the treble it should not exert undue leverage. It may be tied light or heavy, and classic as well as modern patterns are easily adapted to suit this style. The choice may often lie between a tube or a Waddington of similar size, weight and pattern. There are some who consider that the Waddington does not snarl back on the leader as often as a tube does. The treble should remain in alignment with the shank. Early tyings incorporated strands of nylon threaded through the tail eye of the shank, round the back of the treble, and then back through the tail eye, with the ends covered by the body materials. The modern alternative, which is less neat and less time-consuming is to slip a rubber or plastic sleeve over the junction. With the latter system, a damaged hook is more easily replaced.

1 Martin's Thunder & Lightning

COMMENT

The frontispiece to *Salmon Fishing: Philosophy and Practice* by Richard Waddington (1959) shows the patterns tied for him by Alex Martin Ltd. Thunder & Lightning, Akroyd, Silver Wilkinson, Silver Blue and Logie are all easily identified in their new character. The first summer patterns were tied on too big a treble; Waddington was eventually more than satisfied that 16s and 18s were feasible and really did take a good hold. Once the dressing was suitably reduced from the bunchiness of the original examples, he found he used Waddingtons to the exclusion of all other types.

DRESSING

Tag: Fine oval and yellow floss.
Tail: None.
Butt: Black herl.
Body: Black floss.
Rib: Broad oval gold.
Hackle: Orange.
Throat/wing: Long black heron under dyed blue guinea-fowl.
(We have moved away from brittle heron nowadays, and tie with some of the many mobile hairs such bear, bucktail, and the like. The tag, tail and butt are tied on the treble.)

2 Waddington Akroyd

COMMENT

Ted Hunter has stayed within Martin's style here, dressing a japanned black treble and using a nylon strand to ensure the shank–hook alignment. The long mobile fibre of black heron to be found in the traditional pattern is represented by black bear or black bucktail incorporated into the wing. To give the throat effect of the traditional pattern he has used guinea-fowl, which also has 'eye' marking to suggest rare jungle cock sides.
    Again, tag and butt are tied on the treble.

DRESSING

Tag: Oval gold and yellow floss.
Tail: None.
Butt: Black herl.
Body: Rear two-thirds yellow silk, front third black seal fur.
Hackle: Yellow over the yellow fur.
Rib: Broad oval gold.
Wing: Cinnamon bear hair or bucktail under black bear hair or bucktail.
Collar: Well marked guinea-fowl.

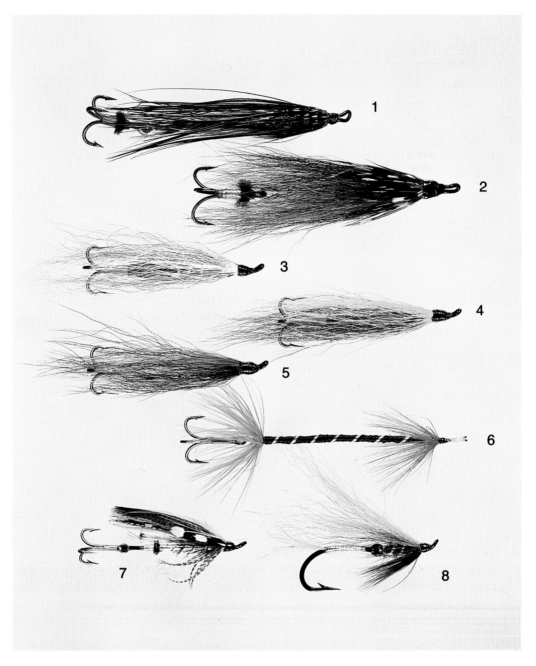

1 Martin's Thunder & Lightning **2** Waddington Akroyd
3 Waddington Shrimp **4** Waddington Green Highlander
5 Waddington Munro Killer **6** Hay's Waddington
7 Wanless Waddington **8** Cebrit Esau

3 Waddington Shrimp

COMMENT

Some Grubs, Shrimps and Prawns have quite complicated dressings. Often the transfer of the pattern to tube or Waddingtons means that the dressing is simplified, with the emphasis kept on some aspects. The colour scheme of the pink-and-white dressings is the essence of this example. In considering the 'size' of a Waddington, the measurement certainly should include the hook; whether the dressing which extends beyond the hook is included depends on how dense it is.

DRESSING

Tag: Fluorescent red.
Body: Black floss.
Rib: Oval gold.
Wing: Red/orange hair strands overlaid by white hair strands.
(The sleeve to keep the shank – hook alignment is secured at each end by a few turns of tying silk.)

4 Waddington Green Highlander

COMMENT

This interpretation has taken the green and yellow theme and emphasised it in giving it to the wing instead of the body. It used to be stated regularly that the Green Highlander fails as a Lowland Scotland pattern. It does, however, provide a contrast and is a variation on other bright flies. It is now readily stocked in tackle shops up and down Tweed, in tubes as well, and some tyings have mylar tinsel bodies.

DRESSING

Tag: Fluorescent red.
Body: Black floss.
Rib: Oval silver.
Wing: Dyed green hair strands overlaid with dyed yellow.

5 Waddington Munro Killer

COMMENT

Although the original design was a summer fly on the Spey, its success in small sizes has led to its being tied very much larger for 'stronger' conditions of water and weather. The pattern, in whatever style, is one of the most recommended patterns on Tweed nowadays.

DRESSING

Tag: Fluorescent red.
Body: Black floss.
Rib: Oval silver.
Wing: A small amount of yellow hair overlaid by a small amount of black. On one side overlay with strands of orange to which a small blue beard hackle is added.

6 Hay's Waddington

COMMENT

This is mentioned in Bill Currie's *Days and Nights of Game Fishing* (1984) and differs from our other patterns in size – 4 and 5 inches, with a second treble being added in the larger sizes – and method of tying. The shank has a length of 24lb nylon spliced firmly onto the appropriate treble, then a whipping overall to give the base for the tying.

DRESSING

Body: Black wool or floss.
Rib: Gold tinsel.
Hackles: Hot orange at head and tail.

7 Wanless Waddington

COMMENT

Wanless started his fixed-spool and light-line writings in 1930 and fifteen titles followed in the next twenty years, calling for a digest in 1953, *Complete Fixed Spool Angling*. In this volume he sketched the style of the flies with which he went spinning. The words 'I have used this type of fly for at least 15 years' give the late 1930s as its inception. He does not look for the symmetrical view of the fly as does Richard Waddington, but dresses the shank according to the usual concept of feather wing on top and throat below, in the style, for example, of the Silver Grey.

DRESSING

For the full dressing, refer to the Silver Grey on page 38. As Wanless followed Pryce-Tannatt, any P.-T. tying would form the basis of Wanless' tyings.

8 Cebrit Esau

COMMENT

In *All Fur Flies and How to Dress Them* (1967) W. H. Lawrie discusses flexible salmon fly hooks. His solution is to cut the shank and then to join the two portions with woven or braided stainless steel. This will be a solid enough base for the dressing, yet will flex when necessary. An alternative is the Cebrit hook (reviewed under 'New Tackle' in *Trout and Salmon* in December 1955). To remain within Lawrie's context, the example illustrated is dressed to one of his salmon patterns. Others are Shaggy Dog, Grey Beard, Black Beard, Blue Beard, and Red Beard.

DRESSING

Tag: Half gold flat.
Tail: Golden-yellow hair.
Body: Half claret seal fur.
Rib: Oval gold over the claret fur.
Throat: Claret fibres under black fibres.
Wing: Brown bear hair with golden-yellow hair over.

DIBBLING,
WAKE FLIES,
DROPPERS AND LOCH
FLIES

Introduction

Go back a couple of centuries – don't bother with the top hat or velveteen waistcoat, but do take up the 18 or 20-foot rod and the crude reel which may be made of wood and fastened to your belt. On it will be wound horsehair line, perhaps with some silk in it. Select your fly – Horseleech or King's Fisher – and present it to the fish. Casting will not be easy: the fly will present a lot of air resistance and the line will certainly not be balanced (in the modern sense) to the weight, length and action of the rod. When the fly alights on the water the iron is unlikely to drag it down, certainly not in fast water, and the line will not be a sinker. The first salmon taken on fly and rod and line would be taking dibbled flies, or surface wake flies – not because the fisherman then wanted the flies to be in the surface but because it was very difficult to make them fish deeper.

Nowadays, we can choose how we fish. Our rod may be 8 or 9 feet, or as long as 16 feet – each will have a role to play. Our lines will have the intrinsic qualities which allow them to float, just to sink, to sink readily, or to sink very fast indeed. We can choose or tie our flies to stay at the surface or sink at a similar rate to our lines. However, if we choose to fish at the surface then the first style of fishing to look at is dibbling.

Dibbling This is a matter of the fisherman's concealing himself from the river and the fish and, with a short line and raised rod point, working his fly so that it breaks the surface over critical spots in the pool, particularly over the fast stream at the run into the deep eddies at the side of it. The style will also apply to lies or parts close to the bank which are regularly adopted by fish but are not fished very successfully with ordinary wet-fly techniques.

Back to history for a moment, and a long quote from Herbert Maxwell's 1898 book. He is speaking of 1867.

Well, at Reedsmouth, the junction of the Reed and North Tyne, there lived in the days I speak of a certain Dr Begg, who rented the fishing of a couple of casts on the main river. 'Begg' is a name derived from the Gaelic signifying 'little', and certainly it was appropriate in this case for the worthy doctor would not have measured more than five feet in his stocking soles. When I first met him early in October 1867, he had killed upwards of 150 salmon and grilse with the fly, during that season. And such flies! All of nearly the same pattern – fat fuzzy bodies, generally of grey rabbit or monkey wool, enormously over-winged on small single hooks, and tied on collars of undyed treble gut. He very seldom left his house before midday when, if the water was in order, he would get into a pair of enormous wading trousers, button his long, yellow 'Piccadilly weeper' whiskers into his coat, clap on a cowboy hat stuck all over with hairy salmon flies, take his spliced rod of the Castle Connell type off the rack, and stroll down to the river. Wading in almost to the armpits, he would begin on a fine stream which ran at the foot of his garden . . . flinging his flies (he always used two of these monstrosities at once) across the current at right angles and bringing them round to within a few yards of where he was standing. No low point and deep fly with him! On the contrary, he gradually *raised* the point of his rod after delivering the cast, trailing the flies along the surface of the water, so that when he had finished the circuit his rod was quite erect.

The style of Begg's flies is not very different from the King's Fisher fly described on page 26, and which was how one imagines all pike flies – mostly composed of peacock moons. A bulk of fur is not streamlined. Long wings and tail also produce a lot of drag, irrespective of the material. Chaytor, writing in 1910, condemns some flies: 'Many of the costly shop flies are so overloaded with feathers that when in the water they are only a sodden lump, and all life and movement are destroyed.'

In dibbling terms, there seem to be some good qualities here; and so it is with many flies today: they are more fully dressed than seems fashionable for standard floating-line fishing, yet they will probably have a role in dibbling. There is still a mass of Durham Rangers, Dusty Millers, Green Highlanders, Butchers and so on, on eyed hooks – not necessarily masterfully tied or of exhibition quality – that should be earning their keep. Since doubles and trebles cause more drag in the water, there are advocates of their use in this style of fishing. A tube fly in large diameter can be quite bluff, with its treble hook adding its quota of water resistance, and long trailing *hair* will add plenty of drag – behold the Collie Dog!

Only in recent years has dibbling received fresh publicity. We learned a lesson on the Aberdeenshire Don twenty-five years ago, but clearly the lesson has lain dormant! A certain Edinburgh gentleman was a habitué of the Forbes Arms Hotel at Bridge of Alford. He was eminently successful in high summer with minute flies, yet he always insisted that we should dibble some pools like the Deepstane before fishing down in a more orthodox manner. He did not specify a particular fly – just suggested that it should be a little larger. He stood, as memory has it, not much over five feet in his 'stocking soles'. His name was Dr Gordon Bruce. Quite a number of coincidences, particularly as he would follow his dibbling by wading extremely deeply down each pool!

Surface Wake Flies   If we are going to make a distinction, dibbling takes place with a short line while a surface wake fly is cast to normal distances and as it 'fishes' it stays in the surface film. The floating line is best; for dibbling it matters less since the rod point is used to control the fly. But the riffled fly, which is knotted on at an angle so it will not swim true, is controlled by carefully mending line and manipulating the rod point. The patterns are not critical, though the design may accommodate this asymmetrical tying-on and plenty of drag. Lee Wulff ties a longer wing and includes bucktail if the fly is to be riffled rather than fished in the orthodox wet-fly way. British fishermen have known of the technique a long time, but seem reluctant to try it. It certainly can be successful. We were invited to the Dee at Abergeldie. The beat was taken for dry-fly fishing for salmon. One fisher would fish orthodox wet fly for comparison and by choice: the others would do what they were told! The dry fly rose salmon, and caught sea trout. The only salmon killed was on the riffling hitch, and the true wet-fly fisher had no action at any point of the week.

Droppers   The dropper comes about halfway between the two techniques described above. A high rod point will make it dibble. It may earn itself a fish or may attract the fish to take the tail fly. Probably it does not double the chance of a fish, but it certainly enhances it. The deficits are: the fly which has not been taken may become snagged; the tangles which *may* ensue *will* try the patience of the most phlegmatic angel.

Loch Flies   Loch-fishing for salmon is not really a matter of chucking and chancing: there is more to it than that since some fishermen seem to have far better results than others. It seems that the ideal salmon lochs have shallow areas preferred by salmon. The Hebridean lochs at Amhuinnsuidhe have favoured shallows, as does Loch Lomond, and there are very specific good lies as well as good general lies. Wind direction and strength have a major bearing on a day's sport, as does the number of fish resident and how fresh they are, of course. In general salmon and sea trout tend to run together and much of the fishing will be non-specific: it may be a sea trout that takes or it may be a salmon, though in the Amhuinnsuidhe lochs sea trout outnumber salmon six to one.

It does appear that a slowly fished fly takes more salmon than one fished faster and that pattern is not of paramount importance. However, and this is quite a qualification, if the fly is fished slowly and bobbed as long and as tantalisingly as possible, even if close in to the boat, it will attract more salmon than will the fly which is lifted off and recast more quickly. The last few yards of the bobbing in the waves seem particularly important. Now a finely-dressed fly just does not make as good a surface disturbance as a bushier one. So we come to a conclusion that style of dressing may be the most important ingredient. The size for both salmon and sea trout will probably be the same – small, down to a size 12. Singles, doubles and trebles all find favour.

Dibbling and Surface Wake Flies

We show a variety of styles, but in fact any style will do, though flies which stay at the surface naturally are easier to fish with for this technique. Weight in a fly tends to be a disadvantage, but although a treble weighs more than a single, it can cause sufficient water resistence to stay near the surface and suit this style of fishing.

It is worth tying a number of quite small short tubes in the design of the Muddler Minnow head. In other words, a deerhair collar, clipped quite short and neat at the front, and with shaggier trailing elements at the rear. If the fishing circumstances call for a dibbling-style fly, this collar can be threaded on the leader and then whatever fly to hand (single, double or treble) can be knotted on in the usual way.

There is really little hard-and-fast distinction between some of these flies and some of the droppers shown on page 143, as so often a dropper is fished to break the surface. However, some dropper patterns were most essentially an alternative wet-fly offering, in either size, profile or colouring.

1 Muddler Minnow

COMMENT

Let Al McClane introduce this fly: 'like showing a He-trout a picture of a half-naked She-trout a-winking'! From its birth in 1950 as a pattern devised by Don Gapen to imitate a small bottom-living bait fish, it has the widest currency for most fish species fished for deep, in mid-water or at the surface, and presents a wide range of illusions – fish, moth, mayfly, grasshopper, and so on. This is the early tying. The style can be tied in a wide variety of colours.

DRESSING

Tail: A swathe of oak turkey.
Body: Medium flat gold.
Wing: A bunch grey squirrel hair under mottled turkey wing.
Shoulder: Spun deer hair, clipped near the hook eye, and left long and straggly but streamlined to add to the wing and give a throat hackle effect.

2 Yellow Dolly

COMMENT

Take fine red plastic tube, build up a ridge of tying silk at the end and bind on yellow fallow deer tail hair as a skirt, which is flared out by the ridge. Tie off and trim the waste butts. Build a second ridge nearer the head, and repeat process with black fallow deer tail. Trim the trailing yellow and the trailing black so that the black overlaps the yellow. This is Derek Knowles's invention, (widely publicised by Hugh Falkus). The smallest he tied were 3/8 inch long, which he used as a final weapon. Derek was then encouraged to write *Salmon on a Dry Fly* in 1987.

DRESSING

Tying silk: Black.
Hook: 14, 16 or 18 treble.
Body: Red plastic tube.
Skirt: Yellow-dyed fallow deer tail.
Throat 'shawl': Black fallow deer tail.

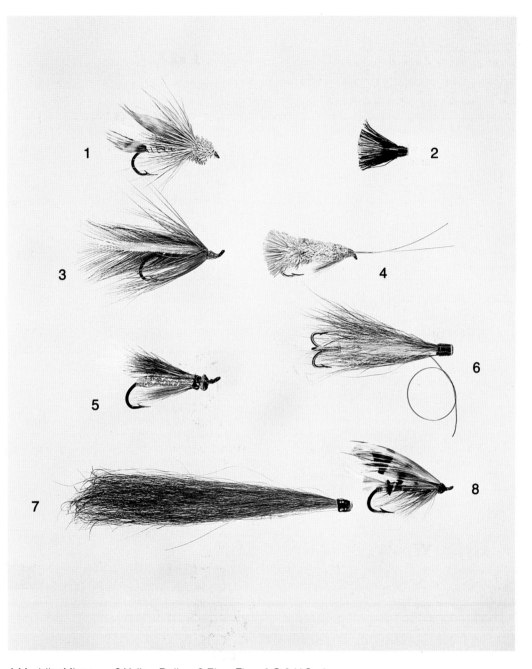

1 Muddler Minnow   **2** Yellow Dolly   **3** Elver Fly   **4** G & H Sedge
5 Blue Squirrel (Hitch-Head)   **6** Riffling-Hitch Tube Fly   **7** Collie Dog
8 Black Ranger

3 Elver Fly

COMMENT

Waddington suggests: 'When a comparison is made between the life histories, range, habitat and abode of the Atlantic salmon and the European eel, we shall see later that there is a very strong case to be made for the hypothesis that much of the salmon's existence is bound up with that of the eel.' The young of the eel, the leptocephalus, is between 1 and 3 inches long and is nearly transparent. The Elver Fly is not Waddington's invention but rather that of Arthur Ransome. There is a 'hopeful' element of imitation about the pattern. Crawford Little suggests the pattern for dibbling.

DRESSING

Body: Black floss – slender.
Rib: Fine oval tinsel.
Wing: Blue vulturine guinea-fowl feathers back to back (can be very long).
Collar: Plain blue vulturine feather.
Cheeks (optional): Jungle cock.
Head: Red.
(The fly is also known as Blue Elver and Ransome's Elver.)

4 G & H Sedge

COMMENT

The trout pattern is a standard sedge imitation with excellent buoyancy. The shape perfectly suggests the insect, and the coloured strands under the shank give a good impression of the tint of the insect's body. Goddard and Henry, the British fly tyers whose initials give the fly its name, use deer hair as the basis, with plenty of flotation supporting the bend of the hook.

DRESSING

Tail: None.
Body: Trimmed deerhair, with a broadly flared skirt at the tail, tapering to a fine head.
Underside: Tie in at the tail strands of thread well dubbed with green or amber seal fur, pull them taut under the clipped deer hair and tie in at the head.
Throat: Greyish hackle strands in beard style.

5 Blue Squirrel (Hitch-Head)

COMMENT

The different construction shows. Wulff devised a plastic material to which fly tying materials could be made to adhere – saving the mechanics of some of the usual tying processes. The 'tinsel' is glitter stuck on, and the head has a rearward groove to take the extra half-hitch of a riffling knot. As Wulff's 'Patent' is hi-tech, intelligent alternatives have to be used for the body. Glitter dust is available from stores like Woolworth's among their Christmas decorations, if it cannot be found elsewhere.

DRESSING

Tag: None.
Tail: None.
Body: Oval or embossed silver.
Throat: Blue hackle fibres tied as a beard.
Wing: Grey squirrel, with topping over.

6 Riffling-Hitch Tube Fly

COMMENT

Any tube pattern will do to illustrate the tying practice. Ideally the tube is plastic, and is chosen in the colour required. The needle is placed in the vice, the tube is pushed over it, and the winging material is applied, trimmed and tied off. Because the leader will not be threaded through at the head we have to make a new hole in the tube, one-third back from the head, behind the wing dressing, and this we do by inserting a heated needle through the wall of the tube, making a hole of suitable diameter.

DRESSING

Body: Black plastic tube.
Wing: Two tufts of black and yellow hair at 180 degrees to each other.

7 Collie Dog

COMMENT

It is difficult to pin down a date for the first use of this pattern. Gillie George Ross was certainly using it on the Oykel in 1972. From the diaries of the Farrer family, who are keen fishers on that river, the success of the pattern from the 1970s is: 1975: 11 out of 15 fish; 1976: 10 out of 10; 1977: 14 to Collie Dog and Stoat's Tail; 1978: 19 out of 20; 1979: 20 out of 21; 1980: 8 out of 10; 1981: blank; 1982: 2 out of 4; 1983: 2 out of 2; 1984: 2 out of 5; 1985: 2 out of 5; 1986: 5 out of 6; 1987: 10 out of 11; 1988: 2 out of 3.

DRESSING

Body: Aluminium tube.
Wing: A long bundle of hairs from a black Scottish collie, tied on top only (the feathering from the back of the hind legs is recommended).

8 Black Ranger

COMMENT

The classic patterns have largely fallen out of favour because of their opacity and lack of action in the water. However, their heavy dressing, particularly those with bodies of dubbed seal fur, is an advantage for this style of fishing: they do not sink readily and are rather bluff in the water. Any of the eyed patterns of this style might reasonably have a turn as a dibbling fly.

DRESSING

Tag: Silver twist and yellow floss.
Tail: Topping and Indian crow.
Butt: Black herl.
Body: Rear quarter, black silk; front three-quarters, black seal fur.
Hackle: Black over the seal fur.
Throat: Blue cock.
Wing: Jungle cock back to back enclosed by large tippets back to back, enclosed by smaller tippets back to back.
Cheeks: Chatterer.
Horns: Blue and yellow macaw.

Droppers

If the dropper is to fish smoothly and easily under the surface it will be tied sleekly in the modern fashion, like the tail fly. If its silhouette is to be different, and it is expected to work well on the retrieve in the surface, then a blockier, bulkier fly will serve better.

It is suggested that the dropper is about four feet from the tail fly, and the dropper link should not be longer than four inches. Experts differ in their opinions as to whether the dropper should be a double or a single – in a strong wind a single would probably tangle least.

Although any patterns can serve for droppers, within the reasoning above, one or two authors have favourites. John Rennie proposes some in *I Have Been Fishing* 1949 and we included John Ashley-Cooper's and Crawford Little's liking for the Black Pennell under Loch Flies, below. Interestingly, Esmond Drury determinedly advised against fishing droppers upstream (*Trout and Salmon*, August 1956).

1 Chaytor's Dropper

COMMENT

'The river was very low indeed, and the weather hot, still and misty. . . . On the Wednesday also I had one rise only and again on the trout rod and some trout flies, which I had taken to in despair of moving a fish with the salmon rod. At the very tail of a long stream, a big fish rose and quickly sucked in the dropper.' Chaytor gives the dressing as a black body with a bright-orange hackle. The dressing alongside is perhaps more in the current style.

DRESSING

Tail: Topping.
Body: Black floss.
Rib: Oval silver.
Throat: Orange.
Wing: Orange-dyed squirrel hair.

2 Rennie's Dropper

COMMENT

'This fly as a dropper was irresistible on the Tweed, and I got quite a number at Cairnton.' Rennie used a dropper in Ireland, the same pattern, relating the loss of a fish on the tail fly which had smashed him round a rock. His dropper was subsequently returned to him by another member of the party who had landed a grilse with the lost dropper caught in the dorsal fin. Later in his book Rennie twice records how well the dropper did him: in his five days he caught a large number of fish; 50 per cent of them were on a dropper.

DRESSING

Hook: Size 9.
Tail: Topping.
Body: Rear half silver, front half black floss.
Rib: Silver over the black floss.
Throat: Blue Charm blue.
Wing: A pair of tippets back to back.

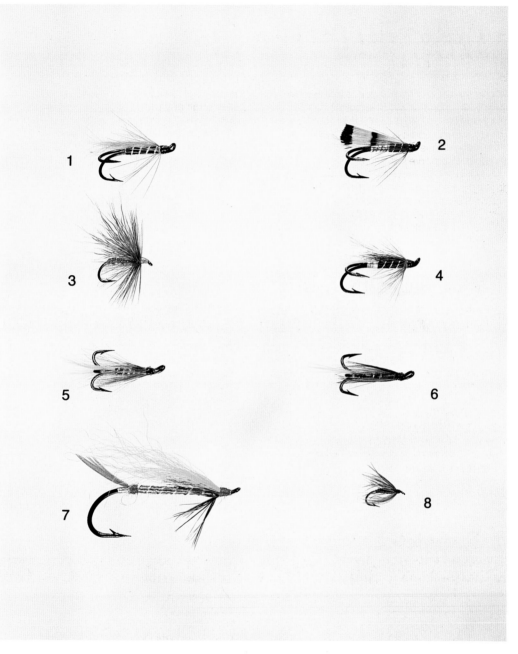

1 Chaytor's Dropper   **2** Rennie's Dropper   **3** Green Peter Dropper
4 Flashing Charmer   **5** Esmond Drury Hairy Mary
6 Esmond Drury Thunder & Lightning   **7** Yellow Boy
8 Snipe & Purple

3 Green Peter Dropper

COMMENT

There are two recent references to the worth of this fly: in *Trout and Salmon*, February 1988, and the same month the following year. It brought Arthur some fun when he was fishing Loch Hope from the Altnaharra Hotel, and Peter O'Reilly in Ireland includes it in his choice of patterns. He lists good salmon loughs where this and the following fly do well: Glen, Fern, Melvin, Conn, Beltra, Inagh, Corrib, Caragh, Currane, Leane, and Costello and Screebe Fisheries.

DRESSING

Hook: 8 and 10.
Body: Olive-green seal fur.
Rib: Gold.
Wing: Deerhair.
Collar: Best-quality natural red, with many turns.

4 Flashing Charmer

COMMENT

This is a modern pattern which after a couple of seasons has shown sufficient success for it to be around for a while yet. It is a variation on the Blue Charm or Hairy Mary theme, and is a salmon pattern when tied on salmon hooks, and sea-trout pattern when on trout hooks. Peter O'Reilly favours it particularly for grilse when they are just up in freshwater.

DRESSING

Tag: Fine oval silver and yellow floss.
Tail: Topping.
Body: Black floss.
Rib: Oval silver.
Throat: Kingfisher-blue cock.
Wing: Grey squirrel hair with five strands of pearl lureflash over.

5 Esmond Drury Hairy Mary

COMMENT

This is a very slightly different pattern from some Hairy Marys with brown bucktail wings. Although this particular dressing was not specifically designed as a dropper, the Hairy Mary is often chosen for the role, and modern authors recommend Esmond Drurys, as well as doubles and singles.

DRESSING

Tail: Yellow.
Body: Black.
Rib: Silver.
Wing: Blue hackle fibres with brindled squirrel over.

6 Esmond Drury Thunder & Lightning

COMMENT

The Esmond Drury series are some of the most popular modern summer flies, and as is usual with these patterns they fish any way up, which cannot be said for flies designed for singles or doubles. Orange is always held out to be a good colour to use for water falling after a spate, which equally is one of the best taking times for salmon. This pattern uses feather fibres rather than the ubiquitous hair.

DRESSING

Tail: Yellow hackle fibres.
Tag: Yellow floss.
Body: Black floss.
Rib: Embossed silver.
Wing: Orange hackle fibres under brown mallard fibres.

7 Yellow Boy

COMMENT

'I also killed a good many fish on the Yellow Boy. This is an excellent fly to try on any river, especially if the fish are dour, and can be used in the bright sun or dusk. It is best fished in the large size, and the wing should be made of yak's tail (dyed yellow) which gives the fly brilliancy.' Though this pattern is shown in T. T. Phelps's *Fishing Dreams* (1949), and we like the use of yak's hair, its inclusion in the plate is inspired by the scene in *Flying Salmon* (1947) by G. P. R. Balfour-Kinnear, when the Sheep has to fish a fast run with a large yellow dropper – for two fish!

DRESSING

Tag: Silver.
Tail: Red ibis.
Butt: Red wool.
Body: Blue floss.
Rib: Silver tinsel.
Throat: Jay.
Wing: Yak.
Head: Scarlet wool.
(The dressing is interpreted from the colour plate in *Fishing Dreams*.)

8 Snipe & Purple

COMMENT

Arthur has mentioned regularly that he has taken salmon on his trout single-hander when he was looking for trout. Since his favourite team of flies in late spring and early summer on the Spey is Partridge & Orange, Snipe & Purple, and Waterhen Bloa, we include one of these patterns. It may be more a matter of fishing a small fly on discreet nylon than that the fly which takes the fish has any particular merit, and Arthur never can remember which of the three proves the most successful!

DRESSING

Tag: None.
Tail: None.
Body: Purple floss.
Throat: Small covert feather taken from a snipe wing.

Loch Flies

The flies listed below are mostly old sea-trout standards, with the inclusion of some 'moderns'. There will no doubt be the usual discussion as to the merits of singles or doubles, or even the long-shank light-wire sea-trout trebles.

Most loch fishing is with a suitable modern single-handed rod. The blessing of carbon fibre is that it allows, even makes possible, long days with 11-foot and longer rods, having both heft enough to cast well yet sensitivity enough to deal kindly with small hooks and light leaders. It is, however, necessary to tighten on the fish on perceiving a take, which may be contrary to the nature of a salmon fisher, who normally allows the strength of the stream in a river to do his tightening for him.

Most loch fishers choose to fish a dropper – it will probably be the taking fly as it trips through the waves. Lines are normally floaters, as relatively shallow water is normally better salmon-holding water than the deeps. It is worth taking a sink-tip as a change of tune, but fly line colour *per se* is probably not important.

1 Peter Ross

COMMENT

One of the best sea-trout flies ever, this will certainly take its share of salmon. Look at the Lion on page 47 to see it grown into classic salmon fly. It is a considerable improvement on the Teal & Red, but many of the Teal & . . . patterns are most reputable. The Teal, Blue & Silver is regularly tied on salmon irons to give the Silver Blue, so keenly adopted on the Aberdeenshire Dee.

DRESSING

Tag: A turn of ribbing behind the tail.
Tail: Topping.
Body: Rear half silver, front half red seal fur.
Rib: Oval silver.
Throat: Black hackle.
Wing: Teal.

2 Goat's Toe

COMMENT

This is the dressing for Connemara and the west of Ireland. The alteration as used in the Hebrides, tied by Peter Cowper-Coles, has a red wool tag, peacock herl body and bushy black hackle.

DRESSING

Tail: Red wool.
Body: Red seal fur.
Rib: Bronze peacock herl.
Throat: Long blue peacock.

146

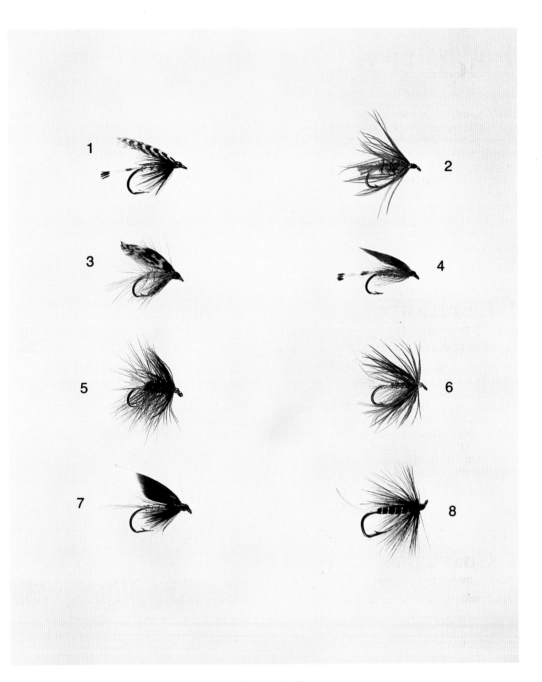

1 Peter Ross **2** Goat's Toe **3** Invicta **4** Grouse & Claret
5 Clan Chief **6** Tartan Fly **7** Jock **8** Black Pennell

3 Invicta

COMMENT

There may be some element of insect imitation here, for the Invicta is widely held to be some representation of a sedge or its pupa. A rich golden tint to the body is found by some to be more taking than lemon yellow. Excellent also are Silver Invicta and Gold Invicta, both tinsel-bodied. All may have red golden pheasant breast feather fibres for the tail. The Haslam is a development of the Silver Invicta, highly rated for salmon, of Welsh origin, with long macaw horns which should cross at the tips and a white wool butt, and without a palmer hackle.

DRESSING

Tail: Topping.
Body: Yellow wool or seal fur.
Rib: Oval gold.
Hackle: Natural red (or ginger).
Throat: Jay.
Wing: Hen pheasant (or woodcock).

4 Grouse & Claret

COMMENT

The huge range of Grouse & . . . and Mallard & . . . follow the same formula: dark throat for darker bodies, natural red or ginger throat for lighter shades. The Mallard & Red and Mallard & Yellow are recommended by McEwan. The Irish vary the patterns with extra grouse, and adapt the trout-fly pattern for salmon use with a good mixed underwing beneath the mallard, calling them Clarets.

DRESSING

Tag: A turn of the ribbing tinsel behind the tail.
Tail: Topping (or tippet).
Body: Claret wool or seal fur.
Rib: Oval gold (or silver).
Throat: Black (or natural red, or grouse, or claret).
Wing: Grouse.

5 Clan Chief

COMMENT

This pattern has elements of the Bibio, the Zulu and Kingsmill Moore's Bumbles. In 1989 Stan Headley refers in one of his regular articles to this tying devised by John Kennedy of Lochboisdale Estate in South Uist, Hebrides.

DRESSING

Hooks: 6–10.
Tag: Flat silver.
Tail: Yellow wool underneath, red wool over the top (or fluorescent).
Body: Black seal fur.
Rib: Medium oval silver.
Hackles: Scarlet and black, wound together.
Throat: Black hen.

6 Tartan Fly

COMMENT

(This is a name of long-standing, an obsolete and complicated style mentioned by Lascelles in 1819.) Our example is the other of John Kennedy's patterns for the Hebrides. The peacock throat should extend well beyond the bend of the hook, and the guinea-fowl should be short enough to allow the peacock to show well.

DRESSING

Hook: 6–10
Tag: Flat silver.
Tail: Topping.
Body: Flat copper.
Rib: Gold wire.
Hackle: Claret cock.
Throat: Blue feather from the neck of a peacock, under red-dyed guinea-fowl.

7 Jock

COMMENT

Bill McEwan enthuses about the turkey-winged flies on his loch – Lomond. Crawford Little also enthuses about it in his selection of loch flies. Ian Wood, author of *My Way with salmon*, was an enthusiast for Loch Lomond, and also a great admirer of white-tipped black turkey for the wings of salmon flies.

This same wing is found on the Turkey & Gold and Turkey & Silver (orange throat hackle and tinsel body). The Turkey & Mixed has a throat of black and a body of orange, yellow and black seal fur or wool.

DRESSING

Tag: A turn of fine oval silver.
Tail: Topping.
Body: Rear half yellow, front half black floss.
Rib: Continuation of the tag.
Throat: Black.
Wing: White-tipped turkey.

8 Black Pennell

COMMENT

There is a wide spectrum of tyings for this fly – it is a classic sea-trout pattern, which is widely used on lochs for salmon as well. Bill McEwan lists a Blue Label, a Blue Pennell to some tyers (as here, but with blue wool body), which is very similar to a Donegal Blue. Ashley-Cooper favoured it as a dropper pattern. He had it tied on single sneck-bend hooks, and found it particularly useful on the Spey in low and clear water for salmon, grilse and sea trout.

DRESSING

Tag: A turn of rib behind the tail.
Tail: Topping, or tippet strands, or orangey-yellow marabou.
Body: Black silk or wool.
Rib: Oval or flat silver.
Hackle (optional): Black – short.
Throat: Black cock – longish.

DRY FLIES

Introduction

Dry-fly fishing for trout has sadly and often been described as purist and snobbish. This is not why fishermen choose to use the dry fly. First, it is an extremely effective way of catching trout; second, it is an extremely enjoyable way of catching trout, as very often the fish, and its style of rising, can be easily seen, so that when it does tilt itself towards the artificial there is a very satisfying excitement.

Equally, dry-fly fishing for salmon can prove extremely effective, and extremely enjoyable, with the chance of a good-sized fish challenging relatively light tackle.

Two books, both transatlantic, by La Branche and by Hewitt, cover most of the ground of the early years of experimentation. Guided by them alone the fisherman would have a very fair expectation of taking fish. Development and further interest in the style is found in a further two books from America – both of the last decade or so, and both by Lee Wulff. He has kindly tied his patterns for our book. Much of the rationale behind their design comes from his own native waters, but with copious exchange of correspondence with others, including the late Gerald Curtis, who regularly fished the Wye and who turned immense practical fishing experience and a fine inquisitive mind to the style.

The dry flies described here are not expected to make surface disturbance. They are largely fished 'dead drift' or walking on their fibres on top of the surface.

The usual artificial dry-fly development has taken place. Salmon look much like large trout, so therefore are to be offered larger trout flies. In the early days of the style patterns did not stray much from 'natural' colours, which means that in the first two decades of the twentieth century greys, browns and whites were the norm. Traditional trout floaters, which had marked elements of insect representation, were tied and they worked when conditions were right. A fair generalisation about 'right' conditions would be a good stock of fresh fish, holding and taking lies which are not too deep, and a water temperature of about 60 °F which rises by 5° or 6° at some time in the course of the day.

The fly has considerable impact when placed over fish in fairly shallow water, and fish sharing lies tend to be more competitive than loners.

Grilse can be particularly competitive, which proves disappointing if larger, slower-moving salmon can be seen to be nudged out of the way.

The rise in water temperature does seem important, and at 66 °F some rivers prove unattractive and ineffective with a wet fly in traditional light summer styles of fishing. At this point the dry fly can prove extremely taking. The wet-fly taking lies may not prove to be the dry-fly taking lies, and in some pools there may be a 'magic' inch where fish will take only if the fly is presented with exceptional accuracy.

The pioneers of this branch of the sport saw a need to fish fine – 3- or 3½-pound gut. Modern nylons can achieve far higher breaking strains in finer diameters, but discretion can be critical: fish may *rise* to a fly on nylon leaders which are coarser than they like, and then, as soon as the point diameter has been reduced sufficiently, *rise and take* confidently.

Subsequent development of 'dead drift' dry-fly fishing has been the introduction of deer hairs – adding buoyancy and bulk – and the inclusion of elements of brighter colours. This latter is not necessarily as an extra attraction to the fish but as an aid to visibility for the fisherman. The use of squirrel and other hair for winging and tailing has helped the other style of dry-fly presentation, that of walking the fly on fibre points over the surface without creating a wake. A horizontal wing and tail of stiff hair helps the fly to balance and tread the surface lightly. The most specialised of the floaters is Lee Wulff's Surface Stone Fly. Side-casting is recommended as the buoyancy element is too slight to float after a heavy vertical landing. This pattern has within its concept very much of direct insect imitation.

There do not seem to be as many problems connected with dry-fly pattern selection as with selection of wet-fly patterns. There are different shapes and profiles, but size seems to be the key. Initially a large pattern, even up to 2½ inches in diameter, may raise a fish. Thereafter it will be a matter of finding a pattern small enough for a confident take. Sometimes the answer is a complete change of profile as well as of size. Delicacy and persistence are both vital ingredients of this style. The ability to throw right- and left-hand curves into the cast to defeat drag is a benefit. Long casting is not at a premium, but timing the strike correctly is – too long a delay and the fly is spat out; too quick a strike and the hook does not take a hold.

History of Dry-Fly Fishing for Salmon The earliest easily found reference to successful dry-fly fishing for salmon in Britain seems to be Chaytor's account of taking a fish on a Mayfly – 23 May 1896. This predates Ashley Dodd's account of various experiments on the Test in 1906. The latter, however, offers the first discursive mention with conclusions being drawn. Thereafter more material springs from North America and North American exponents of the technique have come to this country to try our fish, bringing their ideas with them. The books of George La Branche, Edward Hewitt and Lee Wulff illustrate development of the style across the Atlantic; and on this side we look to Jock Scott and articles rather than books until we come to Derek Knowles's *Salmon on a Dry Fly* in 1987.

There are more mentions of dry-fly fishing here and there. W. J. M. Menzies tells us in his *Salmon Fishing* (1935): 'I am told that in some rivers in Norway grilse are caught in tidal water by a dry fly. . . . This is somewhat at variance with dry fly fishing for salmon in this country, but here it has usually if not always been tried in the non-tidal part of the river.' We have not tried a dry fly in salt water, but certainly have done so in non-tidal waters. Clearly this is a prospect for those of us who have access to the estuaries.

In the British Isles the only published book devoted to the use of a surface fly is Derek Knowles's *Salmon on a Dry Fly*. The Knowles style is to dress a tube in truly diminutive sizes, with flared skirts, so that it presents, under line tension, too much resistance to fish below the surface on a floating line. It is cast upstream, across, or downstream and is kept moving faster than the current to make surface disturbance. His experience is that small trebles down to 16 and 18 are reliable, but that 20s can pull open even on 6lb nylon. Size seems all-important, with his smallest practical patterns at ⅜ inch proving regular catchers of fish. In our view, however, this is wake-fly fishing rather than the dead drift of the true dry fly, so the pattern is given in the earlier section – the Yellow Dolly on page 138.

Fishing Hints Try shepherd's-crook casts, to avoid the cast landing over the fish before it sees the fly. Reduce or delay drag in every way. Try the lazy S, placing slack line between you and the fly. Drop the rod point and direct it downstream – even pay line out through the rings.

Use the lightest tackle suitable in the circumstances. Be as discreet as possible. Frightened trout usually turn away; salmon when frightened do not always move off but rather cease to rise. Short casts are more easily controlled than are long ones, subject to the proviso of being discreet. Persistence is important, with plenty of contrasts to hand, in both silhouette and size.

Deer Hair Research both in the States and in Britain has not discovered the earliest date for deerhair-bodied flies. Possibly in unchronicled ages American Indians tied to their hooks strips of deer hair on the skin, for added attraction. Dr James A. Henshall was perhaps the moving force in seeing the capabilities of the material for bass bugs.

Deer hair is composed of cellular pockets within each strand, and has positive buoyancy. If the hair is clipped from the skin in small bunches it can be applied to a hook shank to give a bottle-brush effect, which then needs trimming. The hair compresses under the firm hold of the tying silk and radiates evenly from that point. It has sufficient substance to be a 'sculptable' material, so the trimming can produce the shape required as well as merely improve the rather hairy appearance.

Henshall died in 1925, and though his 'invention' was known it was not applied greatly to game fishing until the success of the Muddler Minnow in 1948, and the greater popularity of amateur fly-tying over the years. The technique of spinning on deerhair is described in most of the tying manuals, and is no longer considered advanced. We do have a note that in some form deerhair was in use in 1869: 'choicest caribou fly' is mentioned in Robert Roosevelt's *The Game Fish of the Northern States and British Provinces*, and in Britain 'Bickerdyke' tried for some form of protective patent on the material before the turn of the century. Henshall was an honorary life member of the Fly Fishers' Club, elected in 1887. His involvement with deerhair clearly did not cross to the British fishing scene, although red deer, roe deer and fallow deer, all part of our natural fauna, have hair of a style suitable for fly tying.

Dry Flies 1

This is a Canadian and American group. It starts with the initial five drawn from La Branche. The first efforts with a trout fly pattern, the Evening Dun, led to the development of flies which floated better and longer, making them true salmon patterns. La Branche had a friendly acquaintance with Hewitt and they obviously fished together on occasions. Hewitt was not very precise about his fly patterns but he too sought high float and easy visibility for the fisherman as well as the fish. His photographic plates illustrating the impression made by a surface fly as it comes into the fish's view should make us wonder a bit more about the 'footprint' of our dry flies, and how close to nature our endeavours with hackles come. The Bivisibles and Neversinks (which became Loch Ordie dapping flies) are his contribution to the dry-fly box. As Lee Wulff was perfecting his Wulff patterns, alternative high floaters were being devised which used deerhair, particularly for the body. Nowadays it seems that the Irresistible and the Rat-Faced MacDougal are interpreted interchangeably.

1 Pale Evening Dun

COMMENT

'The next morning we sat on the bank of the pool near the camp and watched the fish – and there were a great many. . . . Suddenly, toward the head of the pool in rather swift water, I saw the gentle breaking of the surface, which had we been on our home waters would have been a certain indication that a large trout was feeding. . . . He rose regularly and was unmistakably feeding – or at least taking insects from the surface – for all the world like a huge trout. . . . Nothing in our boxes, however, even approximated [the insects] in size, the smallest we had being a No. 14 Pale Evening Dun. . . .'

DRESSING

Tail: Two or three whisks of barred Plymouth Rock.
Body: Lemon mohair lightly dressed.
Legs: Glossy barred Plymouth Rock cock hackle.
Wings: Light starling.

2 Colonel Monell

COMMENT

Ten patterns were created, all of which rose and killed fish the next season. Four of them seemed more effective than the others. Except in the size and the extra quantity of hackle which was added to improve their floating qualities they differed at first but slightly from trout dry flies.

Cock hackles being of finer quality than hen, they were used exclusively. Dyed feathers were avoided because of an apparent tendency to absorb water. The range was therefore limited to that provided by nature – greys and browns. It was fortunate that this was so, because these colours seemed to interest the fish most.

DRESSING

Tail: Five or six whisks of grey Plymouth Rock hackle.
Body: Peacock herl with a rib of red – lightly dressed.
Hackles: Grey Plymouth Rock hackles, palmered.

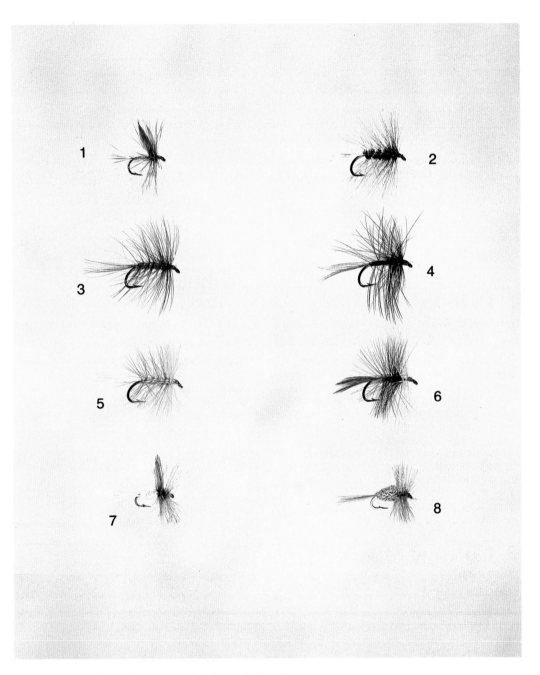

1 Pale Evening Dun 2 Colonel Monell 3 Soldier Palmer
4 Mole Palmer 5 Pink Lady Palmer 6 Bivisible 7 White Irresistible
8 Rat-Faced MacDougal

3 Soldier Palmer

COMMENT

'Tie the hackle directly at right angles to the body.'
All these dry flies should float well. Mucilin or grease can be more effective than more volatile anointments.

DRESSING

Tail: Five or six whisks of hackle.
Body: Red dubbing with a rib of tinsel, lightly dressed.
Hackle: Brown, or brownish-red, tied palmer.

4 Mole Palmer

COMMENT

La Branche's trout pattern is: tail, three or four strands purplish-brown hackle; body, light mole fur lightly dressed and tightly wound; legs, purplish-brown hackle; wings, medium starling or duck (a variation from a wing of light-brown woodcock wings).

   Subsequent to his dressings list, he adds: 'try a clipped palmer hackle for the body to aid flotation, particularly with quill bodies.'

DRESSING

Tail: Five or six whisks of hackle.
Body: Brown dubbing or quill lightly dressed.
Hackles: Dark-brown, lightly mixed with grey at the shoulder, tied palmer.

5 Pink Lady Palmer

COMMENT

The history of this seems tied up with La Branche's purchasing of some King of the Waters patterns which leaked red dye from the body and faded to pink. His trout dressing was not unlike the Red Spinner, but it clearly proved a good fish taker.

   In adapting the trout patterns for salmon, La Branche adopted palmer hackling; and, feeling that wings gave no advantage, but the positive disadvantage of soaking up water, he abandoned them for salmon dry flies.

DRESSING

Tail: Five or six whisks of hackle.
Body: Light-pink silk, lightly dressed.
Rib: Gold tinsel.
Hackle: Ginger.
Throat: Two turns of yellow.

6 Bivisible

COMMENT

Hewitt liked his dry flies from ½ to 1½ inches in diameter. Hackled flies met his approval more readily than winged flies. He used a mixture of albolene and kerosene as a fly-floatant, and believed that a well palmered fly floated well, with the right poise and the right footprint on the water, creating patterns of light and reflection as the hackle points disturbed the surface film.

Bivisibles can be dressed with cock hackles of any natural colour for the body with contrasting turns at throat for visibility.

DRESSING

Tail: Hackle tips from the main palmering hackles.
Body: Fully wound with natural red hackle.
Throat: Two turns of white hackle.

7 White Irresistible

COMMENT

Lee Wulff attributes the origination of the Irresistible to Kenneth Lockwood, who changed the wool body of the Gray Wulff pattern for a clipped hair body. The wings may be hackle point or of hair. The pattern can be tied in a wide range of colours; black and white versions are common. An Adams version is given in the Orvis Index. Reuben Cross refers to it in 1950 in *The Complete Fly Tyer*: 'The Irresistible is a comparatively new and very effective trout pattern, used with good success for salmon in sizes ten to four.'

DRESSING

Hook: 4–10.
Tail: White hair strands or hackle fibres.
Body: Spun, clipped white deerhair.
Wing: Badger hackle points.
Throat: White hackle.

8 Rat-Faced MacDougal

COMMENT

The creation of this pattern has been attributed to Harry Darbee, the Catskill tyer. Subsequently it seems that a great deal of variation has become acceptable in its tying. It is certainly seen with cuckoo hackle point wings, and with wings (of whatever material) slanted forwards and divided.

Thomas Clegg offers this dressing:

DRESSING

Tail: Deerhair fibres, bucktail fibres or hackle fibres.
Body: Deerhair, clipped.
Wing: White calf tail, or hackle points.
Throat/Collar: Ginger saddle hackles, generously tied.

Dry Flies 2

In *Flies*, Leonard lists many standard trout dry-fly patterns for salmon, with perhaps extra hackle to aid floating: Cahill, Cinnamon Sedge, Greenwell's Glory, March Brown, Professor, Montreal, Montreal Silver, McGinty, Pale Evening Dun, Parmachene Belle, Queen of the Waters, Reuben Wood, Silver Doctor, Whirling Dun and Yellow Sally. As Hackles and Bivisibles he lists Black Bivisible, Brown Palmer, Colonel Monell, Grey Palmer, Grey-Hackle Yellow, MacIntosh (brown and grey), Mole Hackle Bivisible, Pink Lady Bivisible, Red Hackle, Royal Coachman Bivisible, Seal Hackle and Soldier Palmer. He also gives Parachutes and Gliders.

Percy E. Nobbs relates in *Salmon Tactics* (1934): 'The maddest fish I ever handled was a grilse lightly hooked outside the head on a small iron; but the fly was a detached-bodied dry fly, and one of its wings completely overlapped one of the grilse's eyes.' The example is for style rather than for a specific pattern. Plainly there are advantages in a natural-looking body with the avoidance of a hook with a long, heavy shank. The bend of a short-shanked hook is obscured by the hackles, a potential extra point of deception.

1 Whiskers

COMMENT

A dry fly credited to Louis M. Butterfield of Stratham, New Hampshire, who owned a camp close to where the River Cairns flows into the Miramichi. This fly took him thousands of salmon and grilse. Many colour combinations and types of hair are used, but here we give Bates's formula for the dressing. The deer hair is tied in first and covered by the yarn and palmer hackles.

DRESSING

Tail: Grey squirrel tail, long.
Body: Angora yarn underbody.
Hackle: Stiff natural red, palmered.
Wing: Generous deer body hair, fan-shaped on top of the hook.

2 MacIntosh

COMMENT

Leonard gave more than 2,000 patterns for the fly tyer. He sent polite questionnaires to local experts, of whom Cartile was one, and published their answers at the end of his book — rather as Mary Orvis Marbury did many years earlier. This pattern is by far the favourite in dry-fly patterns.

This is also known as the Squirrel Tail Dry Fly. Peter Cartile gave it in notes from West Northfield, Nova Scotia, on 28 March 1949.

DRESSING

Tail/wing: Gingery-brown fox squirrel tail hairs extending flat from the hook-shank.
Body: Tying silk only.
Hackles: Three large Rhode Island Red neck hackles, palmered over the silk and may be clipped slightly after the fly is dressed.

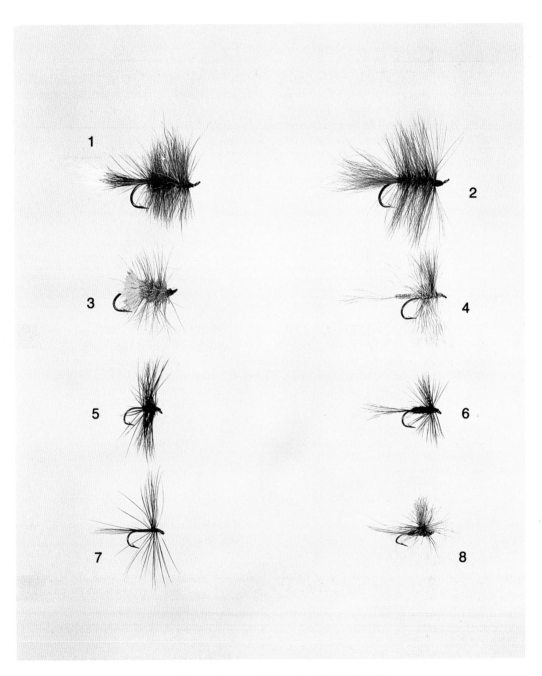

1 Whiskers　**2** MacIntosh　**3** Green Brolly　**4** Detached-Body Dry Fly
5 Skater　**6** Midnight　**7** Spider　**8** Parachute

3 Green Brolly

COMMENT

Derek Knowles devised this hybrid cross
between his Yellow Dolly and a Green Buck
Bug. He hooked an eleven-pound fish on it and
landed it, rose another which came off, and also
clicked two or three more. By using a Minto
Wilson hook he seemed to get the fly to float with
hook point down.

DRESSING

Hook: Single.
Tail/butt: Clipped wound yellow deerhair
protruding as stubs.
Body: Green deerhair clipped close.
Hackle: Natural red wound through the
green body.

4 Detached-Body Dry Fly

COMMENT

Two good examples of detached-body styles
are given in Darrel Martin, the soft body and the
needle body, the latter being the style
illustrated. The thick end of a fine needle is
placed in the vice. Tie in the tail with long waste
butts, which are retained. Take deer or caribou
hair fibres (25 or more) and, allowing them a
long waste butt pointing towards the head, tie
with sufficient wraps. Bend the long ends of the
fibres back over these wraps and use the tying
silk to make ribs starting with two firm wraps.
Withdraw the needle as the detached body is
offered to the hook-shank.

DRESSING

Tail: Four or five small-mammal whiskers.
Body: 25-30 deerhair fibres, undyed or
dyed.
Throat: Grizzle.
Wings: Divided tufts of bucktail (or squirrel).
Collar: Grizzle.

5 Skater

COMMENT

Skaters are like spiders but are more heavily
dressed and lack tails. The angle at which they
ride on the water is with the shank vertical, with
the radiating hackle fibres which support the
weight flat to the water. A base for the hackles is
formed with unwaxed thread. The first hackles
tied in must have their natural curve towards the
head, and the last with their curve towards the
bend. The hackles should be wound as tightly
compressed as possible, and further
compressed by thumb and finger pressure from
both sides.

DRESSING

Tail: None.
Body: None.
Hackle: Top-quality cock hackles.
(Lee Wulff redesigned the skater wing using
bucktail held out from the shank, cocked at
an angle to ensure that the hook point rides
upwards as the fly is skated. His Prefontaine
(page 235) shows this latter style.)

6 Midnight

Lee Wulff has a small black fly which he uses after fishing a large Wulff to give a contrast in offerings to the fish. 'I change this according to the mood I am in when I am fishing over a fish which has risen. I think of flies as the keys to a piano . . . throughout the changes I revert periodically to the fly that brought the first rise.'

Hook: Size 12.
Tail: Black hackle fibres.
Body: Black wool, fat.
Throat: Two black hackles.

7 Spider

The spider is a type of dry fly in which the hackle fibres are very much longer than those of a normal dry fly or Bivisible. Only a few turns are used, and the effect is to give the fly the least solid silhouette. They are always tied on small hooks, usually size 16s. A tail is normally added to cock the fly. Lee Wulff ties his spiders with between two and ten turns of hackle according to flotation and silhouette requirements.

Tail: Hair or hackle fibres.
Body: Tying silk.
Throat: A few turns of extra-long top-quality cock hackle.

8 Parachute

This is a typical example of a style – not a specific pattern. Instead of the hackle radiating at 90 degrees to the shank, the feather is wound round a stub projecting vertically from the shank. The length of each fibre takes the weight of the fly on the surface, rather than just a few hackle points on the underside of the dressing. If a wing is used it can form the stub for the hackle. Bivisible wings help the angler to see a very low-riding fly. White hair or fluorescent-dyed material may be added.

Tail: Hair or hackle fibres.
Body: Wool or the like.
Hackle: Good-quality cock of a natural colour.
Wing (optional): Feather or hair tied vertically.
(J. Edson Leonard considers Gliders – devised by Plympton and Johnson – to be tied with hackle-point wings, while Parachutes have coarse feather or hair wings.)

Dry Flies 3

The Mayfly patterns are shown first: British and North American. Although there is plenty of evidence that British Mayfly tyings have risen, and taken, salmon, some standards could learn buoyancy from across the Atlantic. It has been suggested that Humpies or Goofus Bugs (which name they are given depends on the tyers) appear to the trout as what the trout want to think they are. No doubt salmon find that they look suitably like small terrestrials or mayflies or moths as well. Since dapping is more of a style of fishing than a style of fly tying we give only one dapping fly. The date of development of the Bomber is given by Bates (*ASF*) as 1967, and the river of its birth the Miramichi. *The Atlantic Salmon Journal* of May 1980 refers to a Serge Vincent article attributing the origination to the Revd Elmer J. Smith of Doaktown, New Brunswick. A parallel pattern, Le François Special, derives from the Matane in 1970, tied by Ovila Le François. The Buck Bug shows major similarities except that it is seldom tied large.

1 French Partridge Mayfly

COMMENT

This is a standard mayfly imitation. For better floating, fox, dog or cat whiskers make stronger tail whisks (not from the live animal). Some tyers add an under-throat hackle – olive or natural grey. The final hackle to be applied may be grey mallard breast feather dyed brownish, or Carolina breast feather. Fraser's Golliwog, his pattern for his 1906 fishing on the Test, is a fanwing tying on double hooks.

DRESSING

Tail: Strands of cock pheasant tail.
Body: Raffia.
Rib: Brown tying silk.
Hackle: Yellow-olive cock.
Throat: Two or three turns of French partridge breast feather.

2 Green Drake

COMMENT

The *Fly Fishers' Journal* regularly produces reports of fishermen hooking, rising, losing and occasionally landing salmon on Mayflies in the southern salmon-holding rivers. This pattern will float more confidently, and float through repeated casting, better than the more representational dressing.

DRESSING

Tail: Strips of cinnamon hen.
Body: Cream wool, tapering from thin to thick.
Rib: Light-chestnut silk.
Throat: At least two olive hackles.
Wings: Bunches of brown bucktail or pale squirrel hair, divided and inclined slightly forwards.

1 French Partridge Mayfly **2** Green Drake **3** Humpy (Goofus Bug)
4 Dapping Fly **5** Bomber **6** Buck Bug **7** Scraggly **8** Cosseboom Dry

3 Humpy (Goofus Bug)

COMMENT

In the search for high-riding naturally buoyant dry flies for trout, there was soon a shift from the use of hackles to the use of deerhair, or a combination of the two. The colour of the body varies, and sometimes the other components. The originator seems to have been Jack Horner, and the original name was Horner's Deer Fly. It is a Western pattern. Goofus was the name given to it by Dan Bailey of Montana.

We have taken the formula for this standard from the Orvis Index.

DRESSING

Hook: 8–14.
Tail: Moose body hair.
Body: Colour according to variation, with natural deerhair in strands pulled over and enveloping the top.
Wing: The tips of the body deerhair splayed vertically or split and pointing forwards.
Throat: Grizzle.

4 Dapping Fly

COMMENT

Dapping differs from dry-fly fishing in that the rod is extra-long and the line is extra-light, so that what breeze there is may hold the fly out at a distance, and it alone touches the water with the leader remaining in the air. Live baits – mayflies, daddy-long-legs and grasshoppers – are used as well as artificials. The fly must not be allowed to sink; it must dance on the surface. Tying styles are numerous, with light buoyancy usually being achieved by dense hackling. Hackles of natural colour tend to be stiffer and less absorbent than dyed feathers, so greys, grizzles, natural red and black may be chosen.

DRESSING

Tail: Strong fibres of bucktail, or whiskers.
Body (optional, as a base for the hackles): Floss.
Hackles: Olive, densely palmered.

5 Bomber

COMMENT

This is at present enjoying a vogue, with an eager following. The date of use and thence development is given by Bates as 1967, on the River Miramichi. Forward wing and aft-pointing tail, both in the plane of the hook shank but clearing the eye, are important. The use of *two* palmer hackles allows the fly to stand 'on tiptoe' for the first couple of casts, and thereafter it settles in the surface but with natural buoyancy.

The dressing below is the standard pattern. The colour of all the materials may be varied, and in all combinations.

DRESSING

Hook: Extra-long-shank low-water or streamer.
Tail: Hackle fibres, as for the palmer hackle, or squirrel hair.
Body: Trimmed natural deerhair or caribou hair.
Palmer hackle: Natural red cock.
Wing: Hackle fibres, as for palmer hackle, pointing forwards, or squirrel hair.

6 Buck Bug

COMMENT

This is very similar to a Bomber *but* it is essentially small – not bigger than a size 4 – and has a fluorescent butt, usually fluorescent green.

In *Atlantic Salmon and the Fly Fisherman* Gary Anderson spells the name 'Buc Bug' and observes that it may be difficult to keep afloat, but can kill even when sunk. He suggests that Elmer Smith was the developer of the pattern, in 1970, as expected, on the Miramichi. Subsequently it has proved itself on a wide variety of eastern seaboard rivers.

DRESSING

Tail: None.
Butt: Fluorescent green.
Body: Clipped deer hair.
Hackle: Natural red cock palmered over body.

7 Scraggly

COMMENT

Lee Wulff writes: 'One of my variations is the Scraggly. It floats even higher than the standard Wulff, and it has a bulkier body. It is tied by using chenille or another bulky body material and winding a hackle palmer-style down the body. The body and hackle add bulk and flotation at the same time. I use them for bass as well as for trout and salmon.' As the pattern is a series, we give just one, the White Moth Scraggly.

DRESSING

Tail: Bucktail tips.
Body: Cream chenille.
Hackle and throat: Badger hackle.
Wing: Bucktail separated into two bunches.
Collar: Badger saddle.

8 Cosseboom Dry

COMMENT

There is an inclination to dress some of the standard wet flies in a dry-fly style, rather as some wet trout flies have a dry tying. The Cosseboom in its original style – also called Cosseboom Special – is the example we have chosen. Ideally the body material is non-absorbent and buoyant or extremely well greased. To cock well, most dry flies nowadays are tied with the wings split into separate bunches and angled slightly forwards.

DRESSING

Tail: Grey squirrel, dark with white tips.
Body: Bright green wool.
Wings: Grey squirrel, dark with white tips.
Throat and collar: Bright yellow hackles back and front of the wings.

GRUBS, SHRIMPS AND PRAWNS

Introduction

Though the writers of the turn of the century and earlier were prepared to state that salmon ate shrimps, prawns, small fish and so on in their saltwater stay, they offered relatively few direct shrimp or prawn patterns. Double hooks were recorded by Venables in the late 1600s, yet it seems that their potential in a good shrimp or prawn representation was not taken up. Instead there were Grub patterns on singles, which were to have a role when ordinary flies had passed the fish by without result. Hale gives the following Grub-style flies: Autumn Creeper, Black Creeper, Grub, Glow-Worm, Hop Dog, Spring Grub, Summer Grub, Tippet Grub, Trois Temps, Wasp Grub and Wye Grub. There was no Usk Grub. Kelson gives Ringlet, Hempseed Grub, Heather Dog, Black Creeper Grub, Autumn Creeper, Hop Dog, Gallantine, Glow-Worm, Jungle Hornet, Spring Grub, Tippet Grub, Wasp Grub and Wye Grub. In *Land and Water* there are a few more. Herbert-Maxwell gives but the Ajax, and Pryce-Tannatt has a section of wingless flies: Brown Shrimp, Glow-Worm, Grey Palmer, Jungle Hornet, Silver Partridge, Spring Grub and Tippet Grub. This sums up the major authors. Hardy's catalogue of 1907 does have a shrimp reference, but only in 1934 do we see a highly lauded pattern which we easily recognise as being in the modern style. The Grub style, not far from that of the North American Woolly Worm, might be a reasonable representation of some insects like caterpillars. It tapers from small at the rear to wider at the head. The more pronounced this feature the less like a prawn or shrimp does the lure look, so progress in imitation came when the order was reversed, with long trailing tail hackle fibres, getting smaller in the joint hackle, and smaller still at the head. The shrimp or prawn, incidentally, is a creature with the habit of travelling in reverse gear – tail first.

For a reasonable representation of a prawn we have to wait until Colonel Esmond Drury formulated his General Practitioner in 1953. There was probably never any thought of prawn in the design of flies such as the Durham Ranger, even though to some observers they look rather more like prawns than small fish. In both cases the neck feathers of the golden pheasant are used. The tail hackle for shrimps is usually a golden pheasant breast feather. An alternative, not red but yellow, is its rump feather. Such winging as does take place is to give a smooth shell-back appearance, and the enamelled jungle cock neck feathers are chosen more for this rather than for their contrasting black and creamy white. They are most often tied to form a roof over the body, and like this they seem less vulnerable than mounted vertically. Translucency is an aspect of the uncooked prawn which is thought worth copying. Some tyers choose tinsel – silver or gold – and evanescent hackling like badger. One of the prawn patterns we show has more modern materials. The eyes on natural prawns and shrimps are a protruberant feature. We can reach for naturally marked feather; we can choose feather of the texture we want, and add markings; or we can use bead eyes of various kinds. The bony beak of a prawn, called a rostrum, may be copied and the whiskers certainly should be. Some patterns use the centre stems of poultry hackles with the fibres removed; others rely on the golden pheasant breast hackle. In all logic, if these patterns are to have some element of direct representation a tag on the artificial is superfluous. However, so. ingrained is the habit that many tyings still include it.

We have one anecdote about Shrimps: there was an elderly general who used to fish the River Glass (the upper water of the Beauly). He knew his fishing – he lived beside it – and he had one choice of fly, a size 6 Brown Shrimp. He always outfished other fishermen on his beat and the other bank. It is fair to conclude that a size 6 shrimp is a much bigger dressing than the hook size suggests. Often all the other fishermen were fishing too small. Only when we, as his opposition, moved up to 2/0 or similar fly sizes did we start to approach his catch rate. There is a conclusion to be drawn here: size is most of it. The long mobile hackles, however, do give a wonderfully active appearance in the water, which may be more attractive than any charm a standard summer pattern can offer.

Shrimps and Prawns are alive and well as far as tying imagination goes nowadays. Grubs have largely fallen by the wayside, though Jorgenson is pleased to mention the Tippet Grub and the Jungle Hornet. He does give the Shrimp Fly, the Krabla (which we show on page

191) and the General Practitioner, though this is a small showing. In North America the shrimp and prawn patterns do not have a particularly loyal or inventive following. Fulsher and Krom in their hairwing book manage a Shrimp and Old Swampwater's Shrimp, but both have more characteristics of ordinary winged salmon flies. Gary Anderson, checking through successful pattern lists in fishing logs and diaries, finds that Shrimps feature rarely. The North Americans may choose to look further into this wide grouping of styles when they see how much British anglers rely on them. Since the Irish seem to have adopted the style widely, even adapting some of the classic standards to this style, it is worth listing Malone's Shrimps and Prawns: Bessy Bell, Curry's Blue, Curry's Gold, Curry's Red, Dancer Shrimp, Ghost Shrimp, Grey Thunder Shrimp, Jock Scott Shrimp, Colonel Christie Shrimp, Secret Weapon (not Falkus's), Judy of the Bogs, Kingfisher Shrimp, Quinn Shrimp, Wye Bug.

Grubs

Grubs or creepers seem to be the logical precursors to shrimp and prawn patterns, though no direct attempt seems to be made to represent faithfully crustacea. Essentially they are wingless flies, tied jointed, with a tail hackle, a centre hackle and a head hackle. Cheeks of jungle cock or chatterer are found at each joint in some of the patterns. The Usk in Wales is one of the rivers in which in early times a wingless pattern was considered very effective. Then the style was adapted to copy such insects as wasps. All Grubs have the smallest hackle at the tail, a medium one in the centre and largest at the eye. By reversing the order to largest hackle at the tail and smallest at the eye the tradition of the shrimp pattern was started. A couple of Grub patterns might well have appeared in our 'Added Attraction' section, as their bodies were composed of copper-tinselled chenille. Subsequently the dressing was altered to the more normal oval gold tinsel. In all the literature available to us, we find no references to early Grubs being tied on double hooks, which would greatly enhance their shrimp- or prawn-like appearance.

1 Tippet Grub

COMMENT

Kelson wrote of this: 'An old favourite for a thorough change.' Even relatively simple flies seemed to be varied, so here are Pryce-Tannatt's tying notes: tag, gold tinsel and scarlet seal fur; tail hackle, tippet first, then furnace; body, two similar equal halves – three turns silver thread, then green Berlin wool; centre hackle and head hackle, as above; head, silver thread.

DRESSING

Tag: Silver tinsel and scarlet seal fur.
Tail: None.
Tail hackle: Tippet.
Body: Light-olive-green chenille.
Centre hackle: Tippet.
Body: Light-olive-green chenille.
Head hackle: Tippet.

2 Wasp Grub

COMMENT

Kelson noted: 'A simple but effective low-water pattern in certain locations during the wasp season. On the Usk, for instance, I have been singularly successful with it. The fly is useful on the Dee.' Bainbridge suggested either yellow wool body and black hackle, or black wool body and yellow hackle for his Wasp pattern, of which more is said on pages 256–7.

DRESSING

Tag: Silver tinsel.
Tail: Toucan.
Body: Yellow and black chenille – wasplike, not spiral.
Hackle: Dark-brown coch-y-bonddu over the front half of body.
Throat: As hackle.

1 Tippet Grub **2** Wasp Grub **3** Moisie Grub **4** Glow-Worm Grub
5 Ajax **6** Jungle Hornet **7** Black Creeper Grub **8** Usk Grub

3 Moisie Grub

COMMENT

The Moisie is a river in north-eastern Canada. Although Americans and Canadians such as Wells and Nobbs (in *Salmon Tactics*, 1934) mention that salmon flies like the Jock Scott and Thunder & Lightning look like troutlets or shrimps or small prawns depending on conditions, little endeavour is made to imitate them. Wells records in 1887 that he hooked six fish and killed four (from 21 to 32½lb) on a Moisie Grub.

DRESSING

Tail: Topping.
Body: Rear half, yellow.
Centre hackle: Short black.
Body: Front half, black herl.
Head hackle: Guinea-fowl under grizzle.

4 Glow-Worm Grub

COMMENT

The Trois-Temps is another pattern whose body was copper chenille. As usual, each hackle is larger than the previous one. Pryce-Tannatt's variation is given in brackets.

DRESSING

Tag: Silver tinsel and yellow seal fur (silver tinsel).
Tail: Ibis (scarlet Berlin wool).
Tail hackle: Coch-y-bonddu.
Body: Copper-tinselled chenille (oval gold tinsel).
Centre hackle: Coch-y-bonddu.
Body: Copper-tinselled chenille (oval gold tinsel).
Head hackle: Coch-y-bonddu.

5 Ajax

COMMENT

'This is one of the grub patterns from the Usk. It may be used in all sizes and takes the fish very readily, as I have found in the far North. It is unnecessary to give more samples of wingless flies as they may be made in all colours and of various materials.' So said Sir Herbert Maxwell. Kelson considers the Jungle Hornet to be 'a vast improvement' on the Ajax.

DRESSING

Tag: Silver tinsel and scarlet wool.
Tail: None.
Tail, centre and head hackles: Coch-y-bonddu with jungle cock pair.
Body: Rear half, black and yellow chenille, parallel not spiral; front half, black chenille.

6 Jungle Hornet

Hale, Pryce-Tannatt and Kelson basically agree on the pattern. Kelson claimed credit for the origination though he was probably more its promotor than designer. His variations were a tail of yellow macaw, with or without summer duck, and blue or red chenille substituted for the yellow in the body. The fly may be dressed large or small, and is very useful when the water is slightly coloured.

Tag: Gold tinsel (plenty).
Tail: Ibis (2 strips).
Tail: Centre and head hackles: coch-y-bonddu hackles and jungle cock.
Body: Yellow and black chenille alternating. (Pryce-Tannatt's dressing is: tag, silver tinsel; tail, ibis, and jungle cock back to back; tail, centre and head hackles, coch-y-bonddu with a pair of jungle cock, increasing in size; body, alternate yellow and black Berlin wools.)

7 Black Creeper Grub

A simple dark Grub, recommended by Kelson for use on the Earn and Usk, and upper waters of the Beauly. In the last recommendation it certainly has not been much in use since the mid-1930s if family fishing records may be relied on.

Hale gives the same dressing.

Tag: Silver twist and light blue floss.
Tail: Ibis and blue macaw strands.
Tail hackle: Natural black, cheeked chatterer.
Body: Black chenille.
Centre hackle: Large, natural black, cheeked chatterer.
Body: Black chenille.
Head hackle: Yet larger natural black hackle, cheeked chatterer.

8 Usk Grub

Tied smoothly but bulkily by Molly Sweet. Coombe Richards's version tended to be low-water in slenderness of style. Coombe Richards had a series of shrimps tied by Farlow's – Green, Brown, and Black. He was a keen advocate of these wingless styles for greased-line fishing, and influential in his time.

Tag: Silver thread.
Rear hackle: Golden pheasant breast feather.
Body: Rear half, dull orange (optionally veiled with scarlet cock hackle tips).
Centre hackles: White and orange.
Body: Front half, black seal fur.
Rib: Silver thread.
Front hackle: A pair of jungle cock.

Shrimps

Shrimp patterns seem to have something of a set formula, breast feather for the whiskers, jointed body with silk or tinsel more commonly used than wool or seal fur, an intermediate hackle at the centre, a hackle at the head usually tied as a collar, after any winging, which is normally jungle cock tied roofing the head section of the body. The veiling at the top and bottom and, commonly, the sides, seems standard Irish practice. How necessary it is may be doubted. Ribbing tends to oval tinsel, rather fine, and with plenty of turns to each half of the body. The body sections do not necessarily follow the usual sequence of the rear half being lighter in colour than the front half. Inventors seem to use any combinations, and give patterns of all colours. Shrimps tend to be summer flies, tied smallish on lighter wire hooks and fished with the floating line. If weight is added to the pattern, it is worth using the head varnish colour which to you denotes added weight.

1 Veniard's Welsh Shrimp

COMMENT

The collar hackle is a feature of many shrimps, though a beard may be an acceptable variation. Jungle cock sides/wings are an endeavour to reproduce the scaled back of the crustacean and are regularly included. This pattern was given to John Veniard by Llanwrst tyer R. H. Hughes, for *A Further Guide to Fly Dressing* (1964). Moc Morgan records the inventor as J. D. Jones, also from Llanwrst, a noted fisher on the lower Conway.

DRESSING

Tag: Yellow floss.
Tail: Topping.
Butt: Black herl.
Body: Yellow floss.
Rib: Oval silver.
Wing: Tip of a golden pheasant breast feather.
Sides: Jungle cock.
Collar: White cock.
Head: Black.

2 Curry's Red Shrimp

COMMENT

Malone was in correspondence with Patrick Curry, whom Edson J. Leonard quotes in his book *Flies* (1950): 'May 4, 1949 – I dress hundreds of patterns for my patrons, but when I go fishing for salmon, I confine my stock to three patterns. I consider that's enough, in fact one pattern of my invention kills 95 per cent of all salmon hereabouts . . . I call [it] the Curry Shrimp.' Patrick Curry was then sixty-two years old, and had been fly tying for forty-six years. Malone had his assurance that the veilings were to the sides and not top and bottom. A substitute is usually found for the Indian crow.

DRESSING

Tag: Flat silver.
Tail hackle: Red golden pheasant breast feather. **Rear body:** Red floss.
Rib: Fine oval silver.
Veiling: Indian crow – at the sides.
Centre hackle: Badger cock.
Front body: Black floss.
Rib: Oval silver.
Veiling: Indian crow – at the sides.
Wing: A pair of jungle cock, roofing the black floss. **Collar:** Long grey badger cock.
Head: Red.

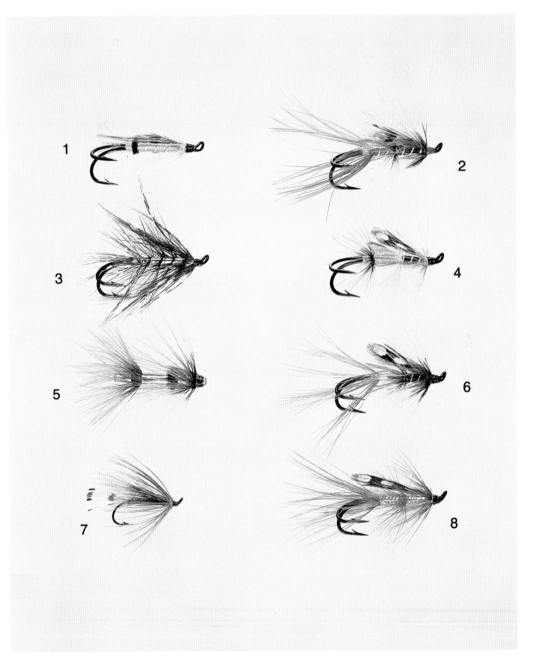

1 Veniard's Welsh Shrimp   2 Curry's Red Shrimp
3 Lochdhu   4 Ghost Shrimp   5 Gold Shrimp   6 Jock Scott Shrimp
7 Stewart Shrimp   8 Quinn Shrimp

3 Lochdhu

COMMENT

This Thurso pattern takes after earlier Grubs in its use of the speckled guinea-fowl feather. It was mentioned in *Trout and Salmon* in February 1974, in conjunction with the Tarantula for the same river (of which the dressing is: tag, oval silver; tail hackle, black and white guinea-fowl; body, pale-grey darning wool; rib, oval silver; hackle, cock dyed light-blue; head hackle, two or three turns of greyish mallard).

DRESSING

Tail hackle: Black and white guinea-fowl.
Body: Flat silver.
Rib: Oval silver.
Hackle: Black cock.
Head hackle: Three turns of black and white guinea-fowl.

4 Ghost Shrimp

COMMENT

Tinsel has two qualities; it reflects light and gives off sparkle, thus drawing more attention to the pattern; or it reflects faithfully the immediate surroundings to provide camouflage. When a pattern is tied with fairly ethereal hackle and tail – white – or with badger or furnace hackles, which become lighter in tone at the ends of the fibres, the result should be fairly spectral.

DRESSING

Tag: Flat silver.
Tail hackle: Furnace cock.
Rear body: Old-gold floss.
Rib: Oval silver.
Veiling: Red toucan.
Centre hackle: Short white cock.
Front body: Black floss.
Rib: Oval silver.
Veiling: Red toucan.
Wing: Jungle cock.
Collar: Long white cock.

5 Gold Shrimp

COMMENT

A pattern like this can be converted to tube or Waddington most satisfactorily, so we show it in that style, though the normal style is on the double hook.

DRESSING

Tag: Gold wire.
Tail hackle: Long badger cock dyed orange-red.
Body: Rear two-thirds flat gold.
Joint butt: Black herl.
Body: Front third flat gold.
Rib: Fine oval over the front of the body.
Throat: Red-orange cock under long badger cock.

6 Jock Scott Shrimp

COMMENT

Malone maintains that this is 'a useful pattern for all waters'. The wing is tied to be vertical, rather than roofing the body. Fluorescent yellow wool is thought to be an improvement on yellow floss for the body. E. C. Heaney's Secret Weapon is almost identical. The Colonel Christie Shrimp is similar, but has yellow, not red, veiling.

DRESSING

Tag: Silver tinsel.
Tail hackle: Red golden pheasant breast feather.
Rear body: Yellow floss.
Rib: Silver thread.
Veiling: Scarlet swan.
Centre hackle: Badger cock.
Front body: Black floss.
Rib: Silver thread.
Veiling: Scarlet swan.
Wing: Jungle cock, back to back.
Collar: Long badger cock.

7 Stewart Shrimp

COMMENT

This is one of the earlier shrimps, and has had a long currency and popularity. This pattern departs slightly from the Shrimp norm in not having a centre hackle. The example is shown on a single hook to illustrate how much less the style of a shrimp is apparent when not dressed on doubles or long-shank trebles.

DRESSING

Tag: Fine silver oval.
Tail: Tip of tippet feather.
Body: Rear half red, front half black floss.
Rib: Fine oval silver.
Wing: Grey squirrel dyed orange-mottled.
Collar: Golden pheasant breast feather.

8 Quinn Shrimp

COMMENT

We were both on the Castle Grant beats of the Spey. Two Irishmen were our fishing companions and both their boxes were full of Shrimp patterns, many derived from classic and traditional flies.

This is as close to a Silver Wilkinson as a shrimp pattern can be contrived. We will not illustrate more in this vein since tyers will see how all the classics can be adapted to the shrimp style.

DRESSING

Tag: Silver.
Tail hackle: Red golden pheasant breast feather.
Body: Flat silver. **Rib:** Silver wire.
Veiling: Bright-blue hen hackle fibres at sides.
Centre hackle: Pale-magenta cock.
Body: Flat silver. **Rib:** Silver wire.
Veiling: Bright-blue hen hackle fibres at sides.
Wings: Jungle cock, back to back.
Collar: Magenta cock under grey badger.

Prawns

Prawns seem to excite fly tyers into greater realms of imagination and innovation. Orange is certainly the most popular colour, and the leader in design and popularity is Esmond Drury's General Practitioner, kindly tied for us by his family. He had noticed that many of the golden pheasant feathers approximate closely to the orange of a cooked prawn, and the 'GP' initially stood for golden pheasant.

Though indiarubber has been used for a long time in fly tying it degenerates fast; latex is much more stable, and flanges cut in a broad V shape suggest themselves for a prawn imitation. The natural pale beige may be coloured with indelible marker pens, for base colour and for markings, so, though the style may be established on the orange version, colour options are widely available. Body material is largely seal fur, normally tapering from broad at the bend of the hook to narrow at the eye. Freshwater shrimp tying practices may be used, with Raffene or an equivalent stretched over the back to give the shellback appearance. Eyes are often incorporated. Weight may be added, as prawn patterns are often fished in larger sizes, and fished deep.

1 General Practitioner

COMMENT

This is the highly popular pattern originated by Esmond Drury, and tied for us by Kate Drury. It is a fly which won ED a number of whisky bets on the Test in 1953. The use of the natural prawn was not permitted on the beat, so ED created a fly to imitate one. If he caught a fish he was to receive a large whisky and soda but if he failed it would be Coca-Cola. By fishing upstream he took the first fish. He doubled stakes for the second, which was taken on the third cast, and broke in the next fish, which saved the stake of four whiskies!

DRESSING

Whiskers: Ten good bucktail fibres dyed orange – long.
Head of prawn: Two golden pheasant feathers, one upside down, one the usual way up. **Body:** Orange seal fur.
Rib: Oval gold. **Hackle:** Orange cock.
Back: Overlapping golden pheasant breast feathers convex side up, in three sections.
Eyes: A V-section of tippet to give the effect of black eyes, added to the back of the first of the back segments.
Head: Red varnish.

2 Latex Prawn

COMMENT

The body should be well picked out to represent legs. The eyebrow has three parallel black lines on top, and the back sections have a broad black line running up the tail. An indelible marker pen does this.

Red washing-up gloves may provide suitable material.

DRESSING

Underjaw: A latex flange with a V cut in the trailing edge, and the tip of a golden pheasant breast feather.
Top jaw: A short rounded latex flange.
Eyes: Black beads on twisted copper wire.
Whiskers: Strands of bucktail dyed orange.
Eyebrows: A large latex flange.
Body: Orange seal fur.
Back: Three rounded flanges of latex.
Tail fins: The fourth flange of the latex for the back extending well over the eye over a golden pheasant breast feather.

1 General Practitioner   **2** Latex Prawn   **3** Peter Deane's Red Francis
4 Purple Practitioner   **5** Chilimps   **6** Deerhair Prawn
7 Hair-Backed Prawn   **8** Polythene Prawn

3 Peter Deane's Red Francis

COMMENT

Peter had a client who wanted a shrimp/prawn pattern, but it had to be different from other shrimp/prawns. The invention proved so successful that one of Peter's tyers was fully occupied tying that pattern and that pattern alone. Her name Frances became somehow transmuted to Francis, and the fly remained christened thus.

The pattern comes in freshwater colours of black, red, yellow and green; for bonefish there is a very catching blue tying.

DRESSING

Rostrum: Two strips of cock pheasant tail.
Whiskers: Stripped grizzle hackle stems, three to each side.
Body: Crimson wool, tapering from thick to thin.
Eyes: Black beads.
Hackle: Natural red, clipped flush on back and sides.
Head: Red.

4 Purple Practitioner

COMMENT

Also referred to as the Purple Prawn fly, it follows the recipe for the General Practitioner, but is purple throughout. The classic purple is the potato dye. The pattern came into being as more and more natural bait fishermen found that the purple-dyed prawn was attracting greater attention than ordinary boiled pink prawns or dyed red ones.

Purple is a favoured colour in Ireland – much more so than in the rest of the salmon-fishing world.

DRESSING

Whiskers: Ten good bucktail fibres dyed purple – long. **Head of prawn:** Purple-dyed golden pheasant breast feathers, one upside down, one the usual way up. **Body:** Purple seal fur. **Rib:** Oval gold. **Hackle:** Purple cock. **Back:** Overlapping golden pheasant breast feathers dyed purple, convex side up, in three sections. **Eyes:** A V-section of purple-dyed tippet to give the effect of black eyes, added to the back of the first of the back segments. **Head:** Purple varnish (or nail varnish).

5 Chilimps

COMMENT

The original was tyed in Sweden by Mr Olle Törnblom on 28 April 1942. It is intended to imitate a shrimp; the name is a mis-pronunciation of 'shrimp'. Variations include a silver rear half of the body and the addition of eyes. Since it is all-orange, we have placed it within the prawn section.

DRESSING

Tail: Orange hackle tip set on vertical edge.
Body: Red wool, tapering from thick to thin.
Rib: Flat gold.
Hackle: Hot orange.
Throat: Hot orange, thick and sweeping back.
Wing: None.

6 Deerhair Prawn

COMMENT

Deerhair is sculptable and possesses buoyancy, the latter quality negatable by the inclusion of weight. Keep the concept that a prawn has broad shoulders and a narrow tail.

DRESSING

Rostrum: A swathe of orange swan.
Whiskers: A bundle of stripped orange hackle stems.
Eyes: Nylon, with the ends heat-blobbed and blackened.
Tail hackle: Long orange cock.
Body: Orange-dyed deerhair, muddler style, clipped short underneath, with 'legs', if required.
Rib: Broad oval gold.

7 Hair-Backed Prawn

COMMENT

This is more a variation on the General Practitioner than a new concept. The insertion of a small amount of hair at intervals along the back serves to give the idea of the scaly segmentation. Colour is to taste – hot orange, reddish or even purple. The illustration is the hot-orange pattern.

DRESSING

Rostrum: A swathe of orange hair.
Eyes: Nylon with the ends heat-blobbed and blackened.
Tail hackle: Long orange cock.
Body: Orange seal fur.
Rib: Broad oval gold.
Back: Tufts of orange-dyed squirrel hair – plain or mottled – tied in at regular intervals and just overlapping.
Beard: Defeo-style orange hair hackle, not too long.

8 Polythene Prawn

COMMENT

The polythene overbody of trout flies such as Sinfoil's Fry and the Polystickle has a role in salmon flies. The French devised some splendid sea patterns of prawns, obviously adaptable to freshwater use for salmon. What follows is a fair interpretation. A live prawn of a natural colour is extremely translucent. Many wrappings of fine polythene represent this well, and a touch of colour on the shank shines through suitably. The choice of colours is wide; the dressing given is the one illustrated in the plate.

DRESSING

Whiskers: Strands of stiff hair or bucktail.
Eyes: Nylon, heat-blobbed and blackened.
Rostrum: A swathe of orange swan.
Underbody: Orangy-red.
Rib: Oval silver.
Overbody: Wound clear polythene.
Tail vanes: Extensions of the body material, fanned out over the hook eye.

SCANDINAVIA AND ICELAND

Introduction

Scandinavia Denmark cannot in all fairness be considered a major salmon-fishing nation, but its inhabitants prove most expert and very considerable artists at the fly-tying bench, and keen travellers, seeking salmon in other lands.

Finland has three effective salmon rivers, the Tenojoki (better known as the Tana), the Naatamojoki and the Tornio. The first-named provides part of the boundary with neighbouring Norway, and is famous for its size and its big fish, for from the Norwegian side came Postmaster Hendrikson's 79lb salmon. Harling is very much the style there. Flies are tied large, because of the cold water – we are talking of a river 250 miles north of the Arctic Circle – so 2/0 to 6/0 are good working sizes. Local patterns are tied slender and spare.

Sweden has declined as a salmon fishery. Hydroelectric systems have affected many main rivers, and pollution and sea fishing have depleted the fish which stay within the Baltic, rather than take to the high seas. Its sea trout remain famous, with the short and prolific Em more remarkable for this species, in large sizes, than for its salmon.

Norway, however, still has a great name for its salmon. Some rivers produce huge fish, but in small numbers; some rivers produce both good-sized and numerous fish; and some rivers good bags of smaller fish and grilse. Where the leases are held year after year, the rivers tend not to make the news, whatever the catches, so much as the rivers with beats to let more publicly. The Vosso, also known as the Evanger and the Bolstad River, has been publicised recently for both its immense fish and the fact that one of the authors of this book, Arthur, has been a regular visitor over the past twenty-eight years.

No doubt the Napoleonic War was a tiresome interruption to some of the major titled and landed British families. The enjoyment of the qualities of Norwegian rivers for the sport they could offer was their monopoly even then. Most Norwegians were extremely friendly and grateful for the rent – they fished with nets and not for sport. The records over the years are truly staggering; the Vosso, as ever, is well documented. Cyril Mowbray Wells, a housemaster at Eton, was a tenant of the Bolstad beat from 1920 to 1939, and then from 1946 to 1950. During that time he caught every

pound weight of fish between twenty and fifty-eight pounds, except fifty-five pounds. He did not classify fish below twenty pounds, and on his eightieth birthday caught his eightieth fish of forty pounds or over. His own average weight was twenty-seven and a half pounds and, though he himself never caught a fish over sixty pounds, some of his guests managed to do so.

Charles Ritz in *A Fly Fisher's Life* captures the tremendous excitement of fishing these mighty rivers. He writes particularly of two: of the Aaro (or Aroy), 'this unbelievably fast and dangerous water'. The style of playing a fish is simply said but not so simply done – holding its head to the stream and not letting it run – control must be established at the outset. Leaders were three strands of 25-pound nylon braided together. Backing was 75–100 pounds BS. Then he wrote of the Alta, a consistent river for fly fishers, with an average weight of about twenty-four pounds, but with forty pounders not uncommon. Good bags have been recorded as follows: Roar Jöraholmen with 44 salmon in 24 hours; the Duke of Roxburghe with 39 salmon and grilse in one day in 1860; Mr Harewood with 26 salmon in one day in 1876; and the Duke of Westminster with 33 salmon weighing 792 pounds in one day in 1926. Tackle for these mighty rivers with their mighty fish was available 'off the shelf'. Ritz determined to take medium-length and light-weight gear, to the incredulity of the gillies, but he spoke of traditional weighty materials. With modern carbon and boron, long days of casting with big rods are not the travail of the times (1950s and 1960s) in which he fished. He related that the fly on the Alta is more productive than spinning – which may be because the banks are spun, but the fly is fished from a boat with greater accuracy of presentation. When he wrote, he found that the gillies largely chose the British standard classic flies – Mar Lodge, Doctors, Jock Scott and Thunder & Lightning in particular. Ritz, however, laid in for himself a supply of General Practitioner Prawn Flies, and they were given a good share of his fishing time. American guests brought American Rat patterns, and these also caught fish. Out of 277 fish in 1954, 56 were taken on a Jock Scott, 42 on a Black Doctor, 26 on a Mar Lodge, 37 on a Prawn Fly (among them, most of the forty pounders) and more than 20 on a Rusty Rat.

Then in 1957 Ritz changed to using a tube fly. After that he had nothing good at all to say about traditional flies. However, after discussion with John Ashley-Cooper in 1971, he revised his style of tube flies by reducing the body length. The present Duke of Roxburghe has been known to lie at the bottom of his swimming pool looking upwards at flies drawn over him, and tubes with long trailing wings and short bodies are to be found in his fly box. With years of experience on the Alta, and a fifty-one pounder to his credit, though on a Rat, his judgement should not be discounted for this style of fishing.

Iceland   There are two main areas in Iceland where the rivers can be considered first-class for salmon – in the west, round the capital, Reykjavik; and along the north coast. In all there are about 64 rivers with salmon, of which 20 are of good reputation. There are many other rivers, but if they are glacier-fed then they run too dirty. A notable point about the best rivers is that they run clear and they are uncontaminated. They have a rapid descent and are usually quite rocky. Rain does not affect the fishability and, because there is no artificial drainage, run-off is extremely steady, and rivers are rarely out of condition. The season is quite short: the fish start to run in mid-June in the west, and about ten days later in the north, with the sea trout running a bit earlier. The serious salmon fisher can find sea trout and sea-run Arctic char quite a pest in the estuarine waters. The season is not long, about ten weeks, but catches can be impressive – over 180 a week have been known to come off the Laxa a Asum, with only two rods allowed to fish at any one time. This, of course, was within the legal hours of fishing, for everywhere throughout the country it is prohibited to fish more than 12 hours in any 24, and it is illegal to fish before 7 a.m. and after 10 p.m. The best rivers are the ultimate in fly water as they are so clean and the fish so fresh. More than the occasional commentator has noted how far fish might follow a fly to *seize* it, not just take it. Although day temperatures may reach 80 °F in the shade, the water seldom warms beyond 60°, so very small flies, much smaller than 6s, are rarely called for. Big flies, inches long, do have their moments, but regular comment is that the dry fly is not a serious contender in Iceland. We note, however, that John Rennie visited Iceland and tried a dry fly when conditions were low and bright, and the fish shy. He used a large Tup, a Black Bivisible, and so on, and rose and hooked his fish well, but struggled with a quagmire of a river bank and had to retire utterly frustrated. He recorded success with a Terror when he tried the Nordura, but reinforced the general comment that a standard pattern with a bit of blue in it was the most taking – a Teal, Blue & Silver once being *the* fly with particular success. His observations about travel (his book was published in 1949) relate largely to the whims and caprices of the ponies which had to be hired. Nowadays transport is based more widely on hired cars or cross-country vehicles, and roads, though not very good, do serve some of the fisheries.

John Ashley-Cooper advised that the visitor will be unlikely to find good tackle shops in Iceland, but should bring out enough for his own requirements, and it should all have a certificate of disinfection. The Icelanders do not want outbreaks of ulcerative dermal necrosis or other disease on their rivers. He also pointed out that the user of a single-handed rod may be blown off the river in some of the many changes of weather. Those who use a 12-14 footer might manage with difficulty to keep fishing, but a 15-16 footer will often bring in fish while the lesser rods have to retire. Fishing in Iceland is not cheap – a feature it shares with Norway – but it offers undeniably excellent fishing for plenty of small fish, a foil for the great Norwegian fisheries.

Scandinavia

Jones on Norway (1848) recommended the following flies: The Cadogan, Tom Tickler, Popham, The Major, Baronet, Rainbow, Stunner, Butcher, Jackass, Doctor, Dandy, Fairy, Flower of Kelso, Colonel, Childers, Artful Dodger, Assassin, Baker, Bonne Bouche and Switcher. Most were out of date by the end of the century.

Fraser Sandeman's *Angling Travels in Norway* (1895) gives the following patterns: Sandeman No. 1, 2, 3, 7 and 11, Jock Scott, Durham Ranger, Bulldog, Llanover, Bransty, Saghoug and Gula. His *By Hook and By Crook* listed more flies. More recently, John Veniard, in *Further Guide to Fly-dressing*, listed John Sand's

patterns for Scandinavia: Golden Mallard, Grey Fancy, Namsen, Ola, Ottesen, Peer Gynt, Rallaven, Rottenikken, Scarlet Pimpernel, Sheriff, Stens Fancy, Thunderjet, Tumma Vaeltaja, Atsingin Keltainen and Kola Fly.

Hardy's catalogues list Jock Scott, Durham Ranger, Silver Grey, Dusty Miller, Black Doctor, Black Dose, Blue Doctor, Thunder & Lightning and Mar Lodge. Flies recommended for Finland were Silver Doctor, Silver Scott, Murdoch, Silver Rower and Black Prince. Bates wrote that some classics in use were Lady Amherst, Green Highlander, Black Rat, Silver Rat, Rusty Rat, Red Abbey and Cosseboom, as well as many others.

1 Vi Menn Flua

COMMENT

This fly is named after a weekly magazine with regular pages on fishing and outdoor life. The editor asked Olaf Olsen, well known in Norway as the King of the River Laerdal, to tie the first fly. From its inception in 1977, this fly has had a good reputation on Norwegian rivers. It is at its best when there is a little colour in the water, and before it gets dark in the evening.

Recommended sizes are 2/0 to 4.

DRESSING

Tag: Oval silver.
Tail: Topping and hackle fibres dyed red.
Butt: Red herl.
Body: Two-thirds black floss, one-third red floss (all black).
Rib: Flat silver and oval.

2 Valdum

COMMENT

This fly is named after a beat on the River Gaula, a favourite river of the tyer, Børre Pettersen. He tried it first in 1984, and since then has had good catches of salmon and sea trout on it. Since then it has for him become a general pattern on all rivers, mainly on doubles in sizes 4, 6 and 8.

DRESSING

Tag: Silver twist and red floss.
Tail: Hackle fibres dyed red.
Butt: Black herl.
Body: Flat silver.
Rib: Black floss.
Throat: Black cock.
Wing: Black swan (black squirrel tail).
Sides: Jungle cock.

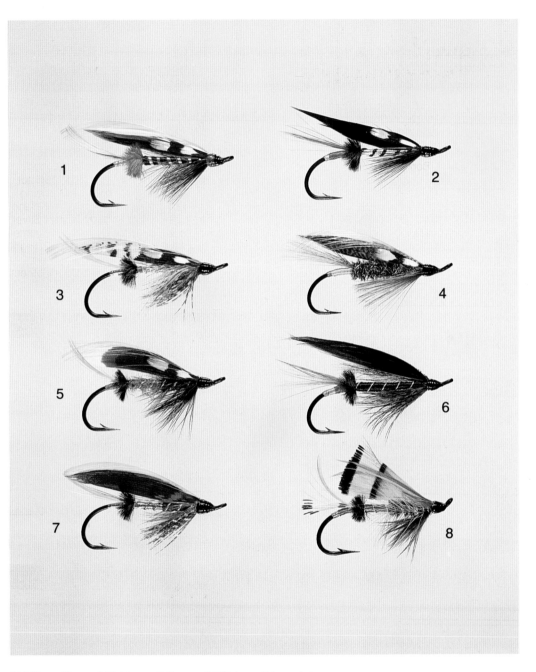

1 Vi Menn Flua   **2** Valdum   **3** Tana   **4** Pålsbu   **5** Laerdal
6 Børre Flua   **7** Gullnøkk   **8** Gaula Variant

3 Tana

The River Tana is the largest and the most productive in Norway. It is in the extreme north-east and is fished in high summer when it is light day and night. Børre suggests that for this reason patterns should be bright, and that this tying should have a sparse hackle and a long wing. He uses it on single hooks in rivers clear as gin.

Tag: Flat gold.
Tail: Topping.
Butt: Black herl.
Body: Flat silver.
Rib: Oval silver.
Hackle: Yellow cock, over the front half of the body.
Throat: Guinea-fowl.
Wing: Strips of Amherst tail, set upright with topping over.
Sides: Jungle cock.

4 Pålsbu

This is one of the oldest Norwegian patterns, orginally tied for trout, but adapated very well for salmon. In August when the rivers are warm and low it seems particularly effective on cock fish. Børre cannot explain the reason. The body should be thick and bulky, so is tied with at least five strands of herl.

Tag: Gold twist and yellow floss.
Tail: Red hackle fibres beneath shorter brown partridge fibres.
Body: Bronze peacock herl.
Rib: Fine oval gold.
Wing: Bronze mallard and topping.
Sides: Jungle cock.

5 Laerdal

This is another invention of Olaf Olsen, famous for his fly tying and a legendary gillie until his death in 1984. The pattern is not as famous as the river of that name, but it has produced good catches for Børre when the sun comes and goes in a cloudy sky. It also can work well between daylight and dark night.

Tag: Oval silver.
Tail: Topping.
Butt: Black herl.
Body: Rear half grey, front half black (wool or seal fur).
Rib: Oval gold.
Throat: Black cock.
Wing: White-tipped black turkey strips, set upright with topping.
Sides: Jungle cock.

6 Børre Flua

Børre Pettersen is one of the best-known salmon fly tyers and fishermen in Norway, and has held courses on tying and casting for some years. He is head of the Department of the Environment in Norway, and has played a key role in protecting the salmon. Having been Member of Parliament from 1969–73, he is now President of the Norwegian Anglers and Hunters Association. His books are *Salmon and Salmon Angling in Norway* (1987), and *Fly-tying in Scandinavia* (1989). This fly is an invention of his as he was wondering how salmon see colour.

Tag: Oval silver, yellow floss, followed by red floss.
Tail: Dyed red hackle fibres.
Butt: Black herl.
Body: Black floss.
Rib: Oval silver.
Throat: Guinea-fowl dyed blue.
Wing: Fibres of guinea-fowl dyed blue under hair from black squirrel tail or vertical strips of black swan.

7 Gullnøkk

Gullnøkk means golden water monster. The fly is one of Børre's favourites when the water is tinged with brown, hot orange being a good colour for a hackle in such conditions, which is a finding in the British Isles as well as elsewhere. This is one of Torgeir Steen's inventions. He was born near the little River Bogna to the south of the Namsen, an area much fished by British visitors who were more than happy to use his flies, as he was a most capable tyer.

Tag: Flat gold.
Tail: Topping and dyed red hackle fibres.
Butt: Black herl.
Body: Rear half flat gold, front half black floss.
Rib: Oval gold.
Hackle: Hot orange over black floss.
Throat: Guinea-fowl.
Wing: Tippet strands under vertical strips of dark mottled turkey, and topping.

8 Gaula Variant

This is not a Børre pattern, but is included as it shows a Scandinavian trend, to dye components to match the tone of the fly. In this case it is the topping which has been dyed. Other tyers dye jungle cock, brown for brown-toned flies, red, blue and so on. As well as seeking tonal harmonies, some tyers look for extra kick, or extra sparkle, on tubes and Waddingtons as well as standard hooks. As is usual, their confections are unnamed, but they can be very bright and have plenty of mobile elements like heron or marabou or both.

Tag: Silver twist and red floss.
Tail: Tippet strands and topping.
Butt: Black herl.
Body: Rear half red floss, front half bronze peacock herl.
Hackle: Yellow cock over the herl.
Throat: Blue dyed guinea-fowl.
Wing: Tippets back to back, slender strands of light-orange and red swan, with blue-dyed topping over.
Cheeks: Kingfisher or chatterer.

Iceland

It appears that Charles Akroyd was the first British fisherman to rent Icelandic salmon fishing, recording his visit in June 1877 in *A Veteran Sportsman's Diary*, 1926. Ernest Crosfield and his brother Shetney took the Ellidaár just after the turn of the century and had splendid catches, with E. Crosfield's catch of 40 to his own rod still a record. From their visit comes the Crosfield fly, which for some reason is determinedly written Crossfield among the American writers. The season is fairly short – and can be extraordinarily generous with large catches of extremely fresh fish, accoutred with all their saltwater teeth, which lacerate the fingers when the fisherman extracts his fly. All the regular standard British patterns were patiently recommended until recently, when slighter streamlined modern patterns do most of the work. Blue flies, or flies with some blue in them, are favoured, and stalwarts such as the Blue Charm and the Silver Blue remain popular.

1 Black Sheep

COMMENT

Sheep variations abound: its feature is the long trailing hairwing, much after the style of the Collie Dog. The name came because the innovation looked so incongruous in an otherwise traditional fly box. The tale is told in the *Atlantic Salmon Journal* and the *Flyfishers' Journal* – but no dressing is given in either. Joe Hulbert 'invented' it in 1977; mostly it is tied on double hooks.

DRESSING

Tag: Fine oval silver.
Body: Black wool.
Rib: None.
Throat: A beard of long sparse blue hackle fibres.
Wing: Yellow under black over bucktail, can be 3 inches long.
Cheeks: Short jungle cock.
Head: Red.

2 Crosfield

COMMENT

In *Ellidaár* 1989 by Ásgeir Ingólfsson the Crosfield is referred to with three dressings. The example illustrated here is the first of these, finished, as seems the practice now, with tag and rib. The wing material is mallard or teal. The second dressing has a darker wing and the third a body of silkworm gut. The hairwing variant has a grey squirrel wing and is recorded in Fulsher and Krom.

DRESSING

Tail: Yellow.
Body: Embossed silver tinsel.
Throat: Blue.
Wing: Grey.

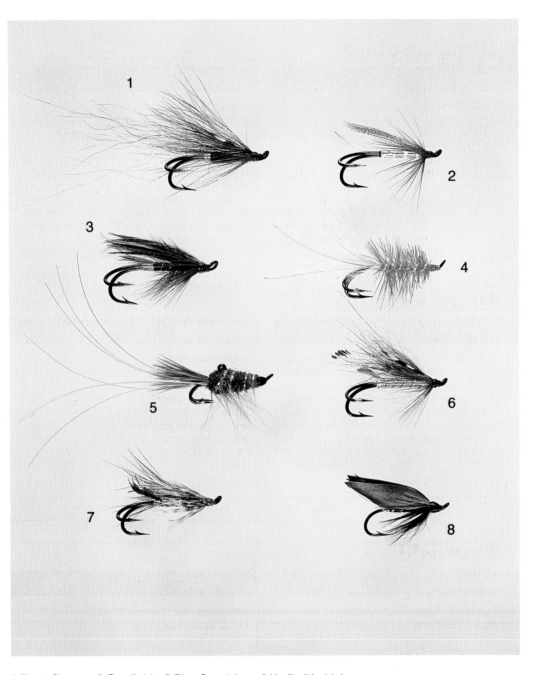

1 Black Sheep   **2** Crosfield   **3** Blue Sapphire   **4** Krafla (Krabla)
5 Francis Prawn   **6** Thvera Blue   **7** Blue Rat   **8** Sweep

3 Blue Sapphire

COMMENT

In *Atlantic Salmon Flies and Fishing* Bates acknowledges that this is Icelandic, without deriving from British classics. It is certainly strongly recommended nowadays.

DRESSING

Tag: Gold tinsel and yellow floss.
Tail: Topping, red and blue hackle tips and strands of guinea-fowl.
Body: Black floss.
Rib: Fine round or oval gold tinsel.
Hackle: Black and blue from second turn of tinsel.
Throat: Extra blue.
Wing: Dark brown turkey or mallard, with an outer wing of blue swan, mottled turkey and brown mallard, with topping over.

4 Krafla (Krabla)

COMMENT

This is an Icelandic pattern, with colour variations. The Green has green antennae, tail and body, with a yellow head, the Yellow & Black has antennae and the rear half of the body in yellow, black tail and front half of the body, and yellow head. Tying instructions are given most clearly by Poul Jorgensen.

DRESSING

Tying silk: Red.
Antennae: Two pink and two white stripped hackle stems.
Tail: White marabou.
Body: Two large reddish-pink and one white saddle hackle wound and trimmed.
Ribs: Oval silver.
Head: Red.

5 Francis Prawn

COMMENT

This is another of Peter Deane's patterns, and his own handiwork. Bates gives Peter's origination as 1970, but our example dates from twenty-five years ago at least. Don't forget the bead eyes (white), secured near the tail. The first trial with the fly took 30 fish in just one day. It has been rechristened the Monster by the Forte family of hotelier fame.

DRESSING

Antennae: Six long stripped grizzle hackle stalks.
Tail: A bunch of medium-long cock pheasant tail fibres.
Rib: Silver thread.
Hackle: Natural red cock, with the butt tied in at tail.
Body: Rear four-fifths, dark-green seal fur, tapering from thick at the tail; front fifth, orange seal fur.
Head: Black.

6 Thvera Blue

COMMENT

Thomas Clegg is rather terse about this pattern: 'for Iceland and northern latitudes, on H6 L/W doubles'. Baboon he considered to be one of the most important modern hair materials introduced into Great Britain by him. He commended it as excellent for its range of sizes – teal is not 2 inches long in the fibre!

DRESSING

Tag: Oval silver.
Tail: Tippet fibres.
Body: Horizon-blue DRF floss.
Rib: Oval silver.
Throat: Blue.
Wing: Silver baboon with any grey-blue natural hair over.
Sides: Jungle cock.

7 Blue Rat

COMMENT

This now seems to be an Icelandic pattern *sine qua non*, certainly for visitors from Stateside. Poul Jorgensen designed it. Joe Bates put the new pattern to good use on the Laxa i Kjos and Nordura. Poul's dressing is given.

DRESSING

Tag: Fine oval gold.
Tail: Four peacock sword strands.
Body: Half pale-blue floss, front half peacock herl.
Rib: Oval gold.
Veiling (or mane): Blue silk over the rear half of the body.
Wing: Grey fox guard hair.
Cheeks: Jungle cock and blue kingfisher (both optional).
Throat: Blue, tied collar-style after the wing.
Head: Red.

8 Sweep

COMMENT

This is a reflection on the older styles of fly so long recommended for Iceland, for instance in Hardy's 1937 catalogue: Blue Doctor, Blue Ranger, Black Goldfinch, Goldfinch, Black Doctor, Butcher, Durham Ranger, Dusty Miller, Mar Lodge, Silver Doctor, Silver Grey, Silver Ranger, Silver Wilkinson, Jock Scott, Silver Scott, Blue Charm and Silver Blue. Modern patterns with a similar strong dark silhouette are Stoat's Tails, Black Bears, and so on.

Hale gives a black body hackle and cheeks of jungle cock.

DRESSING

Tag: Gold.
Tail: Topping.
Body: Black floss.
Rib: Oval gold.
Throat: Black cock.
Wing: Rook or crow.
Cheeks: Kingfisher or chatterer.

SPAIN AND FRANCE

Introduction

Spain   Both of us have had a chance to fish in this delightful country. The rivers which still hold reasonable stocks now only number ten, of an earlier total of fifty or so, with one river on the Portuguese border effectively the most southerly salmon-holding river of their natural range. But for the interest in salmon fishing of General Franco the number of salmon and effective salmon rivers might be even fewer than it is now. We fished the Cares, with excursions to other rivers. We were both entranced by the scenery and setting: hawks, kites and eagles abound, butterflies bask in the early summer sunshine and the meadows stretching down to the river banks were a tapestry of many species of wild orchids. Truly memorable was one simple single-span Roman bridge over the Cares well up from its junction with the Deva, which added a sense of history to the splendour of the Picos de Europa mountains which we had to pass through to reach our fishing.

The Cares and the Deva offer a wide variety of water, not much ideal for the fly fisherman. An all-technique fisherman, like a good Welshman, would probably find himself not too disadvantaged. The honest earthworm is a favourite bait, and long rods trot worms along the bed of the river, with their anglers gently walking them down at a suitable pace. Live prawns – well, certainly not *preserved* prawns – are threaded onto single hooks and they too prove vastly effective. The history of fly fishing is short – well within the century if de Piña's definitive work of 1945 is to be relied upon. Both British and Brittany dressings are suitably effective. A small sample of traditional patterns (from the turn of the century) depicted in the colour plates have been tied to give a Spanish flavour. It is extremely interesting to note how much reference is made to floating and *semi-hundida* – half-drowned – flies throughout the text; and very little mention is suggested of major North American influence, if any. The UK patterns mentioned in the text are Jock Scott, Dusty Miller, Thunder & Lightning and Silver Wilkinson; the Beauly Snowfly is referred to. Black Doctor is added to the others above for the Santander region. In one case an engagingly phonetic 'Yock Scott' is written. Joseph Bates in his two pertinent books lists some modern exhibition tyings – in the traditional and classic style – from Belarmino Martínez, a tyer from Pravia, Asturias. They are the Martínez Special, Silver Orange, Naranxeira, Pas River, Navia River, Esva River and Eo River, the last also found in Fulsher and Krom as a hairwing.

Acknowledgement is most gratefully given to John and Judith Head of the Barn Book Supply in Salisbury for their help in obtaining for our reference *El salmón y su pesca en España* (1945) by D. Pablo Larios y Sánchez de Piña, Marqués de Marzales.

France   France is a sad tale nowadays. Once French rivers which debouched into the Channel or the Atlantic had generous runs of salmon. Within the decades of industrialisation – leading to the need for barrages (without passes) for water power and the consequent by-product of industrialisation, pollution – the salmon-bearing rivers have been vastly reduced in numbers. Some rivers in Brittany and Normandy still offer worthwhile fishing, and the salmon is not quite extinct on the French side of the Pyrenees in the Gave d'Oloron. Its demise, altogether, in France cannot be far away, despite the fanaticism of its devotees. The Rhine, now so totally polluted, has denied the Moselle fish their spawning areas for many long years. The great Loire is now nearly deserted by these fish. While the rivers were in private ownership there was some concept of preserving stocks. At the time of the 1789 Revolution the private rights of the nobility were abolished and public fishing instituted. A further problem was a hereditable right of fishing in estuary and tidal waters to the *Inscrits Maritimes*, the naval enlisted at the time of the Napoleonic wars. They proved difficult to control and could and did overfish to the detriment of stocks. A reasonably modern discussion of the Brittany fishings is found in the books of Pequegnot and Phélipot. We can assure you that the French take their salmon fishing extremely seriously. In fact, in Spain the river wardens felt that the French were the most likely to win the Salmon Fly Fishing Championships of the World of 1982 because they were so thorough and so able.

As in most fishing areas, the patterns of artificials are governed by the availability of local materials for dressing them. Observations of water colour and light lead to harmonious designs and the result in French rivers is cautious, sombre, mobile patterns with grey hackles and wool or fur bodies. 'Gaudy' influence did insinuate itself, and the feeling of there being new magic in new patterns is never lost if current French magazines are to be believed, with French visitors to Scotland singing the praises, and giving the dressings, of leading contemporary Scottish patterns like the Munro Killer. The classic standards such as Jock Scott, Green Highlander, Thunder & Lightning, Doctors, and so on, have reached with success all the corners of the salmon fishing world, so may be used in the Brittany rivers, but it would probably be of interest on a wider scale to use the local tyings.

Modern tyings have adopted 'modern' materials such as marabou, and the inclusion in wings of strands of differing mobility – some of hair, some of marabou, some of hackle fibre – to give mixed wings of differing character so that some part will appear alive in different conditions of water flow and turbulence. *La Pêche* of January 1987 gives the Atlantica series created by Guy Plas and they exemplify this mixed-winging principle. Guy Plas has established quite a name for himself as a fisherman and a fly tyer, with 49 salmon (531lb) in a week on the Hofsa in Iceland. The patterns illustrated in *Pêche à la Mouche en Bretagne* by the two authors mentioned above show great resemblance to the flies in Great Britain in the 1700s and early 1800s – before heavy use of the plumage of the golden pheasant became current. Their ninth fly could easily be the bittern-winged pattern of Bainbridge of 1816. A palmer hackle (or *chenille*, as they call the hackling style) over a woollen body, not necessarily ribbed, and with minimal application of material, all from farm, field or river bank, is the characteristic style. Translucence and mobility are stated to be important. Shape, colour and size are all-important, and the techniques are a compromise between the sunken fly and the greased line. These authors report little successful employment of a dry fly in the Breton rivers, despite seeing fish take insects at the surface. However, some trout fishers have taken salmon on a dry fly. Some of the Breton rivers seem to have a tint which is best complemented by the fly – greenish or greyish in some, orange in others. The old aphorism seems still to be quoted in this region: *'Temps sombre, mouche sombre – temps clair, mouche claire.'* The authors also recommend changing down a size or so after a refusal but recognise that a much bigger fly sometimes proves effective in such circumstances. As seems apparent in most salmon waters, success stems probably more from how the fly is fished than from a specific feature of its own.

Spain

If the newspapers are to be believed, there is an extra excitement to salmon fishing in Spain nowadays. In a word – wolves. It may be necessary to keep a wary eye out behind, for apparently the local citizenry in the Picos de Europa are extremely worried about the increase in numbers of these predators. This is the mountainous area in the north of Spain where some of the better rivers such as the Deva and the Cares are to be found. The large loping Alsatian dog may not be exactly that, and it may have greater ambitions on you than just your sandwich lunch.

The illustrations in de Piña of the dry-fly patterns for salmon all show a similar feature: the hook point is offset, a characteristic of dry flies which has found considerable favour with enthusiasts of this style of fishing in both Great Britain and North America.

1 Eo River

COMMENT

Joseph Bates obviously had some enjoyable correspondence with Señor Martínez, whose work is quite intricate in both hair- and featherwing patterns. The inventor's note on how and when the fly should be used is: for light currents at any time of the year.

DRESSING

Tag: Oval gold tinsel.
Tail: Topping and two small jungle cock.
Butt: Bright-red wool.
Body: Rear three-quarters, embossed gold; front quarter, yellow chenille.
Rib: Oval gold over all.
Throat: Pink hackle under guinea-fowl.
Wing: Pink, yellow and red bucktail under peacock sword fibres under a small bunch of brown bucktail.
Sides: Jungle cock.

2 Mosca 'Camino' 2

COMMENT

The first of de Piña's plates includes six flies. The caption reads: 'Salmon flies used at the beginning of the century by bank fishers of Santander and Asturias'. Two show a style of mane, two are simple whole-feather wings, and the other two are simple vertical strip wings. A throat hackle is not applied to any of them. Two of the hooks are pronounced Limerick in shape, both down-eyed; the others have a gut loop and a round or Sproat bend.

DRESSING

Tail: None.
Body: Creamy-white.
Rib: None.
Throat: None.
Mane: Strands peacock herl, two fifths of the way up the body.
Wings: Strands of peacock herl, their ends aligning with the ends of the mane fibres.

1 Eo River **2** Mosca 'Camino' 2 **3** Mosca 'Camino' 4
4 Mosca 'Flumen' 1 **5** Mosca 'Flumen' 4 **6** Mosca 'Biri' Turbón
7 Mosca 'Biri' Pedresa 8 Mosca 'Biri' San Martín

3 Mosca 'Camino' 4

COMMENT

This is one of the strip-wing tyings, another confection by Enrique G.-Camino.

DRESSING

Tag: Gold twist.
Tail: Topping with tip of tippet.
Body: Orange.
Rib: Gold.
Wing: Grey mallard and topping.

4 Mosca 'Flumen' 1

COMMENT

This is taken from the sixth of de Piña's plates, and all four flies show the same style, with a strong element of imitation of nymphal forms. The treatment of the tail is singular, and in British tying to our recollection found only in the Garry Dog. This winging style is much as recommended in Hewitt's Nymph on page 260, or the Defeo patterns on the same plate. The text gives no indication of their date.

DRESSING

Tag: Gold twist and yellow floss.
First tail: Four or five strands of teal.
First butt: Yellow floss, *not* proud of body.
Second tail: Two strong strands of feather (? cock pheasant).
Second butt: Black.
Body: Red.
Rib: Peacock herl.
Throat: Teal.
Wing: Two grey partridge wing coverts tied three-quarters of the shank length.
Head: Red.

5 Mosca 'Flumen' 4

COMMENT

From the same plate we have interpreted the last fly. The winging is more generous and in its style calls to mind the Pencilled Snipe pattern which Stoddart listed in 1853 for the Tweed, though as a spring tying. All the patterns are shown on a round-bend style of hook with a down eye.

DRESSING

Tag: Gold twist.
First tail: Teal fibres.
First butt: Red floss.
Second tail: Two strong feather strands.
Second butt: Yellow floss.
Body: Black floss.
Rib: Gold.
Throat: Teal.
Wing: Pencilled snipe feathers from underwing of bird (or cuckoo hen hackles).

6 Mosca 'Biri' Turbón

We have names at last! Plate X gives six dry flies for salmon: Rivadagua, Rinchona, Turbón, Reina, Pedresa, Negra madura. The first two are tied without tails, with a quill body and generous throat hackling, the Rinchona having forward-pointing separated wings. Hook points are widely offset. The middle flies of the plate are illustrated almost twice the size of the others, and are given a generous tail.

Tag: Gold.
Tail: Brown mottled feather strands – long.
Butt: Black.
Body: Rear fifth yellow, front four-fifths grey dubbing.
Hackle: Grey over the grey dubbing.
Throat: Teal, spreading forwards.

7 Mosca 'Biri' Pedresa

This is illustrated on a square-bend hook. By the amount of dressing it is unlikely to be *semi-hundida* – half-drowned.

Tail: Brown speckled fibres.
Body: Finely dubbed grey.
Hackle: Cuckoo over the rear two-thirds, yellow over the front third.
Throat: Natural red, directed well forwards.

8 Mosca 'Biri' San Martín

The wet 'Biri' flies are very much within a simple style of classic. Ornamentation is there, but the wings are kept quite simple. None of the illustrations shows married fibres, they are more a random translucent bundle. Whole feathers like tippet are used, and there is something of Blacker's Irish patterns about the way random strands of feather veil the sides of the tippets. The patterns are: Narceiras, Clareta de mayo, Mandea (which is like a simple Jock Scott), Eumesa (like a Black Ranger), San Martín and Indio plateado, silver-bodied with a very full throat hackle and no wing.

Tag: Silver twist and yellow floss.
Tail: Topping.
Butt: Black.
Body: Black.
Rib: Broad gold, widely spaced.
Wing: Blue-dun hen hackle points and fibres with teal over.
Collar: Natural red hackle.
Cheeks: Kingfisher.

France 1

The Brittany waters are relatively slow, so their fishermen find the single hook preferable. It is easier to cast without snarl-ups and can be tied less bulkily than doubles. The wire should also be fine, but not so soft that it opens up under strain. They feel there that low-water shanks offer more leverage than ideal. However, preference is for an up-eye. Romilly Fedden writes: 'The local patterns of salmon flies will doubtless come as somewhat of a shock to the visitor when first he arrives in Brittany. They are indeed gaunt, clumsy-looking creatures in effect, destitute of what we understand as "wing". Only experience can teach that they are here more successful than our customary full-winged patterns' (*Golden Days* 1920). He continues: 'Though the local expert did not favour the Popham, the Jock Scott or the Black Doctor, he liked their colours: and the wing he tied was negligible – more or less flush with the shank of the hook. There is a pattern much like the Toppy of the Tweed, but with the wing most unobtrusive and tied horizontal to the body.' His local friend preferred to fish deep, but later on we see that he also 'backed up'. What seems extremely apparent is that local advice on these hard-fished rivers is vital.

1 Mouche noire de l'Odet

COMMENT

The Odet is the most important of the three small rivers of Quimper (the others are the Steir and the Jet). Fish catches have dropped from 508 in 1934 to 80 in 1981, with an average weight of about ten pounds. A good stretch is fishable with the fly, but the season is early; after mid-April chances are reduced, unless there is plenty of water to let the fish over the dams. This pattern gained its good reputation from the beginning of the century. Some tyers feel that two hackles are enough for the wing.

DRESSING

Hook: 4–8
Body: Black wool.
Tail: The tip of the hackle.
Hackle: Black, palmered.
Wing: Four black cock hackles.

2 Mouche du Trieux (Père Le Gall)

COMMENT

Phélipot considers that chewed-up and tattered flies are often those most appreciated by the salmon. It may be they have extra life and mobility in the eddies and currents. It seems wise to tie with a mixture of fibres, some stiff, some more supple, so that some movement of 'life' is possible in all conditions of water. Le Trieux, running some 72 kilometres and draining an area of 506 square kilometres, used to be one of the best Brittany rivers. Though the fish do not often top twelve pounds, without netting and estuary fishing and pollution the catches would be better than *five or six* a year.

DRESSING

Tying silk: Black.
Tag: None.
Tail: A tuft of cinder-grey hackle.
Body: Tangerine-coloured wool.
Rib: None.
Hackle: Cinder-grey hackle, stripped on one side.
Throat: None.
Wing: Four hackles of cinder-grey colour.

202

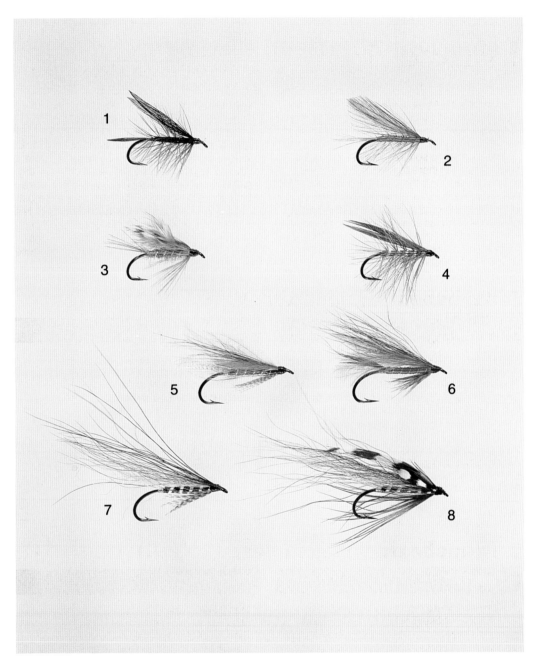

1 Mouche noire de l'Odet   **2** Mouche du Trieux (Père Le Gall)
3 Mouche d'Ellé (Henri Clerc)   **4** Bretonne No.2   **5** Onde-Verte
6 Reine d'Eau   **7** Mouche Debedat No. 1   **8** Mouche Debedat No. 2

3 Mouche d'Ellé (Henri Clerc)

COMMENT

In spring hooks of size 4 and 6 are chosen, from April onward patterns are tied more slender on 6s and 8s, and even down to 12s. The Ellé has big fish running it, over twenty pounds, and in earlier years fish of about forty pounds were encountered.

DRESSING

Tag: None.
Tail: Red golden pheasant fibres.
Body: Boar's hair.
Rib: Tinsel.
Throat: Natural cinder-grey hackle.
Wing: Fibres of peahen wing.
Sides: Tufts of downy fibres from the base of peahen feathers.

4 Bretonne No.2

COMMENT

Bates is sad that France has no patterns for him to include which demonstate 'Art' in fly dressing. All too often the dressings are of sombre simplicity, with the Pyrenean patterns differing only slightly from other French ones. A constant feature is the wing of badger hair or strips of mallard flank feather or both. Bodies are usually wool or dubbed rather than sleek.

DRESSING

Body: Dark-green wool or floss.
Rib: Fine flat gold.
Hackle: Natural red.
Wing: Dark-bronze mallard.

5 Onde-Verte

COMMENT

The hundredth issue of *Connaissance de la pêche*, January, 1987, is a good one for the salmon fisher! It gives the fifteen patterns which Guy Plas designed for Atlantic salmon. Drawing on thirty years' experience of fishing widely different waters, he has introduced some colour to many aspects of traditional French patterns. One aspect of his style is his composite tail – under-fibres and over-fibres. Another is his use of winging materials with different suppleness.

This fly is a good choice for when the water is cold and beginning to warm again.

DRESSING

Tag: Silver twist.
Tail: Under-tail, bright yellow fibres; over-tail, medium-grey *pardos* fibres (or substitute partridge).
Body: Green floss or wool.
Rib: Silver wire or fine oval.
Throat: Medium-grey *pardos* fibres (or partridge), as a beard.
Wing: Greenish hairs with bright-green tips, under yellow and grey herls, under black hair.

6 Reine d'Eau

COMMENT

Pardos are the brown coq de Léon poultry feathers. The old Spanish tyers knew them in 1624, and present French salmon-fly tyers value them just as highly. They are discussed extensively and illustrated in *Fly tying Methods* by Darrel Martin (1987), showing the colour divisions. There are no finer imitations, natural or synthetic, for tails, legs or wings than these feathers, taken from the bird's back. Brown *pardos* are divided into *corzuno, sarrioso, langareto, aconchado,* and *flor de escoba.* Greys (*indios*) are divided into *negrisco, acerado, plateado, rubión* and *palometa.*

DRESSING

Tag: Gold twist.
Tail: Black hairs under very dark *pardos* with red reflections.
Body: Red floss or wool.
Rib: Gold wire or fine oval.
Throat: Very dark *pardos* with red reflections.
Wing: Blackish-yellow hair under bright-red herl under black hair.
(The bright glint and sparkle of *pardos* is their great attraction. English partridge can only give part of the effect as a substitute.)

7 Mouche Debedat No.1

COMMENT

'A fly does not need 36 components to be beautiful. The fibres should not clog together: test in your toothglass, bathtub, or swimming pool and induce a current as well if possible to see how the fly looks. Varnish fragile elements.' Dr Guy Debedat explained his views on salmon flies in *Pêche Magazine*, November 1987.

DRESSING

Tag: Silver twist.
Tail: Topping.
Body: Black floss.
Rib: Flat silver.
Underwing: Evenly distributed fine red and yellow bucktail – long.
Throat: Teal or wigeon in beard style.
Overwing: Fine black bucktail, long, with coarse black moose hair over.

8 Mouche Debedat No. 2

COMMENT

All his three patterns show the same style: single hook, long tail, fibres of wing extending all round the shank and extending nearly half as long as the shank again beyond the bend. His third illustrated pattern (very similar to Derek Knowles's Yellow Badger) is: tag, gold twist; tail, topping; body, yellow wool or seal fur; rib, flat gold; underwing, pale natural badger hair evenly distributed; throat (beard), bunch of guinea-fowl.

DRESSING

Tag: Silver twist.
Tail: Topping.
Body: Black floss.
Rib: Flat silver.
Underwing: Evenly distributed fine red bucktail – long.
Throat: A bunch of long black heron fibres, as a beard.
Overwing: Blue and black bucktail with peahen wing over.
Sides: Jungle cock.

France 2

Thierry Willems, a regular contributor to *Pêche* magazine, has brought together this useful selection of French salmon flies for this plate. He is a frequent visitor in pursuit of Scottish salmon, particularly from the River Spey, and is up-to-date with modern patterns from the British Isles, as well as thoroughly conversant with the flies and tyers of his native France.

His favourite fishing quarry are trout, sea trout, salmon and pike, and he rates fly fishing and fly-tying very highly!

1 Elorn

COMMENT

This fly is named after the river in north Brittany, whose source is thirty-six miles from its outlet to the sea at Brest.

A high point in the records is the catch of 550 fish in 1966, most of them coming off the lower stretches. In 1976, twenty were taken. At one time salmon were so numerous that, fresh or preserved, they were a major foodstuff of the poor.

DRESSING

Tag: Oval gold,
Body: Grey wool.
Rib: Oval gold.
Throat: Grizzle.
Wing: Grey squirrel hair under peahen.

2 Fox & Grey

COMMENT

The fox is another locally available source of fly-tying material: it is surprising that it has not been taken up by British fly-tyers. In the United States, they freely use fibres of grey fox.

Not many of the French tyings include jungle cock.

DRESSING

Tail: Topping.
Body: Grey wool dubbing.
Rib: Oval gold.
Throat: Grizzle.
Wing: Fox.
Sides: Jungle cock (small).

1 Elorn **2** Fox & Grey **3** Scorff **4** Aulne No. 1 **5** Leff No. 1
6 Aulne No. 2 **7** Boyer Stonefly **8** Tréportaise

3 Scorff

COMMENT

The Scorff is a river of southern Brittany and here also most of the catches are made in the lower reaches. Records from Phélipot's *Rivières à saumons* show a high figure of 800 in 1966, and a low of twenty-five in 1976, with numbers increasing thereafter. There are not the usual quantities of mill pools, but smaller holding areas caused by barrages for fishing for eels, very similar to groynes or croys in Great Britain.

DRESSING

Tag: Claret wool.
Tail: Topping.
Body: Yellow wool.
Rib: Oval gold.
Throat: Sandy dun.
Wing: Strands peahen under short tippet.

4 Aulne No. 1

COMMENT

In Breton, the name of this river in the north is Aon. Once the salmon here were so abundant that the inhabitants of Châteaulin (on its route) were called *Pen Eog*, or 'salmon heads', and the fish was depicted in the blazonings of the city – worthily so, as the salmon harvest constituted a major local wealth.

Catches like those of 1932, when two fishermen from Châteaulin caught between them 320 fish, for the most part on fly, are a far-away dream.

DRESSING

Tag: Yellow wool.
Body: Crimson seal's fur.
Rib: Oval silver.
Hackle: Over front quarter, to include throat – sandy dun.
Wing: Badger hair.

5 Leff No. 1

COMMENT

Despite its small size, surprisingly weighty salmon have been taken from this river. Since 1975, there has been a great clearing up campaign, which has also benefited the trout population. Not all those who fish it stick to the fly, and the worm is highly praised.

The forty or so mills, mostly with dams and without fish passes, no longer have justification.

DRESSING

Body: Grey wool.
Rib: Bronze peacock herl.
Hackle: Over front quarter of the body, to include throat – sandy dun.
Wing: Badger hair.

6 Aulne No. 2

The reasons for the decline in this river are multifold: pollution from agriculture, infestation with pike and other coarse fish, and poor access to the redds.

The average weight ranges between 6½ pounds and 11 pounds.

A notable fishing visitor in the 1930s was Sir Anthony Eden.

DRESSING

Tag: Yellow wool.
Body: Golden-olive boar's hair dubbing.
Rib: Oval silver.
Throat: Sandy dun.
Wing: Fox hair under peahen fibres.

7 Boyer Stonefly

COMMENT

The addition of a topping over a hairwing seems justifiable in France as well as elsewhere. Lee Wulff's use of topping on his hairwings certainly gives the concept authority in the United States.

Paul Boyer also writes for the French fishing press; he is a keen fisher of the Gave d'Oloron in the Pyrenees.

DRESSING

Tag: Yellow floss and oval gold.
Tail: Tippet strands.
Body: Beige floss.
Hackle: Over front half to include throat – pale dun.
Wing: Fox hair under tippet and topping.

8 Tréportaise

COMMENT

This is one of Thierry's designs and tyings, given in full detail in *Pêche* magazine, 18 October 1988. Thierry says that most French designs are from Brittany; since his own fishing is locally in Normandy or Picardy, the waters have different characteristics.

His inspiration is drawn from Scottish patterns, particularly the Stoat's Tail, and he puts on a modest wing so as not to lose the mobility of the fibres.

DRESSING

Tag: Oval silver (or gold).
Tail: Dyed-yellow cock hackle fibres.
Body: Black tapestry cotton.
Rib: Oval silver (or gold).
Hackle: One side only of dun cock hackle.
Wing: Black squirrel.

EXTRA ATTRACTION

Introduction

Many of the patterns given in this book may be attractive enough to take fish regularly. Some will have built into them elements which are thought to be of extra attraction. In this section we look at some of the patterns which either by result or design have this extra element. In some it will be found in the body; in others in the wing; sometimes it never really seems to get further than the mind of the 'inventor'.

Translucence: One added attraction which does not show up in photographs, but which is worth mentioning, is that resulting from painting the hook shank white before the dressing is applied. Trout-fly tyers will recognise this technique from J. W. Dunne's *Sunshine and the Dry Fly*. In brief, a white reflector behind the material gives colour enhancement to the dressing. White Cellire is applied to the shank, and then the floss is wound on with great care: when oiled the body appears to become translucent. This principle may be applied to salmon flies. It may subsequently be difficult to draw conclusions! Our method is to tie in tag, tail, rib, and so on leaving the tying silk awaiting its further duties, then paint the hook shank white. A pale tying silk is used, and the whole concept is that the body should not appear as a black silhouette against the light. Dunne used special artificial silk for his effect; lightly dubbed seal fur is suggested in Taverner's notes on the method in the Lonsdale Library *Salmon Fishing*.

Prismatic is not a word often applied to flies. The earliest reference we found was in *The Angler's Souvenir* (1835) by P. Fisher, Esq. (W. A. Chatto), who commented that 'large flies of the most gorgeous colours – a prismatic combination of red, orange, yellow, green or blue – are sometimes dressed, but they are rather for show than use: though the salmon will unquestionably take a very gaudy fly when a more Quaker-like beauty will not tempt them to rise.' Then our search to find Lord Iris (a fly mentioned in Haig-Brown's *A River Never Sleeps*) revealed it in a list of prismatic flies designed by Preston Jennings of Brooklyn, New York. His idea was to imitate the colours of minnows as they appear by the breaking down of light passing through a prism. The patterns are given by Arnold Gingrich in *The Fishing in Print* and are also mentioned by Donald Overfield in *Famous Flies and their Originators*

(1972). Much the same concept is embraced by T. C. Kingsmill Moore in *A Man May Fish* (1960) when he added a topping to the wing of his already successful Kingsmill pattern. 'My black fly stood surrounded by a halo of pure golden light, a halo which was to prove deserved.' The extra visual effect of a good topping on a wing was remarked on by H. P. Wells in *The American Salmon-Fisherman* (1886). After tank-testing several patterns of flies suspended on strands of copper wire, he observed among other conclusions:

> Then, when those flies were moved which were provided with mixed wings of which the crest of the golden-pheasant formed part, the wings seem to flash with reflected light in a manner and with an appearance not unlike that of the fish. The effect was extremely beautiful to my eye. It was like the intermittent flash of a firefly, lighting up the closely contiguous water with a mellow glow, yellower in colour and by no means so pronounced and incisive as the flash of the minnow . . . something was there softly luminous, and endowed with motion and apparent life.

This observation postdates all the early gaudy Irish flies demanding so many toppings for their wings – the Canaries, Goshawks and Parsons. Perhaps there really was some intrinsic merit in toppings, of appeal to fish rather than fishermen. Lee Wulff, much later, adds a topping to some of his hairwing patterns – such as Haggis, Lady Joan and Cullman's Choice. Our own inclination is to replace yellow body hackles in the patterns which demand them, and substitute the golden champagne sparkle of a wound-on topping. Although this is a conclusion reached independently, authority comes for it in Charles Akroyd's book: '1875 [was] the year in which I produced the Akroyd fly, which I am told by those who are at the present time fishing the Dee with it catches more fish than any other pattern. It is not dressed now [1926] in quite the same way as when I dressed it. Where the fly dressers now use a cock's hackle dyed yellow, I put in two long golden pheasant's crest feathers running all the way down, my idea being that the glitter was more attractive than the dull hackle.' Certainly toppings seem to have more attraction than yellow hackle fibres for salmon fly tails.

Fluorescence   Natural floss silks and wools tend to darken when wet, artificial 'silks' such as nylon can retain their brightness of colouring more clearly, but the most highly coloured are the fluorescent dyed nylons. There is some place for them in tying salmon flies, but the results are certainly not well documented and conclusions may be subjectively suspect. Fluorescence is not phosphorescence: it needs light to reflect light and the colours fluorescing differ slightly from the base colour. Phosphorescents need exposure to light, and they then emit light and glow for a duration until they have been 'recharged' with more light. Wools can be used for bodies, but more normally floss is used. It seems to feature rarely as the material for the entire body but very often as a tip or butt, even on dry flies. The other use is in thin strands as a winging material. It is brighter and less bulky than many sorts of dyed hair strands, and thus can incorporate slim colour in light low-water hairwing dressings. It is ideal when the traditional classic patterns are being adapted to simpler hairwings.

Bates *(ASF)* makes a few points about fluorescence: that pastel or low-tone colours fluoresce better than darker colours; and that too much fluorescence is probably self-defeating, though a pattern with a generous inclusion of fluorescence will fluoresce more in poor light.

Fluorescent materials are available in the following colours (the American name first with the English equivalent in brackets): neon magenta (pink), arc chrome (orange), fire orange (scarlet), phosphor yellow (yellow), signal green (lime), electron white (white) and horizon blue (blue). American fluorescence is far stronger; it is sold as DRF (Depth Ray Fire) or Gantron, while the more muted English material is by Veniard's. Tom C. Saville, Ltd, who marketed Gantron from the earliest days when it came on to the market, also has new Datam Glo-Brite in sixteen shades.

Sparkle   Many tinsels have progressed from straightforward flats, ovals and embossed in silver and gold. They include Mylar, Bobby Dazzle, Glitter Chenille, Lureflash, Luminous Lureflash, Twinkle Lureflash, and Flashaboo. They may be used with ordinary materials, or even in conjunction with fluorescents – with the usual caveat that too much extra attraction may be a detriment rather than a benefit.

Prismatics

Mrs N. K. Robertson discusses fly development with singular perception and useful glimpses of history. She mentions the Kilroy patterns, but does not seem impressed: 'other materials were sought. Dyed raffia in small strips is disappointing – when soaked it becomes limp: silk-worm gut, associated with Baden-Powell, is useful but the goat's beard . . . has had a better innings.' She then enthuses about hair for winging. Kilroy flies have the two elements of interest: the plane of the wings and the finish of the body. Wood commented in 1932 or a little later: 'Your flies are all right . . . your trick with the celluloid coating is a very happy idea and I should think would glisten well.' Wood and his guests had nine fish on Kilroys during April 1933.

Hale's second edition lists the 'RBM' series of Gem flies with metallic celluloid bodies: Amethyst, Cat's Eye, Cornelian, Crysoberyl, Emerald, Garnet, Opal, Pearl, Ruby, Sapphire, Turquoise and Yellow Diamond.

1 Baden-Powell Prismatic

COMMENT

W. Baden-Powell, KC, died in May 1921. He had put a great deal of thought to a salmon-fly style which had extra glitter and translucence. J. Arthur Hutton mentions use of the B-P flies: 'I have tried them on many occasions, though perhaps in a half-hearted sort of way. [A guest] had one fish on a Prism Bow 7 double, and then Woolliams (the keeper) tried a Lemon Grey, and on trying the Prism Bow had two fish.' The flies needed a thorough soaking; even then they were disconcertingly bristly and stiff.

Note that little material protrudes to the sides; the tying above and below is very vertical.

DRESSING

Tag: Silver twist with fine red gut over.
Butt: Tightly wound red wool.
Tail: Strands of fine red gut.
Body: Equal sections of orange, yellow, green, blue and purple dyed gut over silver twist.
Rib: Oval silver (rather finer than expected).
Throat: Fine strands of yellow, orange and red gut.
Wing: Strands of yellow, green and purple gut.
Sides: Jungle cock.

2 Ross Special

COMMENT

This is a pleasurably simple pattern from Fulsher and Krom, so will do nicely to illustrate the concept of a white-painted body underneath the red wool to enhance its colour by reflection. Using Dunne's trout-fishing principle of oiling it before use, it should hold its colour (rather than go too dark) and give an impression of translucence.

DRESSING

Tag: Oval silver.
Tail: Topping.
Body: Red wool.
Rib: Oval silver.
Throat: Yellow.
Wing: Red squirrel tail.
Sides: Jungle cock.

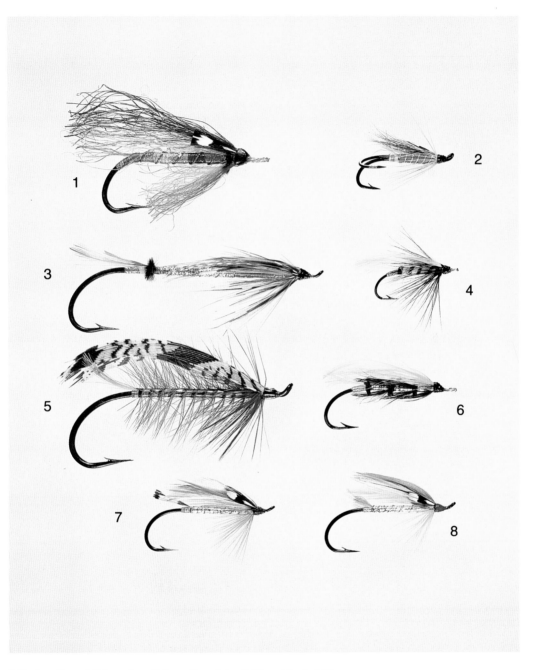

1 Baden-Powell Prismatic   **2** Ross Special   **3** Kilroy Dusty Miller
4 Variegated Sunfly   **5** Speckle Beadle   **6** Black Prince   **7** Lord Iris
8 Lady Iris

3 Kilroy Dusty Miller

COMMENT

The pattern illustrated shows many, but not all, of the features of the Kilroy series. Some have a tail like the wing. The wing is three feathers superimposed, each tied in by the feather stalk so that fibre extends horizontally on each side, with the tip of the feather cut away. The result is very similiar to a short composite Dee strip-wing, and should be highly mobile, yet quite 'broad' rather than 'vertical' in the water. Hardy's tied them, calling them 'Monoplane' and 'transluflecting', and they are illustrated in *Greased Line Fishing* by Jock Scott. Farlow's also tied them, in large and low-water sizes.

DRESSING

Tag: Fine oval silver and yellow celluloid.
Tail: Topping and tip of golden pheasant breast feather.
Butt: Black herl.
Body: Rear two-thirds, embossed silver; front third, red celluloid.
Rib: Oval silver.
Throat: Orange under guinea-fowl.
Wing: Teal, hen pheasant back feather and golden pheasant yellow rump.
Horns: Blue macaw.

4 Variegated Sunfly

COMMENT

To make this into Kelson's Blue variation, the body should be red, black, yellow and blue wool. Its attraction may well lie in its topping wing, and we choose it as our illustration for this reason. Kelson also attributed to it virtues particular to it. It is good in smaller sizes. A thick spindle-shaped body is desirable, not too bulky at the shoulder. Natural black hackle should have better effect than dyed. It was to be used in bright weather.

DRESSING

Tag: Silver thread and pale-blue floss.
Tail: Topping.
Body: Black, yellow and orange wool wound round in parallel.
Throat: Black hackle.
Wing: Six or more toppings.

5 Speckle Beadle

COMMENT

Brown, Yellow, Speckle, Red, Buff and White Beadles make the series in the 'Prismackle' style, designed by C. G. Heyward. He contributed to Farlow's catalogue, and they offered this series as well as Farlow Kilroy 'Skeleton Beadles' and a Beadle Shrimp. The body is broad tinsel with just enough space to allow the palmer hackle stems.

DRESSING

Tag: Silver thread.
Tail: Topping.
Body: Black under silk tinsel, which is very closely wound.
Hackles: One-third reddish-orange, one-third claret, one-third deep-blue.
Throat: Extra turns of the deep-blue hackle.
Wing: Double strips of Amherst pheasant tail, vertically.

6 Black Prince

COMMENT

This is generally used as an 'exaggeration'. Kelson had the splended concept that the fly book has a few vastly over-dressed and overbright flies of appropriate emphasis which are so exaggerated that they do not hook the fish but make it rise and whet its appetite. Then a smaller and more sombre fly of similar style is put over the fish and is taken immediately.

Exaggerations may turn out to be perfect examples of exhibition flies, but they were designed with purpose behind them.

DRESSING

Tag: Silver twist and dark-yellow floss.
Tail: Topping.
Butt: Black herl.
Body: Three equal sections of silver tinsel, each butted with black herl and veiled top and bottom with black toucan.
Wings: Five or six toppings.
Horns: Blue macaw.

7 Lord Iris

COMMENT

We have taken Donald Overfield's patterns for this and the complementary Lady Iris. Both were patented by Preston Jennings, yet he left 'unprotected' his Iris Dunn and Iris Sedge. Haig-Brown's reference is 'Long slim hook, silver-bodied, orange hackle and built wing of blue, green, yellow and red, the furnace hackle laid along and jungle cock cheeks'

DRESSING

Hook: Size 2 low-water.
Tag: Oval silver tinsel.
Tail: Tippet.
Body: Embossed silver tinsel.
Rib: Oval silver tinsel.
Throat: Orange cock.
Wing: Two orange cock hackles, swan fibres dyed red, orange, green and blue, veiled over with badger cock hackles (or furnace hackles).
Sides: Jungle cock.
Head: Red.

8 Lady Iris

COMMENT

The rationale was that the prismatic effect should be apparent in each of these two dressings in the appropriate lights; hairwing derivations might use polar bear hair in the requisite colours for its qualities of shine and translucence. This is the strong-light pattern, while the fly above is for low light.

DRESSING

Hook: Size 2 low-water.
Tag: Oval silver tinsel.
Tail: Topping and Indian crow.
Body: Flat silver tinsel.
Rib: Oval silver.
Throat: Yellow cock.
Wing: Two yellow cock hackles, swan dyed red, yellow, green and blue, veiled over with badger cock hackles.
Sides: Jungle cock.
Head: Red.

Fluorescence

In the early experiments fluorescent materials were substituted for plain ones in some trout patterns, which then took fish when the plain had failed. But when, on other occasions, fluorescent patterns proved utterly useless, it became clear that the material did not guarantee success. It is still an area for experimentation.

Bold or muted applications are possible, with the further choice of vivid or less intense fluorescence, as in the American and British materials respectively. Touches of fluorescence in a tail, such as substituting fluorescent floss for Indian crow or tippet, or mixing one part of

fluorescent to two parts of primrose floss in the body of, say, a Jock Scott may be all thought suitable. The Little Inky Boy in its body colour range is a classic for adaptation: use clear monofil over a fluorescent floss for the body dressing, rather than plain-dye the gut as demanded by its dressing formula.

Luminous Mylar bodies need tying down to keep them strong, and alone may be sufficient in clear water; in coloured water luminous strands may be added to the wing. Peter Nield suggests that takes can be fierce, so it is worth using leader nylon of up to double the normal strength.

1 Black Bear Red Butt

COMMENT

Variations of butt colour are common – Black Bear Blue Butt, Orange Butt, and so on. The Conrad series is very similar, with the same variations, but has silver for the tag and rib. It is very much a North American habit to give a fluorescent tip or butt to some of their simple hairwings as original design rather than a variation on the standard pattern.

DRESSING

Tag: Oval gold.
Butt: Red fluorescent floss.
Tail: Black hackle fibres.
Body: Black wool.
Rib: Oval gold.
Throat: Black.
Wing: Black hair.

2 Cairn

COMMENT

Thomas Clegg gives 44 salmon patterns in the second edition (1969) of his booklet on the use of hair and fur in fly dressing. He includes fluorescence in over half the dressings, as tail substitutes, butt alternatives and body variations. We give his Cairn pattern which was originally designed in small sizes for the lower Tweed with its fluorescent tail.

DRESSING

Tag: Oval silver.
Tail: Arc chrome D.R.F. floss
Body: Claret seal fur.
Rib: Oval silver.
Wing: Parey squirrel tail.

218

1 Black Bear Red Butt   **2** Cairn   **3** Bondatti's Killer
4 Fluorescent Hairwing Silver Grey   **5** Fluorescent Whiskers
6 Ray's Red   **7** Luminescent Highlander   **8** Tritium Fly

3 Bondatti's Killer

The example shown is from the Fulsher and Krom listing; it shows the entire body in fluorescent materials.

Tag: Flat silver.
Tail: Topping.
Body: Rear half fluorescent green, front fluorescent orange floss.
Rib: Flat silver.
Throat: Black.
Wing: Grey squirrel.

4 Fluorescent Hairwing Silver Grey

We have taken the Silver Grey as a typical classic which can be modified for fluorescence in its rewinging. For a thicker wing profile and a heavier dressing, squirrel tail fibres dyed fluorescent colours may be used. The overall impression of the classic is retained, with plenty of mobility.

Tag: Silver thread and yellow floss.
Tail: Topping.
Body: Flat silver.
Rib: Oval silver.
Hackle: Badger.
Throat: Wigeon.
Wing: Combed-out fibres of fluorescent red, yellow and blue floss under grey squirrel tail fibres.
Sides: Jungle cock.

5 Fluorescent Whiskers

On a trip to the Abergeldie beat of the Aberdeenshire Dee we had difficult light conditions – incessant rain and peat stain in the water. We were looking against the light, and any dark floater was extremely difficult to spot on the ripples. The first evening, as we tied for the following day, we added touches of colour to our dry-fly patterns to aid us in keeping an eye on the fly. Fluorescence is just that bit easier to pick out than a plain colour.

Tail: Fibres of fluorescent orange-dyed squirrel tail.
Body (optional): Floss.
Hackle: Natural red.
Throat: Natural red.
Wing: As tail, separated into two bunches.

6 Ray's Red

COMMENT

Fly designers like John Cosseboom had a great belief in the focal attraction of a red head on a salmon fly. The story goes that he had a bet to prove that a red head is superior to a black head on a fly. He took six fish to prove it, and then changed flies with his 'opponent', who then caught five to Cosseboom's one fish on the black-headed fly. The importance of head colour has been maintained in patterns like the classic Doctors and Wilkinsons ever since the middle of the last century. We show a North American pattern for which has been chosen fluorescent rather than plain red for the head.

DRESSING

Tag: Fluorescent rose-coloured wool.
Tail: Hot-orange floss cut flat.
Body: Hot-orange floss.
Rib: Medium embossed gold or silver.
Wing: Grey squirrel dyed hot-orange.
Head: Fluorescent red tying thread.

7 Luminescent Highlander

COMMENT

The intensity with which this pattern glows in the water depends largely on how much light it has been exposed to, and how long ago that was. A really bright torch will recharge it suitably, either for use as the daylight fades, or even in loch fishing where the fly must be fished deep.

The pattern is dressed as a tube.

DRESSING

Body: Rear two-thirds, luminescent Mylar piping; front third, luminescent yellow.
Rib: Broad oval over the yellow.
Wing: In three equal units, orange, yellow and green hair.
Collar: Yellow hackle.

8 Tritium Fly

COMMENT

Ordinary colours lose their intensity the deeper they are submerged (red becomes black at 300 feet). In theory fluorescence will be entirely lost at depth. However, there is evidence from the stillwater trout fishermen that signal green (lime) fluorescent additions are extra-attractive, and that this extra attraction is not lost at normal fishing depths. Tritium tubes phosphoresce – emit their own light. Glow-worms also emit their own light, and there is a record in 1735 of their being borrowed for their light contribution and fished in floats. Tritium's glow is similar to that of lime luminescence.

DRESSING

Tag: Silver twist and fluorescent yellow floss.
Tail: Topping.
Body: Rear half, yellow floss; front half, yellow floss with tritium tube bound under the shank with translucent film.
Wing: Black and white hair.

Sparkle

Peter Nield, fly dresser on the Tweed, has kindly let us have his notes on sparkle and luminescence in salmon patterns, and our observations on these materials stem from his experience. The 'sparkles' have been part of trout-fly tying for some while and when they were first tried in salmon patterns even the traditionalists had to accept their success. The lesson is to carry 'sparkle' patterns in addition to standard patterns. The amount of sparkle or flash to be used will depend on conditions – too much in bright weather may scare fish, and small amounts in coloured water may not be enough. Some colours, like pink, seem to kill trout but remain unproven for salmon, while blue has killing qualities for salmon though not so convincingly for trout. Colour is clearly important. On rivers where night-time fishing is permitted extra shimmer may be an advantage, and there is useful experience from Wales on this subject, but widely drawn from sea-trout fishing. Extra movement of the fly is recommended, rather than just letting it swing round.

1 Black & Gold Flexi (ED)

COMMENT

Mylar piping is a criss-cross network of fine strands woven into a tube over a thread core. It comes in different diameters. With the core removed, it can be slipped over hook shank or tube. The fibres must be held by turns of tying silk otherwise they fray and unravel. An advantage of Mylar is that it does not tarnish like the old-fashioned tinsels.

The extension for aligning the treble must be placed on the tube before the Mylar. The tail end of the Mylar is secured in this case by a red band of tying silk in the place of a butt.

DRESSING

Tube: Plastic, lined aluminium or lined brass, as appropriate.
Body: Gold Mylar tubing.
Wing: Yellow hair under black hair, evenly distributed all round.

2 Blue & Silver Flexi (ED)

COMMENT

If the Mylar tail is extended the pattern does not terminate in an abrupt hard edge and the treble hook is to some extent disguised. One quality of Mylar tube is the impression of fish scales which it can give.

This and the preceding pattern are 'traditional' Mylar patterns with more glitter attraction than plain tinsels. The Esmond Drury Flexi series includes Yellow Belly, Garry, Black & Silver (Collie Dog) and Duke's Killer, as well as the two patterns shown.

DRESSING

Tube: Plastic, lined aluminium or lined brass or copper, as appropriate.
Body: Silver Mylar.
Wing: White hair under pale-blue hair, evenly distributed all round.

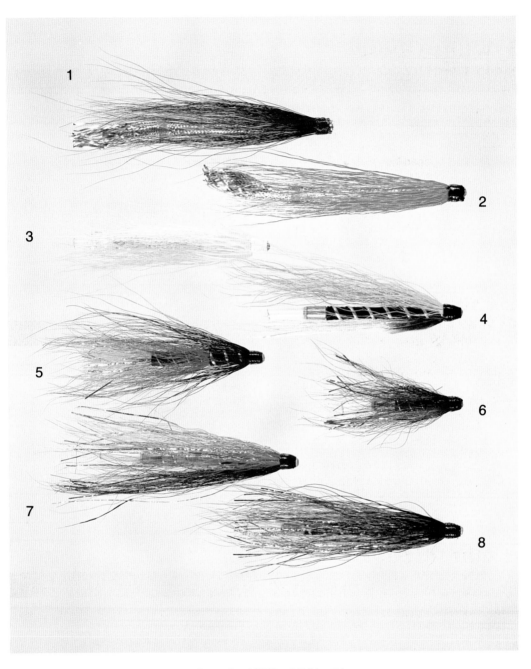

1 Black & Gold Flexi (ED)   **2** Blue & Silver Flexi (ED)   **3** White Ghost
4 Pearl Dog   **5** Shimmering Comet   **6** Shimmering Bruiser
7 Shimmering Jock Scott   **8** Shimmering Willie Gunn

3 White Ghost

COMMENT

The body material is Pearl Mylar piping, which has less of the high sparkle of the gold and silver but gives a discreet faceted glint. Too much 'extra attraction' can be unproductive; just enough may help the pattern to stand out.

DRESSING

Tube: Plastic, or lined aluminium or lined copper or brass.
Body: Pearl Mylar piping.
Wing: One side pale-yellow hair, the other side white hair.
Collar: White cock.
Head: White.

4 Pearl Dog

COMMENT

Pearl is a newer material than the gold and silver Mylars, and is obtainable in piping and filaments. The style of filament here is Lureflash, which has monofilament strands with the tinsel-like strands. The rest of the dressing is recognisably the Garry Dog, seen in other styles on pages 27 and 127.

Leave space on the body tube for the extension which will hold the treble in alignment.

DRESSING

Tube: Plastic, lined aluminium or lined brass or copper.
Body: Black floss.
Rib: Oval silver.
Wing: Red hair under yellow hair, on top of shank.
Throat: Long strands of pearl, equal to the wing length, under short dyed blue guinea-fowl hacke tied in beard style.

5 Shimmering Comet

COMMENT

The basis of this dressing is similar to the Comet on page 127. Limited flash is added, towards the tail only. It must not extend far beyond the hook, or you risk short taking and 'nips' which do not become hooked.

Remember to leave room on the body for the extension tube.

DRESSING

Tail hackle: Yellow hair or hackle with Flashabou strands.
Body: Rear half, black floss with fine oval silver rib.
Centre hackle: Red hair evenly distributed with the tips aligning with the tips of the yellow.
Body: Front half, black floss with broad oval silver rib.
Wing: Black hair evenly distributed with the tips aligning with the tips of the two hackles.

6 Shimmering Bruiser

COMMENT

This example has the extra attraction full-length in the wing. The available range of filament colours is: mother-of-pearl, yellow, copper, bronze, black, lime, red, blue, gold, silver, pink, multi-mix, rainbow pearl, green, purple, deadly mosaic, pink pearl, yellow pearl, purple pearl and pearl mix. Fluorescent strands can also be had.

DRESSING

Tube: As appropriate.
Body: Black floss.
Rib: Oval silver tinsel.
Wing: Blue hair under black hair, with blue Flashabou or Lureflash filaments, evenly distributed.

7 Shimmering Jock Scott

COMMENT

'Experience suggests that the freshness of the fish should be taken into account – while a pattern incorporating such colours as lime, silver and red may tempt a fish fresh from the salt, it might scare the living daylights out of a stale fish in the upper Tweed: a lightly dressed dark fly may, however, have no impact on the fresh fish – Peter Nield's notes.

DRESSING

Tube: As appropriate.
Body: Rear half yellow floss, front half back floss.
Rib: Broad oval silver.
Wing: In four segments – black with black Flashabou, blue with blue Flashabou, yellow with gold Flashabou and red with red Flashabou.

8 Shimmering Willie Gunn

COMMENT

'An example of an unusual use for shimmering flies was found on the upper Tweed in late October 1988 when the river was covered by a thicker than usual carpet of autumn leaves,' writes Peter Nield. 'A reliable favourite for the time of year, Willie Gunn, was failing to tempt fish and many people believed that it was due to the close colour resemblance to the leaves. A little Lureflash was added and the fly was fished with extra movement. Result – fish! The first fish of the week, a bright twelve-pound salmon.'

DRESSING

Tube: As appropriate.
Body: Black floss.
Rib: Broad oval gold.
Wing: Equally mixed hair evenly distributed – yellow, reddish-orange and black – with 'extra attraction' strands of yellow and copper.

PERSONAL STYLES

Introduction

Some of the personal styles illustrated in the next six plates are contemporary and have not yet found their way into books: others reflect the taste of the designer or the user, and perhaps include points in the dressing which may be of interest to both the trade and the amateur tyer.

The authors of this book have differing viewpoints on flies: Arthur feels that it is very much up to the fish once the fisherman has presented his fly in a competent way; John continues to be fascinated by the search for infallible salmon flies, and believes that there is somewhere a thread of reason behind a fish's taking a particular fly.

Crawford Little is a modern writer, not hidebound or overawed by tradition, so it is refreshing to have a modern outlook. One of these days Peter Deane may be encouraged to write his memoirs. We hope he will, for he has been an acquaintance and then a friend for nearly thirty years, and his knowledge and quiet authority back his considerable reputation in the business of fly dressing.

We show a couple of patterns of Peter Keyser's. He really relishes his salmon fishing, and has wide experience, including visits to Iceland. He is a natural fish catcher, and extremely persistent. We have never heard of another fisherman who has followed his fish down through the Falls of Findhorn at Dulsie Bridge and emerged safely with it. He is also the only host we have met who has made his guests fish such long hours that they actually fall alseep deep body-wading!

Just as Hoover has become the trade name to describe all vacuum sweepers, so Esmond Drury's name is automatically attached to all flies tied on long-shank treble hooks. Since their introduction over thirty years ago they have been adopted by a wide spectrum of gillies and fishermen as being unquestionably a most effective design of salmon fly. Their importance must not be overlooked, though in pure *fly-tying* terms there may not be much radical innovation in the patterns which are tied on them.

Esmond Drury had a most illustrious war career, and then he turned his formidable energy to fishing. He saw salmon flies at that time in much the same light as Chaytor did, and he looked to simplification of the patterns and increased hooking and holding potential. His

General Practitioner is a splendid example of ingenuity and an excellent catcher of fish.

During a blitz in Malta in 1941 he discovered from a frogman engaged in harbour work that the least visible colour for a hull of a ship from underwater is white. Bearing in mind that most fish and sea birds have white undersurfaces as a defence from predators below them, he applied this idea to fly lines. White lines, despite criticism, still sell best.

In his obituary in *The Times* in late 1988 there was brought to our memory again his feat of casting a fly from the roof of the Savoy Hotel into the Thames (the police kindly held back the traffic for the attempt). His skills in casting and fishing he handed on in his courses in Lancashire. Mrs Drury has most kindly provided us with our examples of Esmond Drury flies.

Lee Wulff is an institution. He was born in 1905 in Alaska and by the time he was aged two he was out after trout with a piece of bacon on a bent pin. He then became something of an expert at spearing fish to obtain food for the sled dogs. He was nine when he started to tie flies – in his fingers, knowing nothing of vice or hackle pliers.

In the early 1930s he decided to rethink dry-fly patterns, to move away from slim-bodied, sparsely hackled tyings which had to be taken off to be allowed to dry for a while after each fish, in favour of buggier-looking heavier-bodied flies. So started the series of Wulff floaters. At that time he was tying flies to augment a meagre income gained as a freelance artist.

Fly tying is fiddly and time-consuming, so in the 1940s Lee set about finding a simpler method. A suitable plastic was found, and a suitable adhesive, and in the 1950s he was able to take out a patent for a fly-tying technique by which feathers and hair were glued to a pre-formed body. Some of the flies we show are of this style.

We have put in one fly favoured by Francis Francis. That expert fisherman did salmon fishers a great service by listing in the various editions of his *Book on Angling* a vast number of salmon-fly dressings, both as general patterns and as recommended for particular rivers. He managed to combine perceptive and informative detail in a most engaging style, and he expressed the opinion that those who considered but half a dozen fly patterns as sufficient to kill any salmon in any rivers should be compared as chalkers of pavements to Landseer.

Francis Francis was born in Devon in 1822. He changed his original surname, Morgan, to come into an inheritance. He was editor of *The Field* and was a keen supporter of the idea of the Flyfishers' Club. But for his illness he would probably have seen its inauguration in 1883. As it was, he was elected to the committee in 1885, a year before his death from cancer. When he wrote of trout fishing his directions were both broad-minded and forward-looking: 'The judicious and perfect application of dry, wet and mid-water fly fishing stamps the furnished fly fisher with the hallmark of efficiency.' Such words may fairly be taken to heart by the modern salmon fisher.

With the editor's permission we have gone through the pages of *Trout and Salmon* for a few patterns. Some no doubt are real killers, some interesting exercises in fly-tying technique. The magazine gives the public a forum, with most issues mentioning new and old patterns of some sort, for both trout and salmon.

Streamers are included in this section because some salmon fishers have departed from convention and enjoy using very large flies even in bright, low and clear conditions. It is very difficult to cast large and heavy flies on light tackle, particularly on single-handed rods and fine leaders. A well tied and designed streamer has all the size wanted and is active and mobile in the water yet can easily be cast on any tackle.

Tying style differs on either side of the Atlantic. In North America a great number of patterns are tied on extra-long-shank single hooks, or on two medium hooks joined by a short link. The British styles, long called Demons and Terrors, are usually tied on two or three small hooks, with the tail hook sometimes a double, on extended links.

Our examples are nothing like exhaustive – they merely illustrate a very effective style of salmon fly which can on occasions be indispensable.

Esmond Drury

It is easier to think of flies of this sort as Esmond Drury trebles rather than long-shank trebles. He was the champion of this style of dressing, which offers better hooking and holding potential than doubles or singles. Many regular patterns have been adapted to this style – Shrimp, Munro Killer, and others which feature elsewhere in this book – and for this section we have chosen specific and authentic designs from the company.

The advantages of the design are an upturned eye so that the fly can be tied on in a way which ensures that it aligns with the leader; the avoidance of 'skirting' (skating) for which small, light tubes are notorious; and easier casting. The patterns have the same successful reputation for sea trout as they do for salmon, and are a firm recommendation for those fishing in the Falklands. Durability is a feature of their tying, as a special waterproof adhesive is used instead of wax.

We were supplied by the company with a chart of the dressings, so the recipes we give below are absolutely authentic.

1 Green Highlander

COMMENT

Another classic pattern from the north of Scotland simplified for the series. It exemplifies the tying style: no winding of hackles; wings of hair or feather fibres; and, where the pattern permits, the equal distribution of winging materials so that the fly looks similar from all sides.

DRESSING

Tail: Yellow hackle fibres.
Tag: Yellow floss.
Body: Green floss.
Rib: Embossed silver.
Wing: Green hackle fibres under brown mallard.

2 Yellow Torrish

COMMENT

The classic Torrish (a Helmsdale fly) is here simplified to its essentials of yellow and silver with a light-toned wing. This is available more heavily dressed in its larger sizes.

DRESSING

Tail: Yellow hackle fibres.
Tag: Yellow floss.
Body: Silver.
Rib (optional): Silver.
Wing: Yellow hackle fibres with teal fibres over.

230

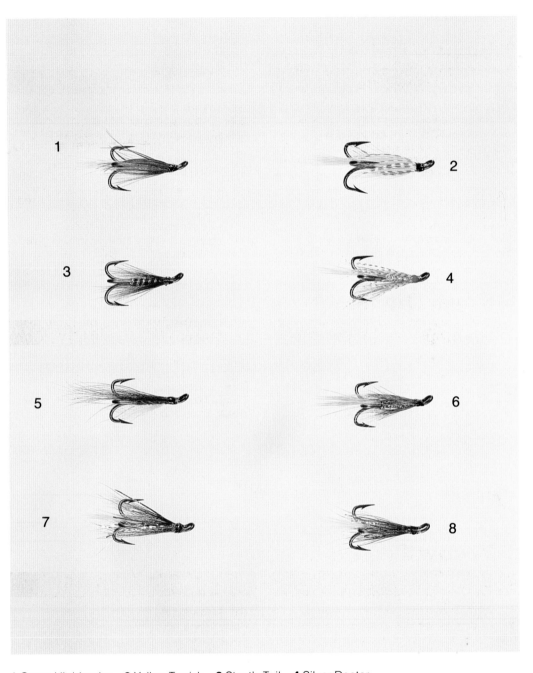

1 Green Highlander **2** Yellow Torrish **3** Stoat's Tail **4** Silver Doctor
5 Tosh **6** Yellow Squirrel **7** Black & Gold Flicker Flash
8 Blue & Silver Flicker Flash

3 Stoat's Tail

COMMENT

The ED Silver Stoat pattern is: tag, none; tail, orange hackle fibres; body, embossed silver; wing, black stoat or black squirrel hair. These are widely used summer flies which are tied by the company from size 4 down to 14. They may also be tied on nickel-finished hooks, as are the ED Silver Blue and ED Blue Squirrel, in hook sizes 8, 10, and 12.

DRESSING

Body: Black.
Rib: Embossed silver.
Wing: Stoat tail hairs or black squirrel.

4 Silver Doctor

COMMENT

The wing is of standard length, to just beyond the bend. The pattern is the classic Silver Doctor, but vastly simplified with emphasis on the red tag and head derived from the original, the blue and silver, and the light winging.

This pattern echoes our feeling that each of the three Doctors in common use should differ in their wings – Black Doctor the darkest, Blue Doctor medium, and Silver Doctor the lightest – rather than all having the same winging. For spring and autumn the company ties the pattern in larger, more heavily dressed sizes.

DRESSING

Tail: Yellow hackle strands.
Tag: Red floss.
Body: Embossed silver.
Wing: Blue hackle fibres with teal fibres over.
Head: Red.

5 Tosh

COMMENT

The pattern is derived from a modern Spey pattern, another tale of the tail of a dog, namely Tosh, belonging to E. Ritchie, gillie on the Delfur beat in 1957. It is an extremely simple pattern both in its original form and in this tying, and should be proportioned with the black wing at least half as long again as the hook shank. Calf tail has a slight crinkle to its fibre.

DRESSING

Tail: None.
Body: Black.
Wing: Half black squirrel, half yellow calf tail.

232

6 Yellow Squirrel

COMMENT

The ED Blue Squirrel is in similar style, with yellow tail, silver body and blue squirrel wing. The tying note given to us is to dress the wing to just beyond the bend of the hook. These summer out-point flies are tied as slender as possible. The squirrel hair has not been bleached, so it retains the mottling through the dye.

DRESSING

Tail: Orange.
Body: Gold tinsel.
Wing: Yellow squirrel.

7 Black & Gold Flicker Flash

COMMENT

This is one of three ED patterns with 'metallic' fibre in the wing. Another pattern is the ED Orange Flicker Flash, which has a yellow tail, black and embossed silver body, and a wing of yellow calf under orange calf with a few strands of gold Flashabou.

DRESSING

Tail: Yellow hackle fibres.
Body: Black floss.
Rib: Embossed gold.
Wing: Yellow calf tail under black squirrel hair, which includes a few strands of gold Flashabou.

8 Blue & Silver Flicker Flash

COMMENT

The squirrel tail has not been bleached. Needless to say, many of these patterns have a tremendous reputation for taking sea trout.

DRESSING

Tail: Yellow hackle fibres.
Body: Embossed silver tinsel.
Wing: Grey squirrel dyed blue with a few strands of gold Flashabou.

233

Lee Wulff

There are one or two giants of American angling scenes: Lee Wulff, for both authors, stands the tallest. His books *The Atlantic Salmon* and *Lee Wulff on Flies* should have a place in every Atlantic salmon fisherman's library. His films and broadcasts fascinate. His mind never stops thinking about fly design and he produces a wealth of ideas: that bodies should be soft so that they are not instantly rejected by the fish; that tube design for game fish (and sea fish) is worth considerable development, either as a soft body or to be tied as a series to make compound flies with differing tone and colour in each segment; or that tubes might be tied with a body broken into two colour segments to give extra colour and flash. With North American restrictions on treble hooks, he has improved tube dressings (in attracting and deceiving styles) for single hooks for all species.

We have taken five of his dry flies and three wet flies to give him a 'guest' page; others of his tyings will be found under suitable headings. The accompanying notes are drawn in part from his correspondence with us and from his books.

1 White Wulff

COMMENT

Probably the best-known of the salmon dry flies, this is used in particularly large sizes as an exaggeration, to make the fish show before a smaller similar or contrasting pattern is tried (though they do sometimes take the larger patterns).

DRESSING

Tail: White bucktail.
Body: Cream angora wool (or rabbit fur).
Throat: Badger hackle.
Wing: White bucktail.

2 Gray Wulff

COMMENT

This is a good natural/terrestrial choice, with a thick body and plenty of hackle to provide flotation. Lee Wulff devised it as a concept fly in the early 1930s, inaugurating it on a salmon river near Malone, NY, with Dan Bailey. He used it with Mucilin grease, and usually in a size 10. (Preston Jennings did not believe that they were sufficiently like trout insects, however, to be included in his *Book of Trout Flies*, 1935.)

The wings may slant forwards, or backwards, or may be left unsplit. If the fly is tied with a palmer hackle it may be called a Scraggly.

DRESSING

Tail: Bucktail fibres of even length.
Body: Grey angora, untwisted so that it does not form a rope, tied smooth and even.
Wings: Bucktail fibres of even length.
Throat: Two grey saddle hackles.

234

1 White Wulff   **2** Gray Wulff   **3** Royal Wulff   **4** Prefontaine
5 Lady Joan   **6** Haggis   **7** Cullman's Choice   **8** Surface Stonefly

3 Royal Wulff

COMMENT

This was very successful tied as single-winged, but it is easier for the fisherman to see the double-winged style, and they float better. Like the other Wulffs, this may be tied with more hackle for extra flotation, and they may even be used as skaters.

DRESSING

Tail: Bucktail fibres of even length.
Body: Rear third peacock herl, middle third red (or fluorescent red) floss, front third peacock herl.
Wings: White bucktail fibres.
Throat: Natural red saddle hackles.

4 Prefontaine

COMMENT

This is a variation of the Skater pattern named after his host by Lee Wulff when they were fishing the Moisie River. It was originally tied on a size 16 hook, with which Alain Prefontaine succeeded in catching a twenty pounder! On a later trip to the Gaspé Peninsula, with the river low and warm, the fishing poor, on a pool 'loaded with fish, [where] no-one had taken a fish for almost a month' Wulff hooked four fish on this fly in one afternoon.

DRESSING

Tail: Hackle tips.
Body: Palmered with at least two hackles.
Wing: Long bucktail 'snoot'.
(The method is: tie in the forward wing first, work down with the tying silk to the bend, to tie in the tips of the hackles; work the tying silk back to the eye, follow with the hackles, tie off.)

5 Lady Joan

COMMENT

Lee Wulff created this when fishing one of the great northern salmon rivers on his side of the Atlantic. He came across some burnt-orange floss and, inspired by a particularly effective trout fly called the Orange Fish Hawk, decided to make an orange salmon fly. Note his style of tight spirals of tinsel, and the inclusion of topping over a hairwing.

DRESSING

Tag: None (or fine oval gold).
Tail: None (or topping).
Body: Burnt-orange floss.
Ribs: Oval gold.
Throat: Soft light yellow, tied as a beard.
Wing: Soft black bear under grey squirrel; with topping over.

6 Haggis

This was devised in Scotland, in 1962, as a dark fly for a dark day, to be fished on a riffling hitch 'through the roughest waters at the pool heads where a normal salmon pattern would swamp if skimmed'. Wulff had two fish from the Dee with it in late June, and considers it one of his favourite and most effective flies. He ties it both *with* black bucktail hairs for extra flotation and *without* when a normal wet fly is needed.

Tag: None.
Tail: None.
Body: Black wool.
Rib: Oval silver.
Throat: Yellow hackle fibres, tied as a beard.
Wing: Black hair with topping over.

7 Cullman's Choice

This was originally called Silver Birch, then renamed for a good friend. The concept again is to surprise the salmon with something it has not seen before – green is more believed in 'over there' than in Britain.

Tag: None.
Tail: None.
Body: Apple-green floss.
Rib: Oval silver.
Throat: White hackle fibres, tied as a beard.
Wing: Black bear with topping over.

8 Surface Stonefly

This is a very low floater indeed, and needs a gentle lateral side cast to make it alight softly, otherwise it will sink. It produces quite a different profile and footprint on the water, and the change from the usual high floater can often convince the salmon. Lee Wulff chooses it when he has had a rise to a Wulff without a hook-up, or when there was no reaction to the Wulff. There is very much an element of insect imitation about the pattern, and it has, as Lee Wulff says, caught him a great number of fish which other flies could not catch for him.

Body: Preformed plastic.
Wing: Bucktail, extending well over the body.
Hackle: Cream badger, wound in parachute style round stub on the body and secured with adhesive.
(Earlier patterns were tied on yellow tubes with ultra-light trebles. A small vertical stub was tied on top of the tube for the parachute hackle fixing.)

Crawford Little

We have chosen a selection of Crawford Little flies because he is a modern writer with a taste for modern flies. He writes regular magazine articles and in his *Success with Salmon*, he lists for warm water, in addition to the seven flies shown here, Hairy Mary, Copper Orange, Kenny's Killer and Shrimp Fly, some described on other pages. Elsewhere he has been asked to comment on fly choice and he suggests the Black Pennell as a good grilse dropper (echoing John Ashley-Cooper), and he likes a Camasunary Killer, which Peter Deane, who has done so much to popularise the pattern, has tied for us in salmon style.

Crawford started his fishing at a very early age. Finding that suitable tackle and suitable tuition were all important, he was the youngest guest on one of Captain Tommy Edwards's game-fishing courses at Grantown, on Speyside. (These courses continue to be run by Arthur, and John has helped instruct for the past ten years.) He then had the chances and the experience to benefit from the excellent salmon fishing in the 1960s before the advent of the latest cycle of ulcerative dermal necrosis (the salmon disease), and the discovery of the salmon's deep-water feeding grounds and their subsequent massacre at sea.

1 Bourrach

COMMENT

Crawford Little notes: '. . . a slim shimmering streak of yellow in the water and quite excellent for fishing fast broken streams in bright conditions. Very definitely a fly to be tied in the long-winged style, or the slimmer profiled hooks or shank.'

It is very similar to the Gillie's Fly given in *Trout and Salmon* of January 1985 by C. W. K. Mundle, the author of *Game Fishing – Methods and Memories* – tail, none; body, flat silver tinsel; throat, sky-blue; wing, buttercup yellow hair.

DRESSING

Tag: Oval silver.
Tail: Blue hackle point.
Body: Flat silver.
Rib: Oval silver.
Throat: Blue.
Wing : Yellow hair.

2 Black Maria

COMMENT

Mrs Robertson in her engaging writings about the Irish Slaney, *Thrifty Salmon Fishing* (1945) and *Further Thrifty Salmon Fishing* (1950), upholds this pattern for its simple effectiveness. Her tying is drawn from a little Breton pattern – tag, not mentioned; tail, 'sans tail'; body, half rich yellow, half black floss silk; rib, sans ribbing; hackle and throat, black (in *FTSF* a teal throat); wing, black (or a wisp of yellow). 'For a pseudo Jock – I give it a turkey tipped-white wing; with an orange hackle it will assume the air of a Thunder.' In *Further Thrifty Salmon Fishing* she changes the yellow in the body to orange as well.

DRESSING

Tag: Oval silver.
Tail: Topping.
Body: Rear half yellow, front half black floss.
Rib: Oval silver.
Hackle and throat: Black over the black floss.
Wing: Black.
(Crawford Little's note is: 'Another of the black and yellow flies that can prove so successful on the Spey. It is reported that 500 salmon fell to this fly in the season at Knockando.')

238

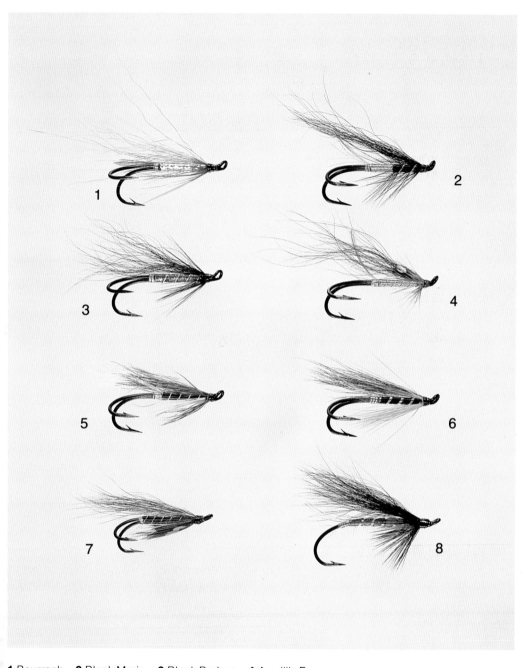

1 Bourrach   **2** Black Maria   **3** Black Brahan   **4** Arndilly Fancy
5 Grey, Blue & Yellow Squirrel   **6** Thunder Stoat   **7** Munro Killer
8 Camasunary Killer

3 Black Brahan

COMMENT

Crawford Little notes both in his book and in *Trout and Salmon*'s 'Flies for 1987' supplement that this is a good fly for salmon and sea trout at dawn or dusk. He gives, as a variant, a green Lurex body.

Fulsher and Krom give an American variant with a red floss body, and they suggest black squirrel for the tail. One more variation of theirs has an orange throat hackle. Clegg suggests fire-orange DRF floss for the body as an alternative, and his pattern has an orange throat hackle.

DRESSING

Hook: Double salmon.
Tag: Oval silver.
Tail: None.
Body: Red Lurex.
Rib: Oval silver.
Throat: Black.
Wing: Black.

4 Arndilly Fancy

COMMENT

A fly Crawford Little connects with that inimitable fly tyer Megan Boyd of Kintradwell, and another fly in the black-and-yellow mould said to be so effective on the Spey. Arndilly is a beat near Craigellachie, on the lower middle Spey. This is very much a modern Spey fly – not possessing traditional Spey features.

DRESSING

Tag: Oval silver.
Tail: Topping.
Body: Yellow floss.
Rib: Oval silk.
Throat: Bright blue.
Wing: Black.
Sides: Jungle cock.
Head: Two-thirds red, one-third black (the head is shown all red in John Ashley-Cooper's *Great Salmon Rivers*).

5 Grey, Blue & Yellow Squirrel

COMMENT

Crawford noted the popularity of the Grey Squirrel on the Annan, near his home. His appreciation of the merits of tricolour flies such as the Munro Killer induced him to make this variant. He regards it as an excellent pattern for fairly low, clear-water conditions and any time when there is more than a blink of sunlight. Though he does not say it, tyers will recognise that the colour intensity of the wing will be heightened with clear blue and yellow, or held back more dully if the blue and yellow are dyed onto grey squirrel tail retaining its mottling.

DRESSING

Tag: Oval silver.
Tail: Topping.
Body: Black floss.
Rib: Oval silver.
Throat: Yellow under blue guinea-fowl.
Wing: Grey squirrel over blue over yellow.

6 Thunder Stoat

COMMENT

Since the original Thunder & Lightning in full dressing contains blue – in its throat hackle of blue-dyed guinea-fowl or barred blue jay – and jungle cock sides, sometimes these elements are added. The major difference between this pattern and the Munro Killer is in style – this pattern is seldom dressed as long and flowing as is the Munro. Dispassionately, there cannot be much to choose between them. Orange is often recommended in times of falling water after a spate, so the two patterns are no doubt interchangeable.

DRESSING

Hook: Double salmon.
Tag : Oval gold.
Tail: Topping.
Body: Black floss.
Rib: Oval gold.
Throat: Bright orange.
Wing: Black.

7 Munro Killer

COMMENT

This fly has as many spellings to its name as there seem to be variants in its dressing. Ashley-Cooper attributes its origination to the late J. A. J. Munro, who for years operated a fishing tackle shop in Aberlour on the Spey. Its throat is normally tied in beard style. Some fishers like a couple of strands of bronze peacock herl over the wing. Some tyers consider that black dustbin bag (stretched) makes a better body than silk. The wing dressing should be long and mobile, according to some fishers and some tyers.

DRESSING

Hook: Double salmon.
Tag: Oval gold.
Tail: None.
Body: Black silk.
Rib: Gold.
Throat: A mixture of orange strands and blue guinea-fowl.
Wing: Black over yellow (or grey squirrel).

8 Camasunary Killer

COMMENT

That great tyer Peter Deane has popularised this pattern. The original design was from Stephen Johnson of Jedburgh, and it was improved by the addition of fluorescent red wool for the front half of the body, rather than running blue the full length. Probably better known as a sea-trout fly, when the hackle should be dressed long.

Peter kindly came out of retirement to dress this and other patterns of his flies for our book.

DRESSING

Tag: Silver wire.
Tail: Topping.
Body: Rear half blue wool, front half fluorescent red wool.
Rib: Oval silver, rather broad.
Throat: Long black hackle, generous.
Wing: Black hair.

Oglebugs and the Like

We have taken a few patterns slightly at random. Either they are of obviously different styles or there is some particular philosophy behind them, or some patterns may spring from a truly simple source of inspiration – availability of material. The Keyser patterns use the tail hair of fallow deer, as Peter is very keen on his stalking.

Within the patterns shown can be found emphasis on shape (in some doubles), on translucency, on the fly body, and on determined variation of design from the accepted norm of fly tying. In the following plate a broad spectrum of design can be seen, continuing this reflection of modern tying design, including extra hooking quality and shrimp derivations.

These are pages which really do not pretend to be exhaustive. Many indeed are the patterns tied by amateurs and professionals which step sideways from the mainstream of salmon flies and which do wonderfully well for their inventors. The difficulty is for a compiler to lay hands on them.

1 Oglebug

COMMENT

Anthony Crossley tied 'buggy' flies; the example on page 89 shows this. There is a look of something furtive and scuttling about some of the tyings, which makes them seem vulnerable and edible. Doubles and trebles often produce a buggy effect, and Arthur says of this fly: 'I like browns and blacks, with an occasional flash of red, when fish have seen regular patterns. Red is a colour which seems to attract migratory fish, and one wonders if there is a link with the colour of the natural ova.'

DRESSING

Body: Black.
Rib: Fine silver.
Wing: Black and red goat hair.

2 Rainbow Warrior

COMMENT

There are other rainbow patterns, but not for the same reason. John's fly was first tied at the time that the *Rainbow Warrior* ship was destroyed in a New Zealand harbour. It seemed to sink without great effect. So, likewise, the first examples of this fly style when presented to salmon. Confoundingly, they now have started to take fish regularly, so perhaps they will have to be renamed.

The winging principle is an update of that of the Owenmore (page 27).

DRESSING

Hook: Low-water double.
Tag: Fine oval gold or silver.
Tail wing: A bunch of plain-dyed orange grey-squirrel hair.
Body: Black floss.
Rib: A continuation of the tag.
Middle wing: Blue-dyed brindled grey-squirrel. **Body and rib:** As above.
Throat hackle (optional): Blue, orange or yellow.
Front wing: Yellow-dyed brindled grey-squirrel.

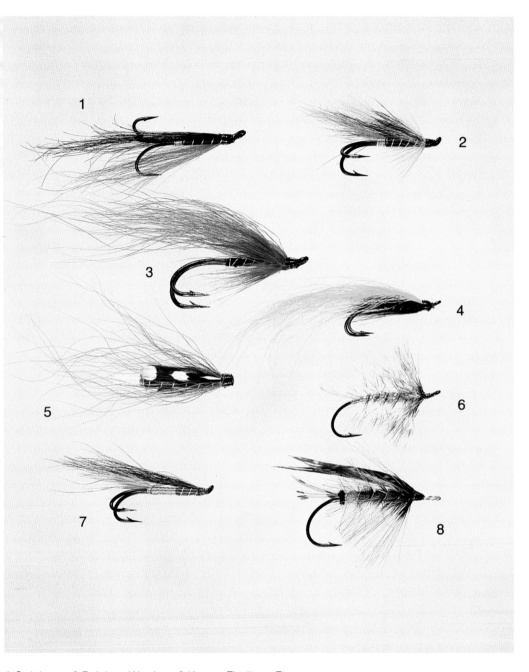

1 Oglebug   **2** Rainbow Warrior   **3** Keyser Findhorn Fly
4 Keyser Spey Fly   **5** Black Dart   **6** Heather Moth
7 Graesser's Tadpole   **8** Francis' Favourite

3 Keyser Findhorn Fly

COMMENT

The Keyser family have a long history of fishing the Morayshire Findhorn. It is a marvellous river of streams, great holding pools, runs and rock-face gorges. Local expertise in knowing exactly where the lies are in every height of water is necessary for success. When we were invited to join their family party, the Keyser patterns outfished all others, even those of similar size and colour. The style is to tie a relatively slender short body, add a generous throat hackle, and then liberal fallow tail hair, not evened out at the tips but tapering.

DRESSING

Tag: A turn or two of fine silver tinsel.
Body: Black floss.
Rib: A continuation of the tag material.
Throat: Blue cock hackle, tied liberally and a little longer than the body length.
Wing: Orange-dyed fallow tail, thick at the shoulder and tapering to twice the length of the shank.

4 Keyser Spey Fly

COMMENT

Peter Keyser took his tyings from the Findhorn to the Spey at Delfur, and other down-river beats. The yellow tying brought him considerable quantities of fish when other anglers were struggling. Peter is persistent in finding the right depth at which to fish: sometimes a sunk line in summer is much more productive than floaters or sink-tips. Some of his patterns have an even more pronounced width at the shoulder, and fine tapering tail – like a raindrop. The wing is made from a variety of hair lengths to achieve this. However this is his pattern which the gillies wanted to copy.

DRESSING

Tag: A turn or two of fine oval gold.
Tail: None.
Body: Black floss.
Rib: A continuation of the tag material.
Throat: Black cock, slightly longer than the body.
Wing: Yellow-dyed fallow tail, quite twice as long as the shank and tapering.

5 Black Dart

COMMENT

We have a West Country pattern here, a rare *English* pattern. Charles Bingham devised this pattern for the River Dart, on which he runs fishing courses. He has two essentials in a salmon fly: the first is that the salmon should take it, so we must consider colour, weight, diameter and length; the second is that the fish should remain hooked till landed. From the illustrations in his book *Salmon and Sea-Trout Fishing*, the wing is sparse and tapering, the few longest strands just reaching beyond the hook. Clearly the body is important, quite as important as the wing in this design.

DRESSING

Tube: Type B Slipstream socketed.
Hook: For a 1–1½ inch tube, Partridge size 8 treble: for a 2-inch tube, size 6 treble.
Tag: No. 16 oval gold.
Body: Black floss over fine lead wire, the lead wire ending before the point where the wing is tied in.
Rib: No. 16 oval gold.
Wing: Orange bucktail evenly distributed.
Sides: Jungle cock, three-quarter length.

6 Heather Moth

COMMENT

This is a Peter Deane fly. It was the brainchild of the owner of the Screeb Fishery in Ireland many years ago. He also owned the Polly and the pattern was devised for that river. Possibly it is called the Heather Moth for its drab appearance; however, 'it has no doubt caught more salmon for my clients in the UK and Eire than any other pattern I have tied in the past forty-odd years'. The Irish occasionally refer to it as Deane's Miracle Fly. Its dressing is adapted to sea trout and to dry-fly use.

DRESSING

Tag: Silver wire.
Tail: Topping (omitted on the sea-trout tying).
Body: Grey wool.
Rib: Flat silver.
Hackle: Grizzle cock.
Throat: Grizzle cock.

7 Graesser's Tadpole

COMMENT

Neil Graesser has two books in wide circulation at the moment, *Fly-Fishing for Salmon,* and *Advanced Salmon Fishing*. This pattern started as a variation on a Collie Dog theme, with more colour, so favourite spring colours were added – yellow and crimson. It received its initiation on the Rosehall beat of the Cassley, which was running at 3 feet 6 inches, an ideal height for March. The first fish to it came from the Upper Platform Pool. Sometimes fish will be utterly contrary in the spring, all coming to a Collie Dog on some days, all to a Tadpole on others.

DRESSING

Tail: Yellow hair tied long.
Body: Rear half yellow floss, front half crimson floss.
Wing: Collie dog hair, extending to align with the end of the tail. Can be tied very long.
Head: Red.

8 Francis' Favourite

COMMENT

'I have killed a good many fish a few years since on the Usk, and all with one fly which thence was called Francis' Favourite.' Forrest's tying on Plate XIX of the 1920 Maxwell-edited edition shows a tail of ibis and tippet, and the rib is not perceptible.

DRESSING

Tag: Medium round silver wire.
Tail: Topping with tippet fibres (or red ibis).
Butt: Black herl (or none).
Body: A few turns of yellow wool or seal fur, the rest dark claret.
Rib: Fine oval gold.
Hackle and throat: Coch-y-bonddu.
Wing: Sections of dark turkey, tied vertically.

Trout and Salmon

Trout and Salmon was established in 1955 and has become one of the most popular magazines for game fishermen. Throughout its history it has included articles on fly tying, both traditional and modern. Trade tyers give their advice and amateurs regularly send in notes of their inventions. The correspondence columns are often used by those who have enquiries about patterns and styles and their inventors. We have therefore drawn on its pages for one or two patterns. Assuming that the circulation of the magazine is nearly 60,000, and there are two or three readers at least of each copy bought, then any fly described will have a wide public, and very much a 'special interest' public at that. If the editor considers the fly's details worth publishing, his judgement will give that pattern wide publicity and considerable authority. We have picked out just a few patterns from the pages of *Trout and Salmon* of recent years. In earlier years Tom Stewart had a regular column, 'Popular Flies', which later were published as *Fifty Popular Flies* in four volumes, and then in one binding as *200 Popular Flies*.

1 Logie Variant

COMMENT

The gillies on the Laggan river in Islay wanted a bit more colour and mobility than is found in the standard light-wire patterns. A palmered hackle, rather than a throat hackle, seemed to meet the requirements. The series adapted hairwing Thunder & Lightnings, Jeannies, Blue Charms, Stoat's Tails, and the wings were also varied in darkness and lightness of tone. *Trout and Salmon* published the story of the design as 'Flies with a Halo'. It was devised with no conscious (or even subliminal) knowledge of the Beadle patterns (page 216), which had much the same principle behind them in the 1930s.

DRESSING

Tag: Oval silver.
Tail: Topping.
Body: Rear third yellow floss, front two-thirds claret floss.
Hackle: Blue over claret.
Wing: Yellow-dyed mottled grey squirrel.

2 Bentley's Folly

COMMENT

In a series of articles in 1988 Bill Bentley enthralled readers with his exploits in Norway. He never expected to catch a real Aaro monster, but could not resist a couple of days on the river. He did take a fish on this fly – all of 8 pounds. The Bentley's Folly rose for him forty fish in different countries and brought twenty-two to the bank. The original hackling was the 'glistening grey hair of a ferocious and villainous monkey from Malaysia'. When the supply ran out a big blue-dun hackle was substituted.

DRESSING

Body: Black floss.
Rib: Gold.
Wing: Orange hair (goat) over yellow, with optional Flashabou in the top only.
Sides (optional): Jungle cock.
Collar: Long blue-dun.

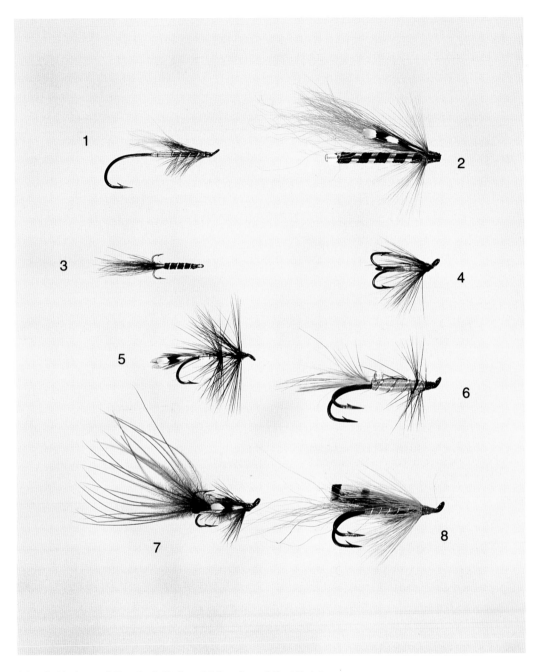

1 Logie Variant **2** Bentley's Folly **3** Microfly **4** Red Twist
5 Delphi Silver **6** Lochy Shrimp **7** Sandy's Shrimp **8** Ally's Shrimp

3 Microfly

COMMENT

In June 1987, Peter Smith wrote about sport in spate rivers on the west coast of Scotland. The best of the fishing is when the river is up and the fish running. However, when the bare bones of the bed are showing there is no need for despair. The requirement is a small but relatively heavy fly. It is fished with sink-tip or slow-sinking line and inched back, or cast upstream and worked back a little faster. In the August 1988 issue he brought his notes up to date with further successes, even adding a fluorescent-green floss tail, feeling that more experimentation was possible even though results were already good.

DRESSING

Tail: Black squirrel or stoat.
Body: Black floss.
Rib: Oval silver.
(We illustrate only the one pattern, the All-Black. The Red & White has a tail of white cock hackle fibres and a body of red floss; the Chinaman, a body of yellow floss. The hooks tied are as small as 16s.)

4 Red Twist

COMMENT

In July 1988 Graeme Harris reported some extensive experimentation to find a reliable sea-trout fly. He ended up with a pattern that took a toll of salmon as well. His intentions were to improve on bad hooking of fish which take 'on the dangle', and have a fly dressed symmetrically from all sides, unlike the traditional tyings with wing on top and hackle below. He considered that hackle had an advantage over hair – in its suitable lengths of fibre, its potential for a slim head, the wide range of easily obtained colours, and simplicity and cheapness of use.

DRESSING

Tying silk: Fine flat Monocord or Cobweb.
Hook: Size 8–16 longshank outpoint treble or 12–16 fine-wire equivalent for ultra-fine use.
Butt: Fluorescent red floss.
Body: Flat silver.
Inner hackle: Dyed red cock.
Outer hackle: Dyed black cock.
(The fly illustrated is one of a series. Body and outer hackle are constant in all. The colour part of the name comes from the butt and inner hackle.)

5 Delphi Silver

COMMENT

In an article in the February 1988 number, 'Sport on a Rolling Wave', Peter O'Reilly gave his favoured patterns for the salmon loughs of Ireland. He propounds the sensible view that a big double may be too heavy to cast easily with a single-hander, and he therefore ties even Shrimps on singles. The Delphi Silver he rates well for low-light conditions and for the last thing in the evenings.

DRESSING

Hook: Size 8 for salmon, 8 or 10 for grilse or sea trout.
Tail: Two jungle cock tied back to back.
Rear body: Flat silver.
Rib: Oval silver.
Centre hackle: Black cock.
Front body: Flat silver.
Rib: Oval silver.
Throat: Black cock.

6 Lochy Shrimp

COMMENT

A design not far from that of Peter Deane's dressing of the Francis Prawn. It achieved for its maker, Michael Shepley, considerable success on the Lochy – 13 caught and 8 lost – in a day's fishing recounted in the January 1989 issue.

Proprietary eyes can be found listed in most fly-tying supply catalogues.

DRESSING

Underbody: Built up with sections of matchstick or wine-bottle lead foil.
Tail: Strands of black, yellow and red marabou.
Whiskers: Two strips of red ibis or substitute quill.
Eyes: Two beads threaded onto 15-pound nylon tied figure-of-eight to the shank with ends heat-blobbed to stop eyes coming off.
Body: Fluorescent pink floss.
Rib: Oval gold.
Hackle: Black, over front half of the body.

7 Sandy's Shrimp

COMMENT

Some of the west coast spate rivers have rapid streamy heads running into large slack holding areas. This pattern was designed to ensure that the dressing stays very mobile. When the stream is insufficient to bring the fly on round, steady 'figure-of-eighting' of the line keeps the fly pulsing like a living creature. Marabou, as we have noted, is a successor to eagle feathers, so we have a relatively modern-style Shrimp using qualities from time-honoured materials. The tail should be at least three times the length of the hook shank.

DRESSING

Hook: 8, 10, 12.
Tail: Black marabou.
Body: Red marabou, dubbed.
Rib: Flat gold.
Throat: Sparse black cock.
Cheeks: Jungle cock.

8 Ally's Shrimp

COMMENT

Alistair Gowans (*T & S*, August 1988) devised a pattern to look a little different from the other flies and tubes in his box, and something shrimpy and semi-translucent, like the creatures he had observed caught by a trawler fishing the Minch. He suggests it is worth a try at any time between late spring and late autumn, and it has notched up successes from the Dee, Tay, Tummel, Tweed and Esks. He tied his pattern to good effect on size 4–10 doubles. Orange as the base colour is his favourite, with red the next best.

DRESSING

Tying silk: Red.
Tail: Strands of long hot-orange bucktail.
Body: Rear half red, front half black floss.
Rib: Oval silver.
Wing: A bunch of grey squirrel with golden pheasant tippets over.
Hackle: Grey squirrel tail, as a beard.
Collar: Long hot-orange.
Head: Red.

Streamers

Bates lists the following streamer patterns as having application for Atlantic salmon: Alexandra, Bloodsucker, Brown Falcon Bucktail, Cains River streamers (a series), Chappie, Cosseboom streamer, Green Beauty, Herb Johnson Special, Lady Doctor, Mickey Finn, Nine-three and Silver-tip Bucktail. In *Trout* Ray Bergman also lists quite some number of streamers. Both these authors are referring for the most part in their books to trout (brook trout, cutthroat or rainbow) tyings, and to landlocked salmon patterns which imitate smelt or small baitfish. The theory that bigger streamers take the biggest fish does not necessarily apply to migratory fish; it is more often a matter of the correct choice in relation to conditions of weather, water height, speed and colour. Those who fish flies of 3 inches or so when normal doctrine suggests sizes 8, 10 and 12 often choose the style as a striking contrast, and they are also able to add life to the fly by vigorous handlining.

1 Royal Coachman Streamer

COMMENT

To our great joy we have found what the Royal Coachman imitates; it is no longer a fancy fly but a direct representation of a mayfly – so considers Preston Jennings, the author of the *Book of Trout Flies* (1935), in a 1956 article in *Esquire*. He suggests the genus *Isonychia*, with the tail bunch of herl representing the egg ball of the gravid female, and the other element of herl representing the thorax. Whether this is so or not does not affect the popularity of the Royal Coachman in wet, dry, nymph, Wulff and streamer styles.

DRESSING

Hook: Long-shank light-wire.
Tail: Tippet strands.
Body: Rear quarter bronze herl, middle red (or fluorescent red) floss, front quarter bronze herl.
Throat: Natural red hackle in beard style.
Wing: White bucktail up to twice as long as the shank.

2 Mickey Finn

COMMENT

One of the most famous streamers with a long history of success, popularised by John Alden Knight in 1932, initially known as the Red & Yellow Bucktail, then the Assassin. Later Gregory Clark (feature writer and war correspondent with the *Toronto Star*) christened it the Mickey Finn. In 1937 the story about it was published in *Hunting and Fishing* magazine at the time the Sportsman's Show was on in New York. It was estimated that between a quarter and half a million of these flies were tied and distributed during the show.

DRESSING

Tail: None.
Body: Flat silver tinsel or Mylar.
Rib: Narrow oval silver over flat silver (none over Mylar).
Wing: One part of yellow bucktail under one part of red bucktail under two parts of yellow bucktail.

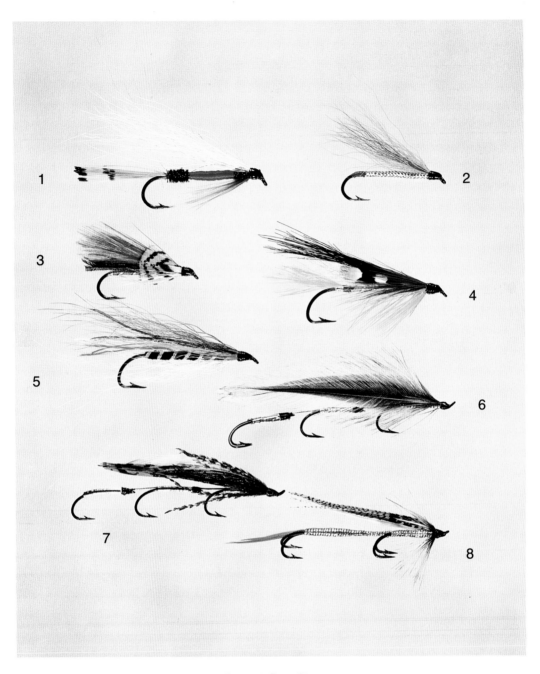

1 Royal Coachman Streamer **2** Mickey Finn **3** Grey Ghost
4 Lady Doctor **5** Herb Johnson Special **6** Badger Terror
7 Alexandra **8** Plain Norsk Lure

3 Grey Ghost

This is the introductory fly in an account in Bates *(ASF)*: 'A Grey Ghost caught by the wind skittered over the surface.' Though it is usually regarded as a landlocked salmon pattern, it has its fans for Atlantic salmon. For the landlocked it may be tied as long as 4½ inches. This pattern was devised by Carrie Stevens at Upper Dawn, Maine, in 1924 to imitate a smelt. She never tied with a vice and was formerly a milliner by trade.

DRESSING

Tag: Narrow flat silver.
Tail: None.
Body: Pale-orange floss, very slender.
Rib: Narrow flat silver.
Throat: A strand or two of peacock herl, strands of white bucktail, and topping with downward curve.
Wing: Topping and four olive-grey saddle hackles.
Shoulders: Silver pheasant body feather.
Cheeks: Jungle cock.

4 Lady Doctor

COMMENT

Bates used this successfully for salmon, though its design related more closely to the requirements of catching trout, bass and landlocked salmon. Joseph S. Stickney of Saco, Maine, designed it in 1926.

DRESSING

Tag: Narrow flat gold.
Tail: Tips of two moderately long and very small yellow neck hackles back to back.
Butt: Two or three turns of bright-red silk.
Body: Bright-yellow silk, slender.
Rib: Narrow gold.
Hackle: Yellow hackle in front of the tinsel.
Throat: Remainder of the hackle.
Wing: White polar bear under black bear.
Sides: Jungle cock.
Shoulders: Red-dyed breast feather one-third as long as the wing.

5 Herb Johnson Special

COMMENT

Herb Johnson designed this fly in about 1950.
It is interesting how little criticism is levelled at streamer hooks in the larger sizes, because there is no end of comment about large single salmon irons. It is probably worth the trouble of tying all streamer patterns in the Demon or Terror style, with small hooks linked. However, it remains important that the fly should be extremely light in weight and mobile and flexible in the water. Marabou is a logical inclusion for a special pulsing fibre action.

DRESSING

Tag: None.
Body: Black wool, fairly full.
Rib: Embossed silver.
Throat: White bucktail as long as the wing.
Wing: A small bunch of bright yellow bucktail with two strands of red and blue fluorescent nylon floss on each side and a strand of peacock herl above, and a bunch of yellow-dyed brown bucktail over all.

6 Badger Terror

COMMENT

In *I Have Been Fishing* (1949) John Rennie writes: 'Terrors. I mention this as they have been the means of my catching a large number of salmon. On the Tummel I got many fish . . . also the Shannon, in Norway, Iceland, Scotland and Ireland much success. . . . Of course it represents a sand-eel, and if the fish have been feeding on this in the sea, then they take it . . . it casts quite well.' Later in the book he suggests a turn or two of throat hackle. Terrors worked extremely well for him and his friends on the Sundal in Norway in 1923.

DRESSING

Hooks: Double, single, single.
Body: Silver tinsel.
Wing: Four badger hackles.
Throat (optional): A turn or two of badger hackle.

7 Alexandra

COMMENT

John Rennie again: 'One rod on the Dee got most of his fish on the "Demon": a contraption of three small hooks tied in the same manner as the "Terror": length of body one a half inches. . . . It is wonderful how large fish may be caught on these very small hooks.' The dressing he gives accords exactly with Hardy's Dr Evelyn Lure the Plain Alexandra. Other 'killers' in this series (which are asymmetric) are the Gold-Tippet Alexandra (tippet one side, herl the other), the Jay Alexandra (herl and golden pheasant tail one side, jay feather the other) and the Jungle Alexandra.

DRESSING

Tail: None.
Body: Silver.
Wing: Generous strands of golden pheasant tail feather on one side, green peacock sword herl half-length on the other side, with topping over all.

8 Plain Norsk Lure

COMMENT

The Norsk lures by Hardy are included here though they were in some ways precursors to Waddingtons. The link between the fore and hind sets of hooks is dressed with body material. 'Any pattern of fly dressed' indicated that the company would produce any of their standard salmon patterns in this style.

DRESSING

Hooks: Two doubles.
Tail: A swathe of red ibis.
Body: Oval silver, covering the link.
Wing: Strips of white swan and speckled bustard.
Collar: Badger hackle.

NYMPHS AND OTHER BEASTS

Introduction

Nymphs   A salmon parr often follows and intercepts larval forms of insects on their way to the surface, as well as taking insects floating down past it. This upward movement, which incidentally is often so fatally attractive to rainbow trout, is an important element in fishing an imitation nymph to an adult salmon. In *Nymphs and the Trout* (1970) Frank Sawyer outlined his experiments with salmon. First was his blue and silver affair on a heavy hook – to get down to mid-water if not lower. He pitched it in upstream on a shepherd's crook cast, took up the slack and then raised the rod point. The resulting fish weighed fourteen pounds and it was from the Test. Later he observed three fish by Ibsley Bridge on the Hampshire Avon weighing about twenty-five, fifteen and nine pounds. With an outsize Killer Bug he 'induced a take' from the middle fish, just like an outsized grayling. A little later, with 10½ foot rod, No. 4 greased line and 8-pound leader, he cast his Killer Bugs tied on size 3 low-water hooks. Five of the seven fish took, and he lost the estimated forty pounder at the last gasp. For the system to work, the Bug has to sink quickly.

Another English reference is that in Henry Williamson's *Salar the Salmon*, in which the nearly fatal fly was likened to a 'nymph' and this appeared to be its attraction to the fishy hero of the tale.

Kelson misses the emphasis of nymphs; he suggests a class of fly – a tribe – the 'impennates', i.e. small patterns with short wings. As they seem, however, to be dressed fully with sides and cheeks in exaggerated size in relation to the proportions of the fly, it is not really possible that they should be considered by us as nymphs within this context.

Hewitt, in *Secrets of the Salmon* (1925) (which nearly became a run-away publishing success when its title was misinterpreted as *Secrets of Salome*), seems to be the earliest proponent of the nymph in salmon fishing. His comments accord well with what Frank Sawyer later observed. He did fish Hardy dry-fly trout leaders of 0.008 inch diameter, which break 'at two and one-half pounds pull', yet his son managed a salmon which weighed 'twenty-five and one-half pounds'. That is probably an indication that terminal tackle must be fine.

In the late season during July and August, one often notices salmon rolling in the pools . . . they seem to be moving very slowly as if looking for food . . . their behaviour however is exactly like bulging brown trout which are known to be taking nymphs of the water insects rising to the surface. I therefore adapted my fly and my whole method of fishing . . . and did not fish in the regular wet-fly style of casting, drawing the fly across the current. I worked the fly as I would a nymph fly for brown trout and immediately had extraordinary results where I had been getting only a few fish before.

Lee Wulff: 'The field of nymph fishing for salmon is one in which very little work has been done. It holds considerable possibility for development. . . . Imitations of the nymph form of the stream insects are effective for salmon but are not often available in tackle shops. . . . It is surprising that those anglers who believe salmon are serious feeders do not carry in their fly-boxes many exact imitations of the nymphs common to the waters they fish.' Rubber or plastic replicas of nymphs were not as effective as less accurate imitations made of feathers or hair or other soft materials, which could give a greater degree of 'leg' movement in the water.

Other American authors mentioning nymph patterns are Gary Anderson and Joseph Bates. Gary Anderson quotes the 1789 edition of Brookes: 'The angler should imitate principally the natural flies found on such rivers where salmon abound.' He writes of Carl Richards and Doug Swisher's book, *Selective Trout* (1971) (which shows wiggle-nymphs and emerger patterns, with considerable likeness to the naturals; their no-hackle flies depend on well-spaced tails and buoyant body materials for floatancy) that any developments they make for salmon might gain for nymphs a greater popularity.

Genuine endeavours to imitate food items which salmon have been seen to take may be the key to increased catches in difficult conditions. There are all the suppositions about salmon – that they do not feed in fresh water, that they do feed but have a ferociously rapid digestion, that they regurgitate any stomach contents upon being hooked, and so on. However, they have been *seen* to take natural baits – of their own volition and unattached to the angler's line.

Prawns and Shrimps are imitations, representations. The Rat flies from North America have some resemblance to stoneflies, as does the Green King from the Spey. There are plenty of recorded instances of the March Brown proving a good pattern when the insect is hatching.

Wasps and Bees have been seen to be taken. Bainbridge had a pattern in 1816, 'a copy from the common Wasp in the natural state which has been selected as being a favourite with the Salmon peal, mort, or gilse; and well-grown fish will sometimes rise at this fly in preference to any other. It is made of the wool of a sheep or other animal, dyed yellow, and a black hackle twisted at intervals over the body: or vice versa, of a black body and yellow hackle.' We wonder if he observed this on Tweedside (gilse is still used for grilse by some Tweed boatmen) for he lived at one time at Gattonside near Melrose.

Lascelles, in his *Letters – Angling, Shooting and Coursing* (1819), gives a wasp or hornet imitation, considering it a capital fly: 'wings: fine fibres of cock pheasant tail (not too stiff), body: yellow worsted ribbed with black, tied full, and a large red cock's hackle or saddle feather black at the roots wrapped several times under the but of the wings for legs'. For a bee there is the proven McGinty pattern.

Butterflies and moths provide a rich field. The Reverend Henry Newland offers a nice Irish one in his 1851 book *The Erne, its Legends and its Fly-Fishing*. In his six patterns, ' "The Butterfly" is distinguished readily from all others by its underwings which, being made of the tippet feather of the Golden Pheasant tied on whole, gives it the appearance of a copper-coloured butterfly'. No doubt large coppers, small coppers, tortoiseshells and commas could be represented with a tippet-tied fly. Kelson also offers a Golden Butterfly, attributing it to Major Traherne, which uses the tippets for body veiling. Kelson was not always logical and was very often fanciful on the subject of what salmon take a salmon fly to represent.

Butterflies were certainly used as a size comparison: Salter in his *Anglers Guide* of about 1823 (5th Edition) suggests 'Salmon are to be angled for at the top with artificial flies of a very large size . . . as big as a large butterfly.' But the anonymous author of the *Anglers' Pocket Book* of 1805 goes one better – 'a real butterfly on the point of the hook improves the bait'. He has another utterance which will follow in due turn.

We rather think we can understand why he chose to remain anonymous!

In 1843 Scrope related seeing 'a white butterfly fluttering up and down on the water and a salmon make a fruitless dart at it. It chanced that I had made some large salmon flies with white wings in imitation of a pattern that was formerly the fashion for trout fishing, and called, I know not why, the Coachman. One of these I immediately looped to my line: the fish no doubt taking it for the butterfly he saw flitting above him, came to it at once and I took him.' Earl Hodgson tells a tale about Sir Herbert Maxwell: 'A friend was fishing on the Inver, in Sutherland. The water was very low. Many fish were lying in a certain pool, but not one would move at a salmon fly, and the fisherman seated himself to rest. Ere long he noticed a white butterfly floating down the stream. A salmon rose quickly and took it.' Earl Hodgson writes at about the same time as A.H.E. Wood made his observations leading to his techniques of the greased-line.

> One afternoon in July 1903, I was fishing an Irish river. The weather for some time past had been exceptionally hot and dry, so that the river had dropped considerably and was very clear. I had no sport all day and sat down to think beside a pool full of salmon that had steadily refused to look at a series of flies, presented to them, as I thought, in every possible way. Shortly afterwards I saw one fish and then another rise to something floating down on the surface of the water. This continued at irregular intervals, and at length I was fortunately able to observe the cause, namely, a sort of white moth similar to those often seen among the heather. As luck would have it, I happened to have with me a White Moth trout fly.

Courtney Williams in *Angling Diversions* (1945) produces a splendid mixed bag of information, including an 1877 account from Frank Buckland: 'Mr Sachs sent me for examination a case containing a selection of salmon flies belonging to Mr Nicholay. The general tint (yellow, green and gold) of these flies gave me the idea that salmon mistake them for a creature generally known as the sea-mouse, a kind of slug with iridescent hairs, very much resembling a fat caterpillar. I will get a sea-mouse and have a hook dressed with the skin.' Apart from the whimsy of this, the interest lies in the reference to iridescence, and to the salmon's saltwater diet: squids and small fishes which illuminate themselves may form part of their feeding at sea.

Traherne's mention of three grilse taken in Norway which were gorged with **daddy-long-legs** probably does not come as a surprise. The insect's struggles on the water are eminently attractive to both trout and sea trout, and enough salmon are caught on the Irish loughs on a Daddy to justify its inclusion in a fly box. To support its use on the Irish rivers we find in *Further Thrifty Salmon Fishing* by Mrs Robertson: 'There remains the deliberate imitation, of which the now popular "Daddy" is the most amusing.' The expected dry trout tying is then applied to a salmon iron.

Grasshopper tying technology has increased greatly in the past few decades, granted that it is mostly for trout fishing. However, Hughes-Parry used a grasshopper with success for sulky salmon on the Welsh Dee, after some words of advice about summer fishing and representative flies. He writes: 'I firmly believe that if men would fish with trout rods and trout tackle they would hook, and probably land, far more salmon than by sticking to the greased-line salmon rod and flies; again and again, on the Welsh Dee, I have seen salmon risen to trout flies when they have refused for days every effort of the greased-line experts.

The three things absolutely necessary are: (1) To keep well out of sight; (2) To fish with as fine a gut as possible, nothing heavier than a 2x and finer if you dare; and (3) To have your flies dressed to represent some fresh-water insect.'

He then tells of salmon taking caterpillars – the green and white variety that come off the 'flannel plant' or great mullein.

About the grasshopper, he devotes a chapter of four pages. He tried first a grasshopper mounted on a 6 hook, with a 8, one-eighth of an inch away. But double-hooked like that, the grasshopper looked like a dead thing. Two grasshoppers were then tried, one on each hook, which was a great improvement. His first salmon came to the surface to take the partially submerged insects, and swallowed the bait. His second fish took a similar set-up, but one which was allowed to sink some six inches or so below the surface.

It is probably more because we have not tried to imitate them and then fish them that they do not regularly take fish, rather than that fish will not take them. Traditional attempts to make imitations float with ordinary hackles have progressed to positive buoyancy, furled polypropylene bodies, Muddler-style bodies and loop-hackle legs.

Our **frog** references we limit to two. The first is from *Favourite Flies* by Mary Orvis Marbury. '[He] impaled a live green frog on his fly hook and floating it down over the salmon, it was taken with a rush.' The other is from Grimble's *Salmon Rivers of Ireland.* 'From the Maigue river Mr Browning, when fishing for pike with a frog, hooked and caught a salmon of twenty-five pounds.'

The **dragonfly** references glow with a gaudy incredibility, until 1950. Up to then their role in salmon fly fishing was imaginary rather than scientific, but prolific all the same. From Walton onwards there is an assumption that they are the natural prey of salmon.

Bainbridge (1816) propounds: 'The most successful bait for salmon which can be used, is the artificial fly. Those made in imitation of the dragonflies are most to be depended upon, as these insects are constantly hovering over the water, consequently, are more familiar to the view of the fish.' W. Carroll, in his *Anglers' Vade Mecum* of 1818, claims that there are 'two kinds of large flies in nature, which are sometimes imitated. The first is the Dragon fly, in some places called the Adder fly.' (Humphry Davy in *Salmonia* (1828), however, is a doubter that the dragonfly is food for the salmon.) Rennie of the *Alphabet* (1833), gave most convincing woodcuts of the natural and artificial – as convincing as a £2 note! He too was a dissenter from the school of artificial flies imitating dragonflies; and *The Practical Angler* (Piscator) of 1842 voices Rennie's suspicions: 'Salmon flies are not often intended to represent any particular insect; the form is normally that of the dragonfly, although of all sorts of colours. Sometimes a fly like the mayfly, only twice the size, is found to answer.' But in 1834 Oliver (Chatto) writes: 'he had on his line a large salmon hook, dressed with silk, peacock's feathers and tinsel, to about the size of kingfisher, to imitate as he said the large dragonfly.' Doubt continues nevertheless.

Then, in the middle of this century, imagination is given a rest. John E. Hutton in *Trout and Salmon Fishing* (1950) states: 'Dragonflies are common objects on many streams in the summer, laying their eggs . . . it is not uncommon to see salmon or grilse taking a dragonfly knocked on the water.' *Lee Wulff on Flies* gives a pattern. That shown is his own tying using his patent plastic body, but the *style* can be reproduced, in other colours and with other materials.

Mouse literature is fine if not abundant. However, it should be prefaced with **squirrel**

literature. Though the villains of the piece are sea-run brook trout, there is a conclusion to be drawn from Hewitt's account:

There were only one or two small salmon, but a number of good-sized sea trout in water six to eight feet deep. They would not touch our flies, and while we were trying to concoct some scheme to make them rise, a red squirrel jumped into the water from the opposite bank and began to swim across the river. The largest trout made for him at once and coming behind him caught his tail and pulled him below the surface. The squirrel broke loose and struggled to the surface again with part of the hair of his tail gone. Again the trout caught him and a second time the squirrel got away with more of his hair stripped off. The third try was near our bank and when the squirrel finally came ashore his tail was stripped like a rat's, and he was completely exhausted. I know now that the hair on a squirrel's tail is his natural protection against sea trout.

We may conclude that it is obviously the right type of material to choose for fly tying.

The same author wrote earlier: 'My son raised a number of salmon on a buck-tailed *mouse* this summer, on the Restigouche, and in fact had several rises in one cast, but he was laughing so at the antics of the fish that he could not hook them. He finally however landed two, just to show it could be done.'

There is early, but doubtful, authority for mice – our anonymous friend of *The Anglers' Pocket Book* of 1805. 'NB water mice and rats are the favourite prey of pike as well as of salmon.' Let the case rest!

Nymphs

There seem to be two ways of looking at salmon nymphs – to tie some sort of accurate representation, or to produce an effect like a nymph, without much attempt at representation. For the first, we can turn straight away to the best trout fly *tying* books, and enlarge and elaborate on a suitable hook. For the second, we turn to trout nymph *fishing* instruction books, to learn how to make our fly behave like a natural nymph. A.H.E. Wood referred to his flies as 'Nymphs', without much elaboration. He did,

however, sometimes fish upstream in some waters, but kept his fly as close to the surface as possible, which is not like Sawyer's method. Frank Sawyer fished an ordinary salmon fly 'like a nymph for grayling' and then used his trout/ grayling pattern specifically for salmon, with success. The clarity of water and steady flow helped him in his observations. Tim Pilcher of Farlow's takes salmon nymph-style, following Sawyer's example, on the River Test.

1 Hewitt Nymph

COMMENT

'The fly below the surface is just like the nymph when it opens its wings at the surface and flies away. I put on one of these flies and a fine leader about 18ft long, and cast out where the fish were rolling, letting it sink a little and drew it slowly towards me by stripping in the line with my hand. The fly had only travelled a few feet before I saw a wake coming towards it, and a salmon took the fly. . . . While the erect style of wing was better than the regular salmon type . . . I could get fish on any of the regular flies or trout flies if they were small enough, Nos 10 and 12' (Hewitt).

DRESSING

Hook: Alcock Model Perfect.
Tail: Two long hairs.
Body: Quill.
Throat: Light-grey blue Andalusian.
Wing: Blue-grey, tied erect, at right angles to the body, with both wings close together like the keel of a boat.

2 Defeo Brown Nymph

COMMENT

In this and the following pattern we have something which is intended to look like a nymph rather than fortuitously happening to do so. It seems that the importance is not in the ingredients of the dressing but the style. We would recommend that intentional Nymph patterns are tied with extra weight (head varnish to indicate accordingly), so that the fisherman can control the pace and depth, and 'induce' a take. The jungle cock feathers are those surrounding the enamelled cape feathers, with a lighter streak down the centre.

DRESSING

Tag: Fine flat silver or gold.
Tail: Brown mallard or hair fibres.
Body: Fiery brown wool or seal fur.
Rib: Oval gold or silver.
Throat: Mallard fibres or natural red Defeo-style hackle.
Wingcase: Jungle cock, or partridge breast tips, short.

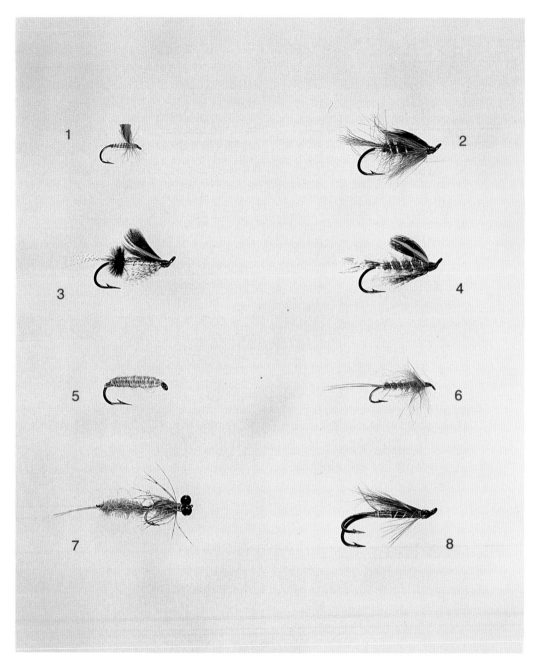

1 Hewitt Nymph   **2** Defeo Brown Nymph   **3** Defeo Silver Nymph
4 Defeo Grey Nymph   **5** Sawyer Bug   **6** Jorgensen's Nymph
7 Wiggle-Nymph   **8** Endrick Double

3 Defeo Silver Nymph

COMMENT

We have drawn from *Atlantic Salmon* by Lee Wulff for these patterns, which are the subject of one of the coloured plates. Bates also gives Defeo Nymphs, which are much the same. This pattern is very much like the Silver Grey, but simplified and given a Nymph style and silhouette. Defeo also has a Jock Scott pattern — body similar to the standard classic, but then only the little stub wings in the nymph style.

DRESSING

Tag: Flat silver
Tail: Grey mallard strands.
Butt: Black herl.
Body: Flat silver.
Rib: Oval silver.
Throat: Grey mallard in Defeo style.
Wingcase: Partridge breast feather tips or jungle cock.

4 Defeo Grey Nymph

COMMENT

Seal fur and some of the modern alternatives such as Antron fibres will possibly be better than wool and natural dubbings — for their extra sparkle. Patterns tied without extra weight might even be tied extra-buoyant in the emerger style, which can be particularly deadly for trout. There is a considerable area for experimentation within the nymph styles.

DRESSING

Tag: Flat silver.
Tail: Whisks of guinea-fowl.
Body: Grey wool or seal fur.
Rib: Oval silver.
Throat: Guinea-fowl in Defeo style.
Wingcase: Tips of partridge breast feathers or jungle cock.

5 Sawyer Bug

COMMENT

A tremendously simple pattern, relying on its easy-sinking profile and the extra weight which is given by underlying turns of fine copper wire. The wool has a special translucency when wet, which makes it such a good material in patterns which imitate underwater life forms.

Mrs Sawyer, who still ties all the Sawyer patterns, most kindly tied this 'original' for us.

DRESSING

Tag: A turn or two of copper wire.
Body: An underbody of copper wire covered with Chadwick's 477 nylon/wool darning wool.
Rib: Copper wire.

6 Jorgensen's Nymph

COMMENT

Poul Jorgensen believes in simplicity – three shades of nymph very much like trout nymphs, pale, medium and dark, with the ingredients selected accordingly. He winds the rabbit hair for the thorax more as a hackle than dubbing. He tints the latex with a suitable marker pen.

DRESSING

Tail: Three pheasant tail fibres.
Body: Blended brownish seal fur.
Rib: Medium gold wound counterclockwise.
Thorax and legs: Rabbit hair, picked out.
Thorax cover: Tinted latex.

7 Wiggle-Nymph

COMMENT

We choose a mayfly-style nymph, or a dragonfly nymph, which has pronounced 'tails', a long body which flexes in the water, and a substantial thorax. Legs are worth including for the extra attraction of movement. The body hinges just behind the thorax. For the rear section we use a loop-eyed hook. Once dressed, the bend is removed and the section is tied to the head section, which is dressed in turn.

DRESSING

Rear hook
Tail: Three strands of cock pheasant tail.
Body: Dubbed olive wool, tapering.
Rib: Hackle with side fibres clipped very short.
Front hook
Body: Darker olive wool, dubbed.
Thorax: Dark turkey tail feather fibres.
Throat: Dyed olive guinea-fowl.
Eyes (for dragonfly): Very protruberant and black.

8 Endrick Double

COMMENT

The pattern seems to be fairly irrelevant, but this actual fly caught the fish! We used to be intermittent visitors to the Endrick, which is a feeder stream to Loch Lomond. Salmon and sea trout ran it freely towards the end of the season, and fish would lie in ranks several fish deep and many fish wide – or so it seemed. In bright low-water conditions wet flies were disdained, and dry flies observed indolently, with the very occasional swirl beneath them. Upstream casting on a floating line, and then raising the rod tip, which in turn raised the fly towards the surface, eventually produced fish.

DRESSING

Tag: Oval silver.
Tail: Topping.
Body: Rear third, yellow-orange floss; front two-thirds, black floss.
Rib: Fine oval silver.
Throat: Blue.
Wing: Stoat's tail.

Other Beasts

The patterns shown here may whet the appetite of fly tyers to think 'natural'. All the naturals mentioned have at some time or another been taken, and imitations of them have also taken salmon.

Naturals we have omitted are worms and maggots. Too many coarse fishermen on rivers like the Hampshire Avon have caught salmon on maggots for the bait to be considered laughable. There may, however, be two difficulties for the tyer – their smell in the water and their movement. The same problems exist in imitating the worm within normal fly-tying techniques. Plastic worm imitations for American black bass have been developed – strong but extremely soft materials are used, and they may be made or subsequently impregnated with scent or flavour. The worm is universally popular (even in rivers in Iceland, which is a country *which has no worms*).

There may be adaptations of trout flies such as Bloodworms (chironomid larvae) yet to be devised for salmon.

1 Wasp

COMMENT

Rather than use wool or chenille, which can absorb water, it is better to use a material which floats. The same style may be adopted for bees, with orangy-brown and dark-brown body bands as appropriate.

Bumble bees have orange or yellowish hinder segments, becoming darker near the head, and they are bigger and more stoutly built.

DRESSING

Tail: None.
Body: Alternate bands of yellow and black deerhair trimmed in Muddler style.
Throat: Two turns of smokey grey hackle.
Wings: Smoky grey hackle points tied flat.
Collar: Two turns of smoky grey hackle.

2 White Butterfly

COMMENT

It must float, and it must have large wings. We can adapt the standard White Muddler Minnow by enlarging its wings. A single strand of 'flash' will add attraction in bright sunlight.

DRESSING

Tail: Broad swathes of white swan or duck.
Body: Silver tinsel (or white).
Wing: Very broad white swan or duck, with a single strand of flash on each side.
Head: Deerhair in Muddler style with a few long fibres to suggest legs and antennae.

1 Wasp   **2** White Butterfly   **3** Daddy-long-legs   **4** Grasshopper
5 Frog   **6** Crayfish   **7** Dragonfly   **8** Mouse

3 Daddy-long-legs

COMMENT

We give just one of many Daddy patterns. Veniard's used to offer a tiny segmented, rubber-like, hollow, preformed body in amber. If you can obtain these, all the better; otherwise raffia may be used for the body, and even fluorescent flosses. Pheasant tail fibres are used for the legs here. They may be stiffened with varnish. Fine nylon strands with thumb knots pulled tight at each joint are an alternative. As the natural struggles on the water, in its endeavours to escape, so the imitation should be given a twitch or two of movement.

DRESSING

Hook: Long-shank, medium to fine wire.
Body: Pheasant tail fibres wound on.
Legs: Knotted pheasant tail fibres.
Wings: Natural red hackle points splayed backwards horizontally.
Throat: Natural red hackles.

4 Grasshopper

COMMENT

There are very many hoppers and crickets, with a wide variety of colour and size, so we show a style and give its tying notes. There is plenty of room for experimentation. It must float well, when required. The natural is known both to land heavily on the surface and to struggle frenetically when in or on the water.

DRESSING

Hook: Wide-gape, medium to light wire.
Body: A detached body formed from a length of polypropylene twisted tightly so that it furls when the two ends are brought together.
Legs: Trimmed and knotted hackles.
Wings: Tufts of bucktail or swathes of grey goose or turkey along the top of the body.
Hackle and throat: Grey or grizzle or natural red hackle.
Head and thorax: Clipped deerhair, with the hackle wound through it.

5 Frog

COMMENT

It is sometimes possible to buy bass bugs of popper-style design, which simulate frogs. It saves making a sculpture out of deerhair. To stay in shape the hind legs must have a strand of wire running through them, which is then bent. During the tying it is worth keeping the legs straight and superimposing the leg material over a rigid needle, which is later removed for the top of the thigh to be tied to the hookshank. Pinch the fibres to make the feet flat and broad, and varnish them.

DRESSING

Hook: Medium-weight wide-gape.
Legs: Bunches of green bucktail with wire inserted.
Body: Sculpted green and yellow bucktail.
Spots on back: Pentel marker or burned with a red hot 'spear' (if required).
Eyes: Optics, glued to the hair.

6 Crayfish

COMMENT

Our pattern is tied in impeccable style by
Fulling Mill Flies Ltd. The claws are bunches of
squirrel tail, light at the tips, and separated into
units by figure-of-eight winds of the tying silk.
The back is tied in as a broad swathe of tail
fibres or primary feathers, and is brought
forwards for tying off after the body has been
made.

DRESSING

Hook: Turned-down eye.
Claws: Tufts of squirrel hair divided widely.
Eyes: Black beads threaded on wire, with the
wire tied in.
Back: A swathe of turkey, tied off to leave a
stub to represent the creature's tail vanes.
Body: Brown wool, seal fur or chenille,
tapering finely to the eye of the hook.
Hackle: Coch-y-bonddu saddle hackle tied
in even spirals in palmer-style.

7 Dragonfly

COMMENT

The looped-hackle style was tied first on
grasshopper imitations, and was then
developed to a moth-style, with wool and
chenille bodies as well as those made of
deerhair. The looped wings proved to give great
floatability, and were practicable for this
dragonfly pattern.
 We have had to adapt the dressing notes. The
one in the plate is an original by Lee Wulff and
uses his patent plastic body.

DRESSING

Hook: Long-shank streamer.
Tail: None.
Body: A yellow tube under much longer
bucktail fibres pointing tailwards.
Wings: Grizzle, looped.
Hackle: Grizzle, tied in parachute style.

8 Mouse

COMMENT

Some tyers with a plaintive touch finish the fly
head (or Mouse's nose) with pink nail varnish.
Trout fly tyers imitate the different mouse
species with appropriate colours. Interestingly,
T. T. Phelps, in *Fishing Dreams* (1949), mentions
the lemming migrations of Norway. Though they
were gorged upon by eagles and hawks of
every kind, there is no mention of their being
part of the salmon's diet.

DRESSING

Tag: None.
Tail: A long strip of wash-leather or string.
Body: Caribou hair wound on in Muddler
style but trimmed below only.
Ears: Shaped wash-leather flanges.
Eyes: Black beads threaded onto wire,
which is twisted.
Head: Shaped clipped deerhair.
Whiskers: Unclipped strands of deerhair left
protruding.

Bibliography

These books have been the basis of our research and many are mentioned in the text. It is a representative selection fairly easily available to those interested in salmon flies and their history. The widest in their application are set in bold.

Adams, Joseph, *The Angler's Guide to the Irish Fisheries,* 1924.

Akroyd, Charles H., *A Veteran Sportsman's Diary,* 1926.

Anderson, Gary, *Atlantic Salmon and the Fly Fisherman,* 1985.

Ashley-Cooper, John, *The Great Salmon Rivers of Scotland,* 1980, 1987.

Ashley-Cooper, John, *A Salmon Fisher's Odyssey,* 1982, 1986.

Ashley-Cooper, John, *A Line on Salmon,* 1983.

Ashley-Dodd, G. L., *A Fisherman's Log,* 1929.

Bates, Joseph D., jnr, *Streamers and Bucktails,* 1950, 1966, 1979.

Bates, Joseph D., jnr, *Atlantic Salmon Flies and Fishing,* 1970.

Bates, Joseph D., jnr, *The Art of the Atlantic Salmon Fly,* 1987.

Bainbridge, George C., *The Fly Fisher's Guide,* 1816.

Balfour-Kinnear, G. P. R., *Flying Salmon,* 1937, 1938, 1947.

Balfour-Kinnear, G. P. R., *Catching Salmon and Sea-Trout,* 1958, 1959, 1960.

Bergara, Juan De, *El manuscrito de Astorga . . . año 1624,* 1984.

Bergman, Ray, *Trout* 1933, etc.

Best, Thomas, *Art of Angling,* 6th edn, 1804.

Bickerdyke   See Cook, Charles H.

Bingham, Charles, *Salmon and Sea Trout Fishing,* 1988.

Blacker, William, *Art of Fly-Making . . .,* 1842, 1843, 1855.

Bowlker, Charles, *The Art of Angling,* 1747, etc.

Bridgett, Robert C., *Tight Lines: Angling Sketches,* 1926.

Brookes, Richard, *The Art of Angling,* 1766, 1778, etc.

Buckland, F. John, *The Pocket Guide to Trout and Salmon Flies,* 1986.

Burrard, Sir Gerald, *Fly Tying Principles and Practice,* 1940, 1945.

Carroll, W., *Anglers' Vade Mecum, 1818.*

Chatto, William A., *Scenes & Recollections of Fly-Fishing by Stephen Oliver, the Younger,* 1834.

Chatto, William A., *The Angler's Souvenir by P. Fisher, Esq,* 1835.

Chaytor, Alfred H., *Letters to a Salmon Fisher's Sons,* 1910, 1919, etc.

Clegg, Thomas, *Hair and Fur in Fly Dressing,* enlarged 2nd ed, 1969.

Collyer, David J., *Fly Dressing,* 1978, 1985.

Collyer, David J., *Fly Dressing II,* 1981, 1985.

Cook, Charles H., *Angling,* 1912.

Crossley, Anthony C., *The Floating Line for Salmon and Sea Trout,* 1939, 1944, 1948.

Crow, S. H., *Hampshire Avon Salmon,* 1966.

Currie, William B., *Days and Nights of Game Fishing,* 1984, 1987.

Daniel, William B., *Rural Sports,* 1801–2, 1805, 1812.

Davy, Sir Humphry, *Salmonia,* 1828, 1829, etc.

Dunne, John J. (Hi-Regan), *How and Where to Fish in Ireland,* 1886, 1887, etc.

Dunne, J. W., *Sunshine and the Dry Fly,* 1924, 1950.

Ephemera   See Fitzgibbon, Edward.

Fairfax, Thomas, *Morgan's Complete Sportsman,* c. 1770.

Falkus, Hugh, *Salmon Fishing,* 1984, 1985.

Fedden, Romilly, *Golden Days,* 1920.

Fitzgibbon, Edward, (Ephemera), *The Book of the Salmon,* 1850.

Fitzgibbon, Edward, *A Handbook of Angling,* 1847, 1948, etc.

Foster, David, *The Scientific Angler,* 1882.

Francis, Francis, *A Book on Angling,* 1867, 1872, etc.

Fulsher, Keith, and Krom, Charles, *Hair Wing Atlantic Salmon Flies,* 1981.

Gallichan, Walter M., *Fishery and Travel in Spain,* 1904.

Gilbert, H. A., *The Tale of a Wye Fisherman,* 1929, 1953.

Gingrich, Arnold, *The Fishing in Print,* 1974.

Graesser, Neil W., *Fly Fishing for Salmon,* 1982, 1987.

Graesser, Neil W., *Advanced Salmon Fishing,* 1987.

Grimble, Augustus, *The Salmon Rivers of England and Wales,* 1913.

Grimble, Augustus, *The Salmon Rivers of Ireland,* 1913.

Grimble, Augustus, *The Salmon Rivers of Scotland,* 1913.

Griswold, F. Gray, *Fish Facts and Fancies,* 1876.

Gudjonsson, Thor, and Mills, Derek, *Salmon in Iceland*, 1982.

Haig-Brown, Roderick, *A River Never Sleeps*, 1948, etc.

Hale, J. H., *How to Tie Salmon Flies*, 1892, 2nd edn 1919.

Hamilton, Edward, *Recollections of Fly Fishing for Salmon, Trout and Grayling*, 1884, 1885, 1891.

Hansard, George A., *Trout and Salmon Fishing in Wales*, 1834.

Harder, John, *The Index of Orvis Fly Patterns*, 1978.

Harris, John R., *An Angler's Entomology*, 1952, 1954, etc.

Hartman, Robert A., *About Fishing*, 1935.

Heaney, E. C., *Fly Fishing for Trout and Salmon on the Faughan*, 1947.

Henderson, William, *My Life as an Angler*, 1876, 1879, 1880.

Herbert, Henry W., *Frank Forester's Fish and Fishing of the United States and British Provinces of North America*, 1849.

Hewitt, Edward R., *Secrets of the Salmon*, 1922.

Hill, Frederick, *Salmon Fishing. The Greased Line on Dee, Don and Earn*, 1948.

Hi-Regan   *See* Dunne, John J.

Hodgson, William Earl, *Salmon Fishing*, 1906, 1920, 1927.

Horsley, Terence, *Fishing for Trout and Salmon*, 1944, 1945, 1947.

Howlett, Robert, *The Anglers' Sure Guide*, 1706.

Hughes-Parry, Jack, *Fishing Fantasy*, 1949, 1955.

Hughes, William (Piscator), *The Practical Angler*, 1842.

Hunter, William A., *Fisherman's Pie*, 1926, 1929, 1937.

Hutton, J. Arthur, *Rod-Fishing for Salmon on the Wye*, 1920, 1930.

Hutton, John E., *Trout and Salmon Fishing*, 1950.

Ingólfsson, Ásgeir, *Elliðaár, Reykjavik's Angling Treasure*, 1986.

Jorgensen, Poul, *Salmon Flies: Their Character, Style and Dressing*, 1978.

Keen Joseph, *Fluorescent Flies*, 1964.

Kelson, George M., *The Salmon Fly*, 1895, 1987.

Kelson, George M., *Tips*, 1901.

Kingsmill Moore, T. C., *A Man May Fish*, 1960, 1979, 1985.

Knowles, Derek, *Salmon on a Dry Fly*, 1987.

Knox, Arthur E., *Autumns on the Spey*, 1872.

LaBranche, George, *The Salmon and the Dry Fly*, 1924.

Lascelles, Robert, *Angling (a series of letters)*, 1815, 1819.

Laurie, William. H., *All Fur Flies and How to Dress Them*, 1967.

Leonard, J. Edson, *Flies*, 1950, etc.

Little, J. Crawford, *Success with Salmon*, 1988.

McClane, Al, *New Standard Fishing Encyclopedia*, 1965.

McEwan, Bill, *Angling on Lomond*, 1980.

Mackintosh, Alexander, *The Driffield Angler*, 1806, 1810, 1821.

McLaren, Charles C., *Fishing for Salmon*, 1977.

Malone, E. J., *Irish Trout and Salmon Flies*, 1984.

Marbury, Mary Orvis, *Favourite Flies and Their Histories*, 1892, etc.

Martin, Darrell, *Fly-Tying Methods*, 1987.

Maxwell, Sir Herbert, *Post Meridiana*, 1895.

Maxwell, Sir Herbert, *Salmon and Sea-Trout*, 1898, 1905.

Maxwell, William. H., *Wild Sports of the West*, 1832, 1833, etc.

Menzies, William J. M., *Salmon Fishing*, 1935, 1938, etc.

Morgan, Moc, *Fly Patterns for the Rivers and Lakes of Wales*, 1984.

Mundle, C. W. K., *Game Fishing, Methods and Memories*, 1978.

Murdoch, W., *More Light on the Salmon*, c. 1925.

Netboy, Anthony, *The Atlantic Salmon: the World's Most Harassed Fish*, 1980.

Newland, Revd Henry G., *The Erne, Its Legends and Its Flyfishing*, 1851.

Nicoll, Henry, *Salmon and Other Things*, 1923.

Nobbs, Percy E., *Salmon Tactics*, 1934.

Oglesby, Arthur, *Salmon*, 1971, 1974, etc.

Oglesby, Arthur, *Fly Fishing for Salmon and Sea Trout*, 1986.

Oglesby, Arthur, *Reeling In*, 1988.

O'Gorman, (?) Cornelius, *The Practice of Angling*, 1845, 1855.

Overfield, T. Donald, *Famous Flies and Their Originators*, 1972.

Peard, William, *A Year of Angling*, 1867.

Pennell, Henry Cholmondeley, *Fishing – Salmon and Trout*, Badminton Library, 1885, 1886, etc.

Pequegnot, Jean-Paul, *Répertoire des mouches artificielles françaises*, 1975, 1984.

Phélipot, Pierre, *Rivières à saumons de Bretagne et de basse Normandie*, 1982.

Phélipot, Pierre, and Pequegnot, Jean-Paul, *Pêche à la mouche en France*, 1971.

Phelps, Thomas T., *Fishing Dreams*, 1949.

Piña, D. Pablo Lario y Sánchez de, *El salmón y sa pesca en España*, 1945.

Piscator   *See* Hughes, William.

Bibliography

Pryce-Tannatt, Thomas, *How to Dress Salmon Flies*, 1914, 1948, 1977.

Ransome, Arthur M., *Mainly about Fishing*, 1959.

Rennie, James, *Alphabet of Angling*, 1833.

Rennie, John, *I Have Been Fishing*, 1949.

Righyni, Reg V., *Advanced Salmon Fishing*, 1973, 1977, 1980.

Righyni, Reg V., *Salmon Taking Times*, 1965.

Ritz, Charles, *A Fly Fisher's Life*, 1959, 1965, 1972.

Robb, James, *Notable Angling Literature*, n.d. 1947.

Robertson, Mrs N. K., *Thrifty Salmon Fishing*, 1945.

Robertson, Mrs N. K., *Further Thrifty Salmon Fishing*, 1950.

Roosevelt, Robert, *The Game Fish of the Northern States and British Provinces*, 1869.

Rudd, Donald G. F. (Jock Scott), *Greased Line Fishing for Salmon*, 1935, etc.

Rudd, Donald G. F., *Game Fish Records*, 1936.

Salter, Thomas F., *The Art of Angling*, 1814, 1833.

Sandeman, Fraser, *Angling Travels in Norway*, 1895.

Sawyer, Frank E., *Nymphs and the Trout*, 1958, 1970, etc.

Schweibert, Ernest, *Trout*, 1979.

Scott, Jock   *See* Rudd, Donald G. F.

Scrope, William, *Days and Nights of Salmon Fishing in the Tweed*, 1843, 1854, etc.

Shipley, William, and Fitzgibbon, Edward, *A True Treatise on the Art of Fly Fishing*, 1838.

Spencer, Sidney, *Salmon and Sea Trout in Wild Places*, 1968.

Stewart, Tom, *Fifty Popular Flies and How to Tie Them*, Vols 1, 2, 3 and 4, 1962 onwards.

Stewart, Tom, *200 Popular Flies* (omnibus), 1984.

Stoddart, Thomas T., *The Art of Angling as Practised in Scotland*, 1835, 1836.

Stoddart, Thomas T., *The Angler's Companion to the Rivers and Lochs of Scotland*, 1847, 1853, etc.

Sutherland, Douglas, and Chance, Jack, *Trout and Salmon Flies*, 1982.

Taverner, Eric, *Lonsdale Library – Salmon Fishing*, 1931, etc.

Taylor, Samuel, *Angling in All its Branches*, 1800.

Traherne, John P., *The Habits of the Salmon*, 1889.

Tolfrey, Frederic, *Jones's Guide to Norway . . .*, 1848.

Venables, Robert, *The Experienced Angler*, 1662, 1969.

Veniard, John, *A Further Guide to Fly Dressing*, 1965.

Voss Bark, Anne, *West Country Fly Fishing*, 1983.

Wade, Henry, *Halcyon*, 1861.

Waddington, Richard, *Salmon Fishing: Philosophy and Practice*, 1959.

Waltham, James, *Classic Salmon Flies*, 1983.

Wanless, Alexander, *Complete Fixed Spool Angling*, 1953.

Wanless, Alexander, *The Angler and the Thread Line*, 1932.

Wells, Henry P., *The American Salmon Fisherman*, 1886.

Wilkinson, Sidney B., *Reminiscences of Sport in Ireland*, 1931, 1987.

Williams, A. Courtney, *Angling Diversions*, n.d. 1945.

Williamson, Henry, *Salar the Salmon*, 1946, etc.

Wood, Ian, *My Way with Salmon*, 1957.

Woods, Shirley E., *Angling for Atlantic Salmon*, 1976.

Wulff, Lee, *Lee Wulff on Flies*, 1980.

Wulff, Lee, *The Atlantic Salmon*, 1959, 1983.

Younger, John, *On River Angling for Salmon and Trout*, 1840, 1860, etc.

Anonymous
The Angler's Pocket Book, 1805.
The Book of the Flyfishers' Club, n.d. 1934.
Where to Fish: (*The Field* or Harmsworth Press).

Catalogues
Farlow, Forrest, Hardy, Ogden Smith, Orvis, Redpath.

Magazines and Periodicals
American Fly Fisher
Atlantic Salmon Journal
Connaissance de la Pêche
The Field
The Fishing Gazette
The Fly Fishers' Journal
Land and Water
Pêche Magazine
Salmon & Trout Magazine
Shooting Times & Country Magazine.
Trout and Salmon

Index

Bold numerals denote page numbers of illustrations.

Index

Index

Index